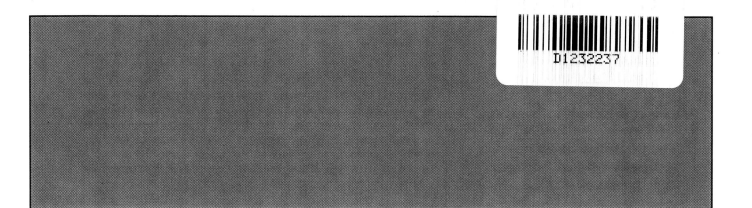

THE PROFESSIONAL PARALEGAL WORKBOOK

Elizabeth Brantlinger Angus

Australia • Brazil • Japan • Korea • Mexico • Singapore • Spain • United Kingdom • United States

The Professional Paralegal Workbook
Elizabeth Brantlinger Angus

Career Education Strategic Business Unit:
Vice President: Dawn Gerrain

Director of Learning Solutions: John Fedor

Managing Editor: Robert L. Serenka, Jr.

Editor: Shelley Esposito

Senior Product Manager: Melissa Riveglia

Editorial Assistant: Melissa Zaza

Director of Content & Media Production: Wendy A. Troeger

Senior Content Project Manager: Betty L. Dickson

Art Director: Joy Kocsis

Director of Marketing: Wendy E. Mapstone

Marketing Manager: Gerard McAvey

Marketing Coordinator: Johnathan Sheehan

Cover Design: dc Design

For product information and technology assistance, contact us at
Cengage Learning Customer & Sales Support, 1-800-354-9706

For permission to use material from this text or product,
submit all requests online at **www.cengage.com/permissions**
Further permissions questions can be emailed to
permissionrequest@cengage.com

ISBN-13: 978-1-4018-8919-7

ISBN-10: 1-4018-8919-0

Delmar
Executive Woods
5 Maxwell Drive
Clifton Park, NY 12065
USA

Cengage Learning is a leading provider of customized learning solutions with office locations around the globe, including Singapore, the United Kingdom, Australia, Mexico, Brazil, and Japan. Locate your local office at **www.cengage.com/global**

Cengage Learning products are represented in Canada by Nelson Education, Ltd.

To learn more about Delmar, visit **www.cengage.com/delmar**

Purchase any of our products at your local bookstore or at our preferred online store **www.ichapters.com**

Printed in the United States of America
2 3 4 5 6 14 13 12 11 10

ED008

To Grace and Kate

Contents

Preface

The Professional Paralegal Workbook was conceived out of necessity. As an instructor of a paralegal certificate program, I use a number of terrific textbooks but found that they lacked certain subject matter and at times were unwieldy as a general reference and exercise book for my students. I developed this workbook to bridge those gaps. I included chapters on criminal, tort, and contract law that discuss the essential elements of the law and include discussion points to facilitate classroom interaction and exercises.

A second goal in writing this workbook was to create a text that students would utilize actively, both in class and during study periods. This *Workbook* contains wide margins for students to write notes and complete exercises, and is easily portable, unlike many of the very heavy hardbound textbooks. This text also functions as a launch pad for class discussions, and through its exercises creates many opportunities for students to review material covered in class for full understanding while studying. The range of subject matter is attractive to most general law courses and is applicable to both the paralegal market and the undergraduate pre-law course. The concise yet thorough treatment of substantive law issues is coupled with interactive and hands-on exercises and discussions. Legal analysis, writing, and research are covered in addition to the treatment of substantive law.

Each chapter contains

- Chapter Introduction
- Boldface Terms/Running Glossary
- Examples woven into text
- Practice Alerts
- Discussion Points
- Key Terms List
- Exercises
- Library Resources
- Online Resources

The Professional Paralegal Workbook is an interactive, portable text that students and instructors can easily utilize in both a classroom and home study environment. It is designed to be a companion text and to enrich a general law course by offering extensive exercises and discussion points. Students will use the *Workbook* as a reference and as a class and study guide. Its wide margins and workbook format encourage the student to make notes and complete exercises to gain a full understanding of the material offered. Instructors will appreciate the many opportunities for classroom discussion and group work as well as the homework and assignment features offered.

I would like to take this opportunity to thank the people who helped in the process of creating this workbook: Attorneys Pam Meotti, Michelle Clay, and Ronald Gregory, for their insight and assistance in creating some teaching materials; Developmental Editor Diane Colwyn; Catherine Erik-Soussi, Director of Academic Programs at Saint Joseph College, and Catherine DeSimas; the University of Connecticut School of Law, especially for all my time spent on the fifth floor; all my past students who inspired me to create this workbook; Todd Angus, who both created the graphics for this text and acted as my most valuable sounding board; and finally my family, Todd, Grace, Kate, Amy, David, Mom, and Dad, for their never-wavering support and very effective cheerleading. Finally, thanks to the many who took the time to review and provide meaningful feedback, especially Pam Bailey, Subrina L. Cooper, Leslie Sturdivant Ennis, Annette Hart, Tim Hart, Deborah Howard, Jane Kaplan, Brian McCully, Kristine Mullendore, Randi Ray, Kay Rute, Judy Streich, and all of the staff at Delmar, Cengage Learning.

ABOUT THE AUTHOR

Elizabeth Brantlinger Angus developed and instructs the Professional Paralegal Certificate Program at St. Joseph College, West Hartford, Connecticut. She is the president of Advance Paralegal, an education and consulting firm located in Simsbury, Connecticut.

Attorney Angus holds a B.A. in Government from St. Lawrence University and a J.D. from the University of Connecticut School of Law. She is a member of the Connecticut Bar. You may contact Attorney Angus with any comments at eangus@sjc.edu.

PART 1

FOUNDATIONS OF LAW

CHAPTER 1

The American Legal System and Terminology

INTRODUCTION

The legal profession helps people through the tangle of law and regulations that comprise the American legal system. How do an attorney and paralegal help their client through the litigation process? Let us follow a typical case through the process.

LITIGATION TIMELINE 1

Transaction or occurrence giving rise to litigation.

On the morning of September 24, 2004, Martha left her home in New London, Neverland, and headed for her workplace 15 miles away. Martha followed the same route she took every day, Route 189 to I-95. Martha stopped for her customary cup of coffee and continued on her way. At her exit off I-95, Martha stopped at the red light and then turned right on red. As she was turning, a large pick-up truck struck Martha's car broadside. Martha was transported by ambulance to a local hospital where she was admitted and hospitalized for one week. Martha suffered a broken leg, a dislocated elbow, and a concussion. She also suffered severe burns to her right arm and leg, a result of spilling her hot coffee during the accident.

The pickup truck was driven by Herb, an employee of Acme Hauling, who was driving toward a job site. Herb resided in New Glasgow, Neverland, and the truck was owned and registered by Acme. Herb was also transported to the hospital following the accident. Herb was treated for minor bruises and lacerations and released the same day. A blood test administered at the hospital revealed that Herb had a blood alcohol level that exceeded the legal limit.

CIVIL LITIGATION

Step 1: Who is liable?

The **adversarial system** is the essence of the United States judicial system. It provides that both sides have a chance to be heard, to present evidence, and to prove or disprove legal arguments. Both Martha and Herb have the opportunity to be heard by the court and both are given equal protection under the law.

After being injured, Martha seeks legal advice to determine whether she can obtain money to compensate for her injuries. This money award is called **damages**. Because Martha is the injured party seeking relief, she is known as the **plaintiff**. In order for Martha to recover damages she must prove that someone is **liable**—that is, responsible or accountable under law—for her injuries. That person is known as the **defendant**, which is Herb in this case. The plaintiff and defendant are known as **parties** to the litigation.

Martha may decide to sue or commence **litigation** against certain defendants in order to recover damages for her injuries. In this discussion, we will focus on Herb's liability. Martha may sue Herb under **tort law**. A tort is a civil wrong for which individuals seek compensation for injuries or harm caused by other individuals' action or lack of action.

Martha, the plaintiff, sues Herb, the defendant.

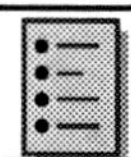

Discussion Point

Who else might Martha be able to sue? Who may also be liable under civil law for her injuries?

Step 2: Where to Litigate

Once Martha decides to sue Herb, she must then determine in which court she may begin the litigation. In order to hear a case, a court must have **jurisdiction** over the case. Jurisdiction is a court's power to consider a case and decide the outcome. There are different types of jurisdiction, including:

- **In personam jurisdiction:** The court has jurisdiction over a party to the litigation. (See detailed discussion in Step 5.)
- **In rem jurisdiction:** The court has jurisdiction over property that is the subject of the litigation.
- **Subject matter jurisdiction:** The court has jurisdiction because of the subject matter of the litigation. For example, housing courts have jurisdiction over all housing matters but do not have jurisdiction in juvenile matters.

More than one court may have jurisdiction over a matter but only one court may be the **venue**. The venue is the actual court that considers the litigation. For example, Martha may file her lawsuit against Herb in two Neverland state courts based upon in personam jurisdiction: in New London where she lives and in New Glasgow where Herb lives. However, Martha must choose only one of these courts as the venue to hear her lawsuit.

LITIGATION TIMELINE 2

Martha may sue Herb in Neverland, New Glasgow court, the venue for the litigation. Neverland court has in personam jurisdiction over Herb because he resides in that jurisdiction.

Each state has its own court system. Generally, there are three types of courts: trial court, appellate court, and supreme court. States differ as to what these courts are named, but their functions are essentially the same, as illustrated in the following section.

- **Trial court**: Hears evidence, and a jury is often the finder of fact
- **Appellate court**: Reviews the record of the trial court and rules on decisions made by the trial judge
- **Supreme court**: Reviews the record of the appellate court and rules on decisions made by the appellate judges

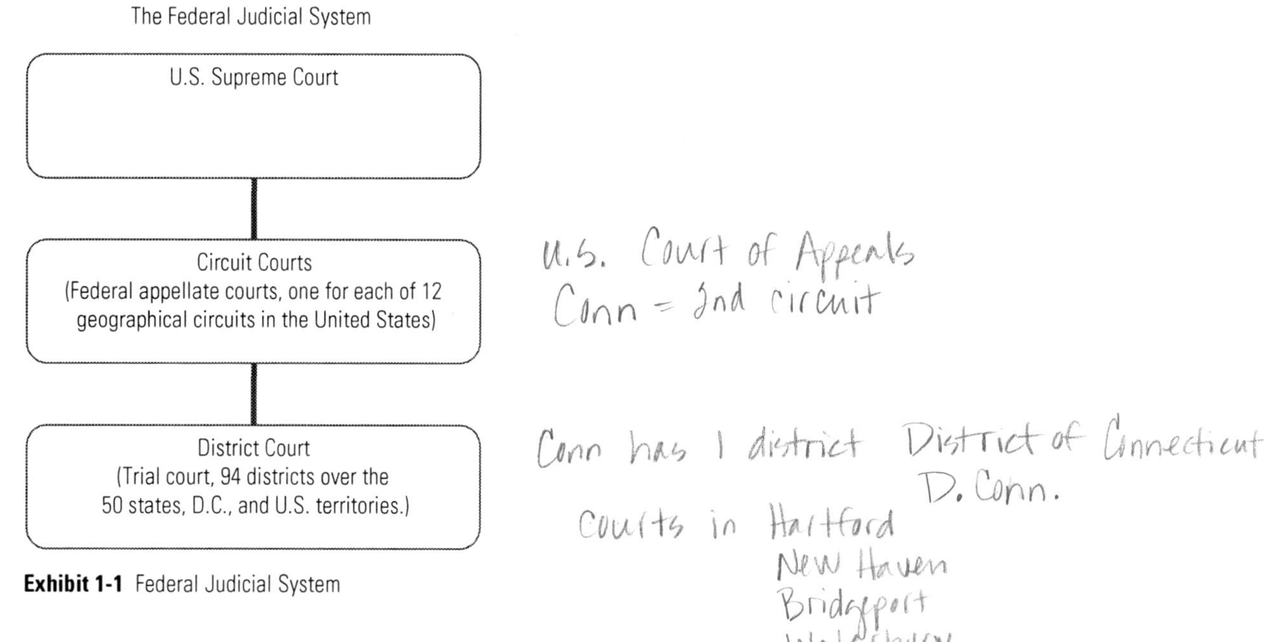

Exhibit 1-1 Federal Judicial System

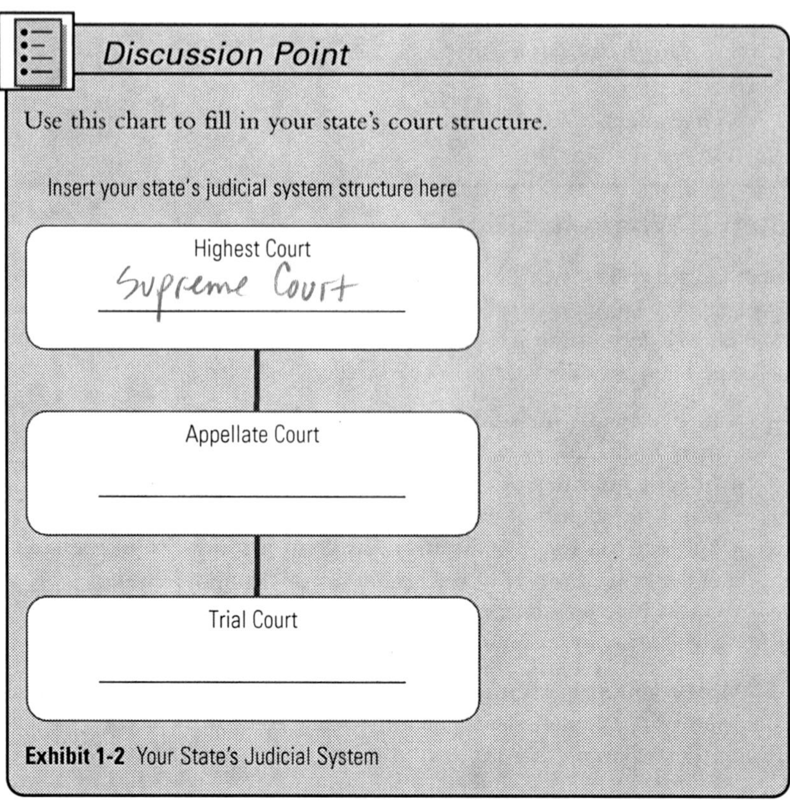

Discussion Point
Use this chart to fill in your state's court structure.
Insert your state's judicial system structure here
Highest Court
Supreme Court
Appellate Court
Trial Court

Exhibit 1-2 Your State's Judicial System

The federal system is similar in structure to most state systems. Federal courts may only hear cases that fall within the jurisdiction set by the U.S. Constitution. This includes jurisdiction over all cases, including but not limited to, cases involving:

- diversity of citizenship. For example, a resident of New Hampshire is involved in a car accident with a resident of North Dakota.
- civil actions arising under federal statute.
- civil actions in which damages sought exceed $75,000.

(Article III, Sec. 2 U.S. Const., Cong. Statute Section 28 USCA Secs. 1251, 1331, 1332)

Step 3: Getting Started

Once Martha has chosen the appropriate venue to consider her lawsuit, she must file certain documents with that court called **pleadings**. Pleadings are the initial documents filed in a lawsuit and begin with the **complaint**.

LITIGATION TIMELINE 3

Martha files a complaint with the trial court alleging that Herb was negligent in driving his vehicle while under the influence and causing the collision. This is Martha's cause of action against Herb.

Practice Alert

Different jurisdictions may call this initial pleading by other names, such as petition. Consult your local rules of practice.

The complaint states the plaintiff's version of the facts of the case including:

- a **jurisdictional statement** that informs the court that it has jurisdiction over the lawsuit.
- a **cause of action** or a legally acceptable reason for suing. Failure to include a valid cause of action may result in the plaintiff's lawsuit being dismissed by the court.

- **allegations** by the plaintiff regarding actions or lack of actions by the defendant.
- **ad damnum, wherefore clause**, or **prayer for relief**, which are the portions of the complaint that requests damages be awarded to the plaintiff.
- a **subscription**, which is he signature of the attorney who prepared the complaint, represents the plaintiff, and is affixed at the end of the complaint.

The complaint must be served and filed with the court within a certain period of time prescribed by law, known as a **statute of limitations**. The statute of limitations differs by tort and by state.

Step 4: Obtaining Personal Jurisdiction

In most jurisdictions, personal jurisdiction over the defendant is required in civil cases. In order to obtain personal jurisdiction, **personal service** must be completed. Personal service is the delivery of the summons and complaint to the defendant ordering him to appear or answer the complaint. This service must be personal, which means that the **summons** and complaint must be placed in the hands of the defendant or left with a person at the defendant's known abode or place of business. Most jurisdictions require **service by a disinterested party**, usually a sheriff or marshal, who must complete an **affidavit of service** after the defendant has been served.

LITIGATION TIMELINE 4

Martha has the complaint and summons personally served to Herb by a marshal.

summons: A formal notice from the court telling the defendant to appear or answer; usually accompanied by the complaint

service by disinterested party: Most jurisdictions require that service be made by a disinterested party, usually a sheriff or marshal

affidavit of service: A sworn statement that party has been served completed by the sheriff or marshal who served the papers and returned to the court to prove that personal service has been completed.

Step 5: Responding to Complaint

Once Herb is personally served with Martha's complaint, he may file a motion to dismiss, an answer, a crossclaim, a counterclaim, or a third-party complaint. These response options are described in the following section.

Motion to Dismiss

A motion to dismiss is a request to end the litigation without a trial. A **motion** is a formal request to a judge. This motion is usually predicated on a claim that the plaintiff has failed to establish a valid cause of action in his or her complaint. Even if the plaintiff proves every fact alleged in the complaint, the facts do not establish a cause of action that entitles the plaintiff to recover damages.

The judge will rule on the motion to dismiss and either deny the motion (the case will continue), dismiss it **without prejudice** (meaning the plaintiff may file another complaint), or dismiss it **with prejudice** (meaning the case is dismissed and the plaintiff may not file another complaint from the same cause of action).

LITIGATION TIMELINE 5

Herb files a Motion to Dismiss Martha's complaint, alleging that she failed to state facts that support her cause of action.

LITIGATION TIMELINE 6

The judge denies Herb's motion.

Answer

An **answer** is the defendant's formal response to the plaintiff's complaint. In the answer, the defendant will respond to each allegation contained in the complaint by admitting, denying, or leaving the plaintiff to her proof.

Within his answer, the defendant may include **affirmative defenses**, which are based on new allegations raised by the defendant that the defendant must prove. For example, Herb may include an affirmative defense of comparative negligence, alleging that Martha was negligent in failing to exercise due caution in turning right on red.

LITIGATION TIMELINE 7

Herb files an answer and submits an affirmative defense alleging that Martha was contributorily negligent by turning right on red unsafely.

Crossclaim

Herb may file a **crossclaim** against a co-defendant. For example, if Martha named Acme Trucking as a co-defendant in her complaint, Herb could file a crossclaim against Acme alleging that their faulty maintenance contributed to the accident, thereby lowering Herb's liability to Martha.

Counterclaim

Herb may file a **counterclaim** against Martha, the plaintiff. The counterclaim alleges a separate cause of action against the plaintiff arising from the same event. The counterclaim is not a defense, such as comparative negligence, but is a separate cause of action. For example, Herb may allege in his counterclaim that Martha was driving under the influence at the time of the accident and veered into traffic.

Third-party Complaint

LITIGATION TIMELINE 8

Herb files a third-party complaint against the manufacturer of the unsafe brake pads installed in his car.

Herb may file a **third-party complaint** against a person not originally named as a party to the lawsuit. For example, Herb may file a third-party complaint against the manufacturer of the faulty brake pads not named by Martha in her complaint.

If Herb fails to respond to Martha's complaint, the judge may grant a **default judgment** whereby the plaintiff's allegation are deemed to be proven and the defendant is liable for damages requested.

Step 6: Gathering Information

LITIGATION TIMELINE 9

Both Martha and Herb gather share information.

The next step in the pretrial process is the fact-gathering stage, known as the **discovery** phase. Both sides gather information regarding the case and are obligated to share that information with each other. Certain tools have been established to ensure that information is shared between the parties.

The shared information found during discovery includes the following:

- **Interrogatories:** written questions answered under oath, in writing
- **Request for admission:** written statements sent to the opposing party that must be admitted or denied
- **Request for physical or mental examination:** written request to allow physician to conduct an examination of the opposing party
- **Request for production and inspection of documents:** written request to inspect or copy documents and other tangible items under the opposing party's control
- **Deposition:** oral questioning under oath recorded by reporter or video
- **Subpoena** and **subpoena duces tucem:** an order from the court to appear for questioning; a subpoena duces tecum requires that the person bring specified documents with him or her

Step 7: Further Attempts to Resolve Dispute Without Trial

After the discovery process has been completed, the defendant may file a motion for **summary judgment**, requesting that the court dismiss the case on the grounds that the plaintiff has failed to provide enough evidence to support her cause of action. For example, Herb may file a motion for summary judgment stating that Martha's medical records and his independent medical examination obtained through discovery fail to support her claim that she was injured in the accident.

Both parties will meet with the judge in a **pretrial conference** to attempt to **settle** or come to a mutual agreement without trial. If pretrial conferences fail to produce a settlement, the court will set a date for trial.

Step 8: Picking the jury

The jury is the finder of fact in a trial and makes the final determination as to liability. The process of picking a jury differs by jurisdiction. Most states question or **voir dire** potential jurors in a group setting, whereas some question them individually.

Each side has an opportunity to ask questions in an effort to determine any **biases** or prejudices of potential jurors that may affect their decision-making capabilities. Attorneys may challenge jurors **for cause** when they can demonstrate such biases exist. Attorneys may also exercise limited **peremptory challenges** with which they may excuse a juror for any reason at all. The "art" of jury selection can be quite complex and some observers believe that a case is won and lost in jury selection.

A trial by jury is not guaranteed in a civil case. In many jurisdictions, judicial economy has resulted in fewer jury trials or smaller juries, from 12 to 6 jurors. The judge acts as finder of fact in the absence of a jury.

LITIGATION TIMELINE 10

Defense counsel for Herb exercises a challenge for cause for a juror who won a suit against Acme Trucking three years ago, claiming the potential juror would be biased against him based on this previous experience.

Step 9: Trial

In any civil trial, the plaintiff has the **burden of proof.** The plaintiff must prove that the defendant is liable for the injuries suffered by the plaintiff by a preponderance of the **evidence**. This standard requires that the plaintiff prove that it is more likely than not that the defendant is liable.

LITIGATION TIMELINE 11

Martha must prove by a preponderance of the evidence that Herb was negligent.

The plaintiff meets this burden by presenting evidence. Evidence is anything that tends to prove or disprove the existence of a relevant fact. Evidence can take the form of witness testimony or as tangible evidence, such as photographs or X-rays. The judge decides which evidence the jury may consider and the jury alone decides which evidence it believes and which it does not.

After the plaintiff presents her case, the defendant presents his. Because the burden of proof is the plaintiff's, the defendant is not required to present evidence but in most cases does.

After both sides have presented evidence, the case then goes to the jury for consideration. Immediately prior to the jury's consideration, the defendant may motion to the judge for a **directed verdict**, whereby the judge determines that based on the evidence presented at trial, there is by law only one way the jury can decide and, therefore, decides for the jury. Judges are reluctant to withdraw the fact-finding role from the jury and will do so only when the evidence or lack of it strongly supports such a motion.

Before the members of the jury deliberate, the judge will give them **jury instructions**. These instructions are written by the judge with input from both parties and include information the jury may use to guide its deliberations. Once the jury reaches a unanimous decision, it is read aloud in court and known as the **verdict**. A **judgment** as to the amount of damages awarded is also announced by the jury.

LITIGATION TIMELINE 12

The jury returns a verdict finding Herb liable for Martha's injuries and returns a judgment for Martha.

Step 10: Post-Trial

After the verdict and judgment are made, the post-trial period begins. The losing party may file an **appeal** with a higher court, requesting that the appellate court review the trial court record for error. The party making the appeal is known as the **appellant** and the person being brought on appeal is known as the **appellee**.

LITIGATION TIMELINE 13

Herb, the appellant, files an appeal based on the record from the trial. Martha is the appellee.

The appellate court will consider the appeal and write an **opinion** of its decision. In that opinion the appellate court may either **affirm** or **reverse** the lower court's decision and may **remand**, or send back, the case to the trial court for further proceedings.

LITIGATION TIMELINE 14

The appellate court affirms the lower court's ruling.

Once a case has completed the appeals process, it is considered fully adjudicated and **res judicata** attaches. Res judicata is the doctrine that provides that litigation must end at some point, and once the parties have been given a full opportunity to have their case heard, they can no longer litigate.

LITIGATION TIMELINE 15

Res judicata attaches and the lawsuit between Martha and Herb has been fully litigated.

CRIMINAL PROSECUTION

LITIGATION TIMELINE 16

Herb, the defendant, is arrested and tried for the criminal offense of driving while intoxicated under State Statute 53-45.

The same event can give rise to both civil litigation and criminal prosecution. In Martha's case, Herb could be criminally prosecuted for driving under the influence of alcohol and could be sued by Martha in civil court for negligence. Criminal law has some special terms to consider.

All criminal defendants are entitled to **due process** protections guaranteed by the United States Constitution. Due process ensures criminal defendants a range of protections including prohibition of unreasonable search and seizure and a right against self-incrimination.

LITIGATION TIMELINE 17

Herb pleads not guilty and is given a trial in state criminal court with due process guarantees.

Criminal defendants may plead guilty, not guilty or nolo contendere (no contest). Prosecutors may make a **plea bargain** agreement in which the defendant agrees to plead guilty and avoid a trial in exchange for a lesser sentence.

LITIGATION TIMELINE 18

The prosecution must prove beyond a reasonable doubt that Herb is guilty of the crime.

The prosecution bears the burden of proof in a criminal case. The state must prove that the defendant is guilty **beyond a reasonable doubt** in order to convict.

LITIGATION TIMELINE 19

The jury considers the evidence at trial and acquits Herb of the criminal charges.

Beyond a reasonable doubt is a very high standard of proof and if the state does not prove the defendant guilty beyond a reasonable doubt, the jury may **acquit** the defendant.

Key Terms

acquit
ad damnum clause
adversarial system
affidavit of service
affirm
affirmative defenses
allegations
answer
appeal
appellant
appellate court
appellee
beyond a reasonable doubt
bias
burden of proof
cause of action
complaint
counterclaim
crossclaim
damages
default judgment
defendant
deposition
directed verdict
discovery
due process
evidence
for cause
in personam jurisdiction
in rem jurisdiction
interrogatories
judgment
jurisdiction
jurisdictional statement
jury instructions
liable
litigation
motion
opinion
parties
peremptory challenge
personal service
plaintiff
plea bargain
pleadings
prayer for relief
pretrial conference
remand
request for admissions
request for physical or mental examination
request for production or inspection
res judicata
reverse
service by disinterested party
settlement
statute of limitations
subject matter jurisdiction
subpoena
subpoena duces tecum
subscription
summary judgment
summons
supreme court
third-party complaint
tort law
trial court
venue
verdict
voir dire
wherefore clause
with prejudice
without prejudice

Exercises

1. "By a preponderance of the evidence" is the standard of proof in criminal actions. ______________
   a. true
   b. false

2. The Fifth Amendment of the U.S. Constitution provides due process guarantees. ______________
   a. true
   b. false

3. A subpoena duces tecum requires that an individual appear in court and bring certain documents with her. ______________
   a. true
   b. false

4. A settlement is when a criminal defendant agrees to plead guilty to a crime in exchange for an agreed upon sentence. ______________
   a. true
   b. false

5. The state in which you reside has a bicameral legislature. ______________
   a. true
   b. false

6. Ad damnum is also known as a(n) ______________
   a. escheat
   b. wherefore clause
   c. petition
   d. none of the above

7. A complaint is ______________
   a. a discovery
   b. part of the voir dire process
   c. part of the summons
   d. a pleading

8. The location of the trial is known as a ______________
   a. jurisdiction
   b. venue
   c. forum non conveniens
   d. circuit

9. The court of original jurisdiction in the State of Connecticut judicial system is the ______________
   a. County Court
   b. Superior Court
   c. Appellate Court
   d. Supreme Court

10. The following term applies *only* to civil actions: ______________
    a. statute of limitations
    b. guilty verdict
    c. state's attorney
    d. none of the above

11. In the Federal judicial system, a case will progress through the courts in the following sequence: ______________
    a. appellate court, district court, supreme court
    b. superior court, appellate court, supreme court
    c. civil court, district court, supreme court
    d. district court, circuit court, supreme court

12. Which of the following is not a discovery document? ____________
    a. request for admissions
    b. interrogatories
    c. motion to dismiss
    d. deposition

13. Which of the following is not a pleading? ____________
    a. affidavit
    b. complaint
    c. affirmative defense
    d. answer

14. The defendant in a civil action responds to allegations made by the plaintiff the complaint by filing a ____________
    a. subscription
    b. answer
    c. affidavit
    d. response

15. Which of the following is *not* a type of jurisdiction? ____________
    a. venue jurisdiction
    b. in rem jurisdiction
    c. in personam jurisdiction
    d. subject matter jurisdiction

Library Resources

Black's Law Dictionary, 3d Edition, Bryan A. Garner, West Publishing, 2006.
The classic law dictionary.

Dictionary of the Law, James E. Clapp, Random House Webster, 2000.
User-friendly dictionary, written for the novice.

Online Resources

United States court system, http://www.uscourts.gov
The United States court system official Web site.

Findlaw, http://dictionary.lp.findlaw.com
Searchable database of legal terms.

Jurist, http://jurist.law.pitt.edu/dictionary.htm
The University of Pittsburgh's browsable dictionary of basic legal terminology.

CHAPTER 2

Torts

INTRODUCTION

This chapter provides an overview of theory and application of tort law. Exercises are included that are designed to illustrate the important elements of tort law.

Most paralegals will practice in the area of civil law. The biggest area of civil law is **tort law**.

tort law: The area of civil law wherein individuals seek compensation for injuries or harm caused by another individual's action or lack of action.

The tort system allows individuals to litigate to resolve their differences regarding damage to their person or property before a court of law. It is important that a paralegal have a working knowledge of the theory of torts as well as its practical application to his or her client's facts.

THEORY OF TORT LAW

Generally, a **tort** is a civil wrong or omission by one individual against another.

tort: A civil wrong or omission by one individual against another.

In order to establish a cause of action in tort, a legal duty must exist between the parties. The plaintiff must then prove that the defendant violated that duty. The many different types of torts are addressed in this chapter. Contract disputes are not tort actions and are bound by separate doctrine discussed in Chapter 3. The person or entity who commits a tort is called a **tortfeasor.**

tortfeasor: The person or entity who commits a tort.

The standard of proof in a civil tort action is **proof by preponderance of the evidence**.

proof by preponderance of the evidence: Standard of proof in a tort action that provides that the evidence presented must make it "more likely than not" that the defendant is liable for the harm suffered by the plaintiff.

This standard is considerably lower than the standard of proof required in criminal law of beyond a reasonable doubt.

A single event can give rise to both a civil cause of action *and* a criminal prosecution. For example, O.J. Simpson was acquitted of criminal charges of murder but was later sued and found liable in a civil court for wrongful death damages.

There are three main categories of torts: negligent torts, intentional torts, and quasi-intentional torts. These types of torts will be described in the following section.

I. NEGLIGENT TORTS

Most tort actions are based in **negligence**.

negligence: Failure to act in a manner that a reasonable person under similar circumstances would, involving an unreasonable risk of injury to others.

In order to establish a valid cause of action based in negligence, the following four elements must be proven:

1. the defendant owes a legal duty to the plaintiff
2. the defendant breaches that duty

3. that breach of duty is the actual and proximate cause of the plaintiff's injuries
4. injuries or damages have resulted from the breach of duty by the defendant

All four of these elements must be proven in order for a negligence action to succeed. It is not enough for a plaintiff to allege merely that an accident occurred and he suffered injuries. The plaintiff must prove each of the four elements of negligence. In a civil claim, the plaintiff must present sufficient evidence to support his claim of negligence or his claim may be dismissed by the judge. This showing of evidence is called a prima facie case.

prima facie case: A showing of evidence sufficient to satisfy a party's burden of proof. In Latin translates to "At first sight."

The rules of negligence were created by judges in order to assure that only valid claims are compensated in court. The following section will describe each required element of negligence.

1. The Duty of Care

The first element to establish in a cause of action in negligence is that the defendant owed a duty of care to the plaintiff. This duty may be determined by statute or by the "reasonable man" standard.

statutory duty: A duty set forth and encoded in a statute.

A **statutory duty** is a duty set forth and encoded in a statute.

An example of a statutory duty may be found in motor vehicle laws. All drivers of motor vehicles are required by statute to drive with their headlights on under certain conditions. A reasonable and prudent driver would turn her lights on when it gets dark; the statute encodes this reasonable man standard.

Connecticut General Statutes Sec. 14-96a, Lighted lamps and illuminating devices required,

(a) Every vehicle upon a highway within this state shall display such lighted lamps and illuminating devices as may be required...(1) at any time from a half hour after sunset to a half hour before sunrise, (2) at any time when, due to insufficient light or unfavorable atmospheric conditions, persons and vehicles on the highway are not clearly discernable at a distance of five hundred feet ahead, and (3) at any time during periods of precipitation, including but not limited to, periods of snow, rain or fog...

"reasonable man" standard: The duty to exercise reasonable care where circumstances would indicate to any reasonable or prudent person that such care is required.

The **"reasonable man" standard** creates a duty in the absence of a statutory duty.

This standard, which was developed through case law, holds that a duty exists to exercise reasonable care when circumstances would indicate to any reasonable and prudent person that such care is required. An example of this standard may also be found in a motor vehicle scenario. A motorist owes a duty to pedestrians not to drive on sidewalks. This duty may not be written in a statute, but a reasonable and prudent motorist would know that it is not safe to drive a car on a sidewalk because they may injure a pedestrian.

This duty of care may vary depending upon the nature of the relationship between the parties and the capacity of the parties involved. For example, a homeowner is sued by a neighbor who attended a block party held on the homeowner's front lawn and was injured after he tripped on a loose brick on the patio. The standard of care would be determined by what other homeowners in a similar situation would reasonably do. A restaurant open to the public would face a different standard of care because that standard would be based on what other restaurant owners would do under similar circumstances.

The reasonable man standard is that of comparable experience, age, and capacity. Therefore if a defendant has special skills such as a doctor or lawyer, their conduct will be measured by a standard determined by others who share that same special skill. For example, a client sues her former attorney for failing to file her complaint in a timely manner. The court would review what other attorneys with similar practices would have done and apply those findings as the reasonable man standard in that case.

2. Breach of Duty by Defendant

In order to prove liability for negligence, the plaintiff must first prove that the defendant owed him a duty and then prove that he breached that duty. The defendant breaches a duty when she fails to conform to standard of care practiced by a reasonable person in her position. If the defendant violated a statute, the plaintiff must prove the defendant violated all elements of the statute that incorporates the elements of negligence. This is called **negligence per se**.

negligence per se: Negligence determined by the fact that the defendant violated a statute that incorporates the elements of negligence.

Upon reviewing Connecticut General Statutes Sec. 14-96a again, one can determine that in order for a person to be found in violation of this statute, it must be proven that

1. a vehicle in the state (duty of defendant to plaintiff)
2. did not display lighted lamps and illuminating devices (breach of that duty)
3. from one half hour after sunset through one half hour before sunrise
4. when insufficient light or unfavorable atmospheric conditions make persons and vehicles indiscernible from 500 feet away
5. any time during periods of precipitation, including but not limited to snow, rain, or fog

The elements of this statute incorporate the elements of negligence and if the elements are satisfied, the defendant is liable for the plaintiff's injuries under negligence per se.

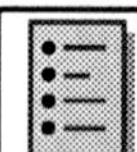

Discussion Point

What other statutes in your jurisdiction can you think of that constitute negligence per se?

If there is no negligence per se, the plaintiff must prove that the defendant failed to conform to the "reasonable man" standard of care. This is proven by the introduction of evidence by the plaintiff to demonstrate what the standard of reasonableness is in that particular case and then prove that the defendant failed to so conform.

The plaintiff may also prove that the defendant breached his duty by proving that the instrument that caused the damage was in the exclusive control or possession of the defendant at the time the injury occurred. This doctrine is known as **res ipsa loquitor.**

res ipsa loquitor: Doctrine that holds that the plaintiff in a negligence action must prove that the instrument that caused the damage was in the exclusive control or possession of the defendant at the time the injury occurred. In Latin translates to "The thing speaks for itself."

For example, the pilot of a passenger plane has complete control over the plane and therefore under res ipsa loquitor, injury to passengers as a result of a crash would necessarily be a result of his breach of duty.

3. Causation

The third element is **causation**.

causation: Plaintiff must prove that the defendant's actions were the probable and sufficiently direct cause of the plaintiff's injuries.

Causation determines the link between the defendant's actions and the plaintiff's injuries. In other words, without proving that the defendant's actions in some way brought about the plaintiff's injuries, the defendant cannot be held liable. Causation is divided into two separate elements, both of which must be satisfied in order for a negligence action to prevail. First, the plaintiff must prove the defendant's action was the "cause in fact" or "actual cause" of the plaintiff's injuries. Second, the plaintiff must prove that the defendant's action was the proximate cause of the plaintiff's injuries.

a. Cause in Fact

"but for" test: Test applied to determine cause in fact by proving that "but for" the defendant's actions, no injury to the plaintiff would have resulted.

The **"but for" test** has been developed by judges to determine cause in fact.

In order for causation to be proven, the plaintiff must first show that "but for" the defendant's actions, no injuries would have resulted.

Consider the following illustration: Plaintiff is a visiting nurse. During a visit to one of her patients on rainy day, she fell down a flight of stairs and was injured. After landing at the bottom of the stairs, she noticed a doormat that had been on the landing was now on the bottom step. She sued the defendant alleging that the plastic mat in front of the defendant's door "constituted a dangerous or defective condition that defendant created or had notice of." However the plaintiff provided no proof to support her contention that the mat caused her to fall, she merely presumed that it caused her fall. The Court stated "From this proof, it is just as possible that the mat was already at the bottom of the stairs when she fell and the accident could be caused by the wet condition of the stairway..." (*Dapp v. Larson,* 659 N.Y.S.2d 130 (N.Y. App. Div. 1997)). The court dismissed the case because the plaintiff failed to prove that, but for the defendant's action (in this case the placement of the mat), the plaintiff would not have suffered her injuries.

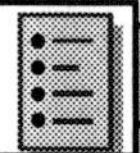

Discussion Point

Consider *Dapp*. What facts could the plaintiff have presented to prove the defendant's actions were the cause of her injuries?

b. Proximate Cause

proximate cause: An act which, unbroken by another a=cause, produces injury and without which the injury would not have occurred.

foreseeability: The duty of a reasonable person to foresee the probable consequences of his actions.

After establishing that the defendant's negligent conduct was the cause in fact of the plaintiff's injuries, the plaintiff must now establish that the negligent conduct was also the **proximate cause** of the plaintiff's injuries.

The test for determining proximate cause is **foreseeability**.

The plaintiff must prove that the defendant, as a reasonable person, should have foreseen that his negligent actions would result in injury to the plaintiff. As discussed earlier, the reasonable man standard is fact specific. In other words, it is a standard of what a reasonable and prudent person would have done under the same circumstances.

A famous case often used to illustrate proximate cause and the foreseeability test is *Palsgraf v. Long Island R. Co.,* 162 N.E. 99 (N.Y. 1928). In *Palsgraf,* a man carrying fireworks stumbled while getting on a train. When assisted by a railroad worker, the package dislodged and exploded causing a heavy scale to strike and injure Mrs. Palsgraf who was standing on the platform. Mrs. Palsgraf sued the railroad. The New York Court of Appeals found that Mrs. Palsgraf was not a foreseeable victim of the railroad employee's negligent handling of the explosive package and therefore was not liable for her injuries, stating "[n]othing in the situation gave notice that the falling package had in it the potency of peril to persons thus removed." Any reasonable railroad employee under the same circumstances would not have foreseen that the action of helping a passenger with a package would result in a scale falling on another passenger a distance away. Therefore proximate cause cannot be established.

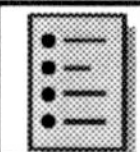

Discussion Point

Using the *Palsgraf* case as a guide, discuss different real-life scenarios in which proximate cause can be established and in which it cannot.

Let us apply both of the causation tests to a simple scenario

- The defendant is driving a car in excess of the posted speed limit = *negligence per se/statutory duty* and injures a pedestrian.
- *Cause in fact* of the plaintiff's injuries = *but for* the defendant's negligent act of driving too fast, the plaintiff would not have been injured.
- *Proximate cause* of the plaintiff's injuries = it is *foreseeable* to a reasonable and prudent driver that driving too fast may be dangerous to those around him.

However, if another person came over to the pedestrian and shot and killed him immediately after the defendant struck the pedestrian with his car, would the driver be liable for the death of the pedestrian? No, because the act of the shooter constitutes an **intervening cause.**

intervening cause: An unforeseeable, independent act that destroys the chain of proximate cause.

Applying our two tests to this scenario, it is clear that

1. a reasonable and prudent driver could not foresee that driving too fast would lead to a pedestrian being shot
2. "but for" the driver striking the pedestrian with his car, the pedestrian may still have been shot dead.

The rationale for applying these causation tests is to ensure that defendants are not held liable for injuries that were unforeseeable or for actions that are so far removed from a resulting injury that legal fairness prohibits the liability of the defendant.

4. Damages

Finally, if the first three elements of negligence are satisfied, the defendant is liable for paying damages to the plaintiff. These damages can include lost wages and medical costs, which constitute **actual damages**.

actual damages: Lost wages and medical costs and other tangible damages suffered by the plaintiff.

Other types of damages include **non-pecuniary damages** such as pain and suffering.

non-pecuniary damages: Damages that cannot be quantified economically such as pain and mental anguish.

Lastly, there are **punitive damages** which seek to punish the defendant for outrageous behavior.

punitive damages: Damages assessed to punish the defendant for outrageous behavior.

All of these damages must be proven to the court through the introduction of evidence. The plaintiff has a responsibility to reasonably **mitigate** any further damages. If she fails to do so, her damage award may be diminished.

mitigate: To make less severe.

For example, a plaintiff sues a large drug company for heart damage she suffered as a result of taking the medication. She may receive money to compensate her for the cost of surgeries she underwent to correct the problem (actual damages) and her husband could sue for loss of consortium (non-pecuniary damages).

If she could prove that the drug company knew that the drug was harmful but continued to market it anyway, she may be able to collect punitive damages. If she continued to take the drug after being advised it was harmful, her damages claim may be diminished by her failure to mitigate her damages.

Scenario 1. A case that satisfies all four elements of a negligent tort.

The defendant, Dr. Feelgood, a cardiologist, operated on the plaintiff, Mr. Chondriac for a heart valve irregularity. During the surgery, the defendant left the operating room to check the score of two football games on which he had placed bets. While the defendant was out of the operating room for 25 minutes, the plaintiff suffered severe blood loss due to a failure by the defendant to fully suture an artery. The plaintiff was hospitalized for three weeks and still suffers from anemia.

Essential element	Facts supporting proof of the essential element
Defendant owes a legal duty to the plaintiff	The defendant, a cardiologist, owes a legal duty to his patient, the plaintiff to operate with the care of a "reasonable" cardiologist under the same circumstances.
Defendant breaches that duty	The defendant failed to act as a reasonable cardiologist by leaving his patient in the middle of an operation.
The breach of duty is the actual and proximate cause of the plaintiff's injuries	Applying the "but for" test; "but for" the defendant's action of leaving in mid-operation, he would have discovered the leaking suture and repaired it, thereby avoiding the injury suffered by the plaintiff. The defendant's negligent action of leaving the operating room was the proximate cause of the plaintiff's injuries because it was foreseeable to a reasonable cardiologist that doing so could cause damage to his patient.
Injuries or damages have resulted	The plaintiff suffered blood loss, three weeks in the hospital, and continuing anemia.

Exhibit 2-1 Case That Satisfies Elements

Scenario 2. A case that does not satisfy all four elements of a negligent tort.

In this scenario, consider the same facts as in Scenario 1, except

- defendant did not leave the operating room.
- plaintiff had rare and previously undiagnosed bleeding disorder.
- excessive bleeding resulted from the bleeding disorder and normal sutures.

Essential element	Facts supporting proof of the essential element
Defendant owes a legal duty to the plaintiff	The defendant, a cardiologist, owes a legal duty to his patient, the plaintiff to operate with the care of a "reasonable" cardiologist under the same circumstances.
Defendant breaches that duty	No breach of duty occurred, as defendant acted as any reasonable cardiologist would have in similar circumstances. Defendant's expert witness, a cardiologist stated "no reasonable cardiologist would be expected to know about this specific rare bleeding disorder".
The breach of duty is the actual and proximate cause of the plaintiff's injuries	Applying the "but for" test; "but for" the undiagnosed bleeding disorder, the plaintiff would not have suffered these injuries—the defendant followed the standard of care therefore his actions were not the cause in fact of the plaintiff's injuries. Defendant's expert witness establishes that it was not foreseeable to a reasonable cardiologist that such bleeding disorder was present, therefore proximate cause has not been proven.
Injuries or damages have resulted	The plaintiff suffered blood loss, three weeks in the hospital, and continuing anemia.

Exhibit 2-2 Case That Doesn't Satisfy

DEFENSES

A number of defenses have been developed through case law, including comparative and contributory negligence; vicarious liability; assumption of risk; and strict liability. These defenses are described in the following section.

Comparative and Contributory Negligence

Comparative and contributory negligence defenses hold that claims in negligence may be defended by alleging that the plaintiff contributed to the injury that is subject of the negligent tort case.

Contributory negligence is a common law doctrine that generally holds if any negligence by the plaintiff is proven, however slight, then the plaintiff is barred from any recovery.

contributory negligence: Seldom applied doctrine that holds that if any negligence by the plaintiff is proven, the plaintiff is then barred from any recovery.

The often harsh and unfair results this doctrine created has led to a more modern and commonly accepted doctrine of comparative negligence.

Comparative negligence is the modern doctrine now followed in most states.

comparative negligence: Modern doctrine that allows that liability for damages be proportionately divided among the parties.

Comparative negligence allows that liability for damages be proportionately divided among the defendant or defendants and the plaintiff. For example, if the jury finds that the plaintiff was responsible for 20% of the damages, the plaintiff would receive only the remaining 80% from the defendant.

Vicarious Liability

A defendant may be held jointly liable for the actions for others under the doctrine known as **vicarious liability**. This doctrine evolved to extend

vicarious liability: The extension of liability for a tortious act based on the legal relationship of the parties.

liability based on legal relationship. These legal relationships commonly include that of parent-child and employer-employee.

For example, a tortious act committed by an employee within the scope of employment may be imputed to the employer based on their legal relationship as employer-employee. In other words, the employer may be liable for the tortious acts of an employee if the act occurred within the scope of his employment.

For example, the defendant works for a pizza delivery business. While delivering pizzas for his employer the defendant collides with another car. The other driver may sue both the delivery person and the business because the driver was delivering pizzas at the time of the accident. If the employee is on personal business at the time of the collision, the employer may not be liable for employees' actions because they were not acting within the "scope of employment."

deep pockets: Term used to describe the defendant with the most money.

This doctrine is often connected with the term **deep pockets**, which refers to a tendency of plaintiffs to look for a defendant with the greatest financial capacity to pay damages. In the example above, clearly the pizza business has more assets and therefore a greater capacity to pay substantial damages than the delivery person.

Other current examples of vicarious liability include suits against the Catholic Church for molestations conducted by priests and suits lodged against the parents of the Columbine shooting perpetrators.

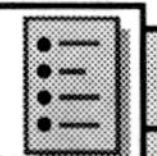

Discussion Point

Discuss current news events containing issues that raise the doctrine of vicarious liability?

Assumption of Risk

assumption of risk: For cases in which it is proven that the plaintiff knew and understood the danger of the activity that resulted in the tort claim and voluntarily engaged in the activity anyway, the plaintiff may not recover damages from someone else for a resulting injury.

The doctrine of **assumption of risk** provides that for cases in which the plaintiff knew and understood the danger of the activity that resulted in the tort claim and voluntarily engaged in the activity anyway, the plaintiff may not recover damages from someone else for a resulting injury.

In contributory negligence states, the defense of assumption of risk may bar the plaintiff from any recovery. States that still adhere to the doctrine of contributory negligence include Alabama, Maryland, and North Carolina. In the more common comparative negligence states, assumption of risk would be considered in determining recovery amount by the plaintiff.

Most instances of assumption of risk involve inherently dangerous activities such as bungee jumping or other extreme activities in which participants would sign a waiver or document signifying their understanding of the dangerousness of the activity. For example, when you purchase a ski lift ticket, the back portion contains a disclaimer for injuries that may result from your participation in this dangerous sport.

> ***BIG SKI MOUNTAIN***
> *I understand and recognize that skiing in its various forms is a hazardous sport with many dangers and risks. I realize that injuries are a common and ordinary occurrence of this sport. As such, I agree, as a condition of being allowed to use the ski area facility and premises, to freely accept and voluntarily assume all risks of personal injury, death or property damage, and release Big Ski, Inc. and its agents, employees, directors, officers and shareholders from any and all liability for personal injury, death or property damage resulting from any cause whatsoever, including their negligence, conditions on or about the premises or facilities, the operations of the ski area including, but not limited to, grooming, snowmaking, ski lift operations, actions or omissions of employees or agents of the area, or my participation in skiing or other activities at the area, accepting myself the full responsibility for any and all such damage, death or injury of any kind which may result.*

Exhibit 2-3 Assumption of Risk Waiver

Strict Liability

The doctrine of **strict liability** provides that in certain circumstances liability may be imposed upon a defendant without any proof of negligence or other fault.

strict liability: In certain circumstances, liability may be imposed upon a defendant without any proof of negligence or fault.

Strict liability is often encoded in statute and is applied in cases in which the inherent extreme dangerousness of the act or event is obvious or apparent to any reasonable party.

The person who keeps an alligator in the bathtub of his apartment would be strictly liable for any injuries imposed by the animal. Because it is so inherently dangerous to keep a large, hazardous animal in an apartment, regardless of "due care" exercised, no prima facie finding of negligence is necessary.

Strict liability is often statutorily applied in product liability cases. Courts have held that a manufacturer is liable if the plaintiff proves that the product is defective. In such cases, it is irrelevant whether the manufacturer exercised due diligence. If the defective product causes injury to the plaintiff, the manufacturer is liable under the doctrine of strict liability.

The next section will discuss intentional torts.

II. INTENTIONAL TORTS

As one can gather from the name of the category, intentional torts share one essential element: that of the intent of the tortfeasor. Unlike the negligent torts discussed in the previous section, intentional torts require that the tortfeasor intend to commit the act of the tort. Intentional torts have clear counterparts in criminal law. Intentional torts may be divided into two types: intentional harm to an individual and intentional harm to property.

a. Intentional Harm to an Individual

i. Battery

battery: The intentional infliction of a harmful or offensive touching of another person.

Battery is the intentional infliction of a harmful or offensive touching of another person.

The intentional element of the tort requires that the touching be a deliberate act on the part of the defendant, which is harmful or offensive.

For example, the defendant grabs you as you are walking through a mall and passionately kisses you. This is an intentional act by the defendant resulting in the offensive touching of your person.

Conversely, if you are riding in a crowded subway car and the person next to you brushes your backside as they move, the element of intent and deliberation in the act is absent and therefore the elements of the intentional tort of battery are not satisfied.

ii. Assault

assault: The creation of the fear of imminent physical harm or intentional touching without physical contact.

Assault is the creation of the fear of imminent physical harm or intentional touching.

Often grouped with the tort of battery, assault does not include any physical contact.

Words and/or actions may create this fear. The fear must be reasonable and imminent. For example, a masked man wielding a gun approaches you as you withdraw money from an ATM and states "Your money, or your life." This is assault. Without touching you, the gunman created a reasonable (the gun looked real) and imminent (the gunman was threatening to shoot you immediately) threat. Assault would have also occurred in this fact pattern if the gunman brandished the gun without the verbal threat.

iii. False Imprisonment

false imprisonment: The restriction of a person by physical restraint or through threat to a person or his property.

False imprisonment is the restriction of a person by physical restraint or through threat to a person or his property.

This restriction must be against the will of the plaintiff and must be for an unreasonable period.

Police detainment can constitute false imprisonment if there is no compliance with constitutional guarantees. Individuals may be liable for false imprisonment if the elements of the tort are satisfied. An example of false imprisonment is bank robbers holding customers of the bank hostage. The robbers lock the hostages in the locked vault (physical restraint) and threaten to shoot if they attempt to escape (threat to person). If those same hostages were placed in a conference room with open windows on the first floor with no guard and no threat to shoot if they escape, then the elements of false imprisonment would not be satisfied.

iv. Intentional Infliction of Emotional Distress

intentional infliction of emotional distress: The defendant intends to cause severe emotional distress upon the plaintiff through his outrageous conduct.

Intentional infliction of emotional distress is the tort of the defendant **intentionally causing severe emotional distress** in the plaintiff.

The intentional element requires that the plaintiff demonstrate that the defendant intended to cause severe emotional distress by his outrageous conduct. (Note that a plaintiff may claim negligent infliction of emotional distress as well, which requires a showing of reckless imposition of severe emotional distress.)

An example of intentional infliction of emotional distress may be found in a dispute between neighbors. The tortfeasor, angry with his neighbor over piles of leaves that blow into his yard, takes the neighbor's dog and kills it in plain sight of the neighbor and his family. The tortfeasor intended to kill the dog in order to shock his neighbor. Note that the neighbor had a close relationship with the dog because it was his pet and he experienced severe emotional distress upon the dog's death. If it had been a stray cat, the neighbor may have been upset, but because he did not have a personal relationship with the animal, severe emotional distress could not be claimed.

We now shift from intentional injury to persons to intentional injury to property.

b. Intentional Harm to Property

i. Trespass to Property

Trespass to property requires that the plaintiff show that the defendant entered the plaintiff's real property (land) without authorization.

trespass to property: The entering onto another's land without authorization.

Trespass to property can be a temporary use of another's land or even the falling of a tree branch into another's land can constitute trespass.

A good example is a farmer allowing his sheep herd to graze on a neighbor's pasture. By entering the neighbor's land without authorization, the farmer is depriving that neighbor of the full use and enjoyment of his land.

ii. Trespass to Personal Property

The same elements of trespass apply to **trespass to personal property** except that instead of land, the tortfeasor is trespassing on the personal property or chattels (any personal property, from motor vehicles to furniture) of the plaintiff.

trespass to personal property: The use of another's personal property without authorization.

iii. Conversion

The tort of **conversion** is the intentional, permanent taking of another's personal property.

conversion: The intentional, permanent taking of another's personal property.

The key difference from the tort of trespass is that conversion permanently deprives the rightful owner of his property.

An example of conversion is stealing a car (the tortfeasor takes the car and permanently deprives the rightful owner of use of the car) whereas trespass would be taking a car on a joyride (while the tortfeasor deprives the owner of the use of the car for a time, it is not permanent). The criminal law counterpart to conversion is theft.

iv. Nuisance

There are two types of nuisance: private and public. Private nuisance affects and unreasonably interferes with the use and enjoyment of the property by its owner. Generally, only a limited amount of people are affected by the **private nuisance**.

private nuisance: A nuisance that affects and unreasonably interferes with the use and enjoyment of property by a limited amount of people.

A **public nuisance** interferes with the use and enjoyment of property by many and can include a large community.

public nuisance: A nuisance that affects and unreasonably interferes with the use and enjoyment of property of a large amount of people.

An example of a private nuisance may be found in the case of *Clinic & Hospital, Inc. v. McConnel* (241 Mo.App. 223 (1951)). In *Clinic & Hospital*, a music shop was located next door to a doctor's clinic. Every day the record shop would continuously play music from 8 a.m. to 8 p.m. or later. The music was audibly loud in the doctor's building and caused patients to become upset and require extra sedation and treatment. The doctor sued the music shop under the theory of private nuisance. The court found in the plaintiff's favor stating "[a] business which is lawful in itself may become a nuisance where it is not operated in a fair and reasonable way with regard to the rights of others in the use and enjoyment of their property."

An example of a public nuisance may be found in the case of *Anderson v. W.R. Grace & Co.*, (628 F. Supp. 1219 (D.Mass. 1986)). The book and movie, *A Civil Action,* are based on this case. The plaintiffs, a group of residents of a town in Massachusetts, alleged that the defendant contaminated local groundwater by disposing of hazardous chemicals that seeped into the water supply. These toxins caused severe health problems for the residents. The court held that the residents could sue the defendant under a public nuisance theory.

We now move to the category of harm to non-physical property or quasi-intentional torts.

III. QUASI-INTENTIONAL TORTS

Quasi-intentional torts involve damage to one's reputation or expectation of privacy. The categories of quasi-intentional torts are described in the following section.

a. Defamation

defamation: The communication of an embarrassing and/or damaging message about another's reputation to a third party.

slander: The oral or spoken form of defamation.

libel: The written form of defamation.

Defamation of character occurs when a tortfeasor communicates an embarrassing and/or damaging and untrue message about another's reputation and character to a third party.

There are two types of defamation: **slander** is the oral or spoken form of defamation and **libel** is the written form.

The damaging statement must be published or communicated to a third party and the statement must damage the reputation of the plaintiff within his community. An individual may be defamed as well as a corporation or group.

The ultimate defense to any defamation claim is that the statement is true. If the plaintiff in a defamation action is a public figure, the defendant may defend against the claim by stating that the statement was made to satirize or without malicious intent.

b. Invasion of Privacy

invasion of privacy: The unauthorized use of the plaintiff's likeness or name, or the unreasonable disclosure of the plaintiff's private affairs, for the pecuniary advantage of the defendant.

The tort of **invasion of privacy** includes the unauthorized use of the plaintiff's likeness or name, or the unreasonable disclosure of plaintiff's private affairs, for the commercial or pecuniary advantage of the defendant.

An example of the tort of invasion of privacy is the publishing of photos taken with a telephoto lens in someone's back yard for commercial advantage. The plaintiff has an expectation of privacy in their own backyard. Consent to the use of the likeness or the disclosure is a defense to the tort.

c. Intentional Misrepresentation

intentional misrepresentation: The false representation of facts to the plaintiff that the defendant knows to be false and supplied with the expectation that the plaintiff will rely on those falsehoods to his detriment.

Intentional misrepresentation, also known as fraud, occurs when the tortfeasor supplies false representation of facts to the plaintiff, that the tortfeasor knows to be false, with the expectation that the plaintiff will rely on those false facts to his detriment.

The misrepresentation must be of material facts that the tortfeasor intends for the plaintiff to rely on and the plaintiff must be ultimately harmed by their reliance on the tortfeasor's misrepresentation.

An example of intentional misrepresentation is an infomercial that states that a diet pill will guarantee weight loss. In this example, intentional misrepresentation is present if

- the infomercial represents that the pill will create weight loss in all who take it while its manufacturers know that it is only a sugar pill and will not aid in weight loss (misrepresentation of material facts).
- plaintiff takes pill to lose weight (reliance on misrepresentation).
- plaintiff gains weight and develops diabetes (harmed by reliance).

Key Terms

"But for" test

Causation

Deep pockets

"Reasonable man" standard

Actual damages

Assault

Assumption of risk

Battery

Comparative negligence

Contributory negligence

Conversion

Defamation of character

False imprisonment

Foreseeability

Intentional infliction of emotional distress

Intentional misrepresentation

Intervening cause

Invasion of privacy

Libel

Mitigate

Negligence

Negligence per se

non-pecuniary damages

Prima facie case

Private nuisance

Proof by preponderance of the evidence

Proximate cause

Public nuisance

Punitive damages

Res ipsa loquitor

Slander

Statutory duty

Strict liability

Tort

Tort law

Tortfeasor

Trespass to personal property

Trespass to property

Vicarious liability

Exercises

Read each of the following exercises carefully. Identify any possible torts and discuss the elements of that tort and why you believe those elements have been satisfied. Don't forget that more than one party may be liable.

1. Sis is walking on a public park path. Ryan comes from behind her and says "Move over or I'll punch out your lights!"

2. Using the same fact pattern as above, adding: Sis looks behind her and sees that Ryan is 8 years old.

3. Sally is at her friend Coco's apartment attending a party. On her way out to the deck to get a beverage, Sally is told by Coco to "avoid the hand-railing because it is loose." After getting her drink, Sally becomes engaged in conversation with her physics professor, Dr. Brown, and leans back on the railing. She plummets down two stories and suffers numerous injuries.

4. Rich and Crispin have been neighbors for years. Over those years, they hosted a weekly poker game, alternating their homes as site of the game. The games commonly lasted into the early morning hours with loud music and conversation audible throughout the immediate area.

Rich suffered a large loss during one game and he and Crispin had a falling out resulting in Rich withdrawing from the game. The following week, Crispin hosted the game without Rich. Rich was kept awake until 3 a.m. by the noise.

5. Amy develops a hand cream based on a recipe handed down to her by her grandmother, Melba. After using the hand cream, Amy's chronic case of severe eczema improved. Wanting to share her cream with other eczema sufferers, Amy begins manufacturing and marketing the cream on eBay. She calls it "Melba's Magnificent Miracle Cure" and states in her advertising "Melba's will cure whatever ails you."

For a number of months, Amy's profits rise steadily and she receives many testimonials regarding the efficacy of the product. Approximately eight months after the release of the product, many users begin to develop a purple rash in areas where the cream was applied. Numerous consumer safety organizations begin investigations into the product. Shortly after appearing on the Today show extolling the virtues of the product and calling the investigations "witchhunts," Amy withdraws all cash from company accounts and flees to Brazil.

6. Two 14-year-old boys bring shotguns and homemade bombs to their middle school and shoot and injure five people. After being subdued by police, they are interrogated and their homes searched pursuant to a warrant. In the locked bedrooms of both boys, police find more firearms, a large assortment of knives, and bomb-making material and guides. The boys live with their families, in homes owned by their parents. Both boys had been disciplined at school the month prior to the shootings for making threatening remarks to fellow students but the school declined to expel them.

7. Marshall was a famous 1970s rock star. During his time as a rock star, Marshall was a heroin user and alcoholic. After leaving his band in the late 1980s, he became a respected record producer and a follower of Guru Shwazili, who advocated healthy living. He had lived with his girlfriend, Susie, for the four years preceding his death from AIDS in 2001.

In 1999, Marshall visited his doctor, Cassandra Block and learned that his blood had tested positive for the HIV virus that causes AIDS, and that this condition placed him in one of the high-risk categories for contracting full-blown AIDS. Approximately one year later, Dr. Block informed Marshall that he was showing signs of full-blown AIDS despite administration of available and appropriate medications. When Dr. Block made this diagnosis she was aware that Marshall lived with Susie.

During the time Marshall and Susie lived together, they had frequent sexual relations. Both followed the teachings of Guru Shwazili and ate only raw vegetables and abstained from drugs and alcohol. Marshall never informed Susie that he had tested positive for HIV or had developed full-blown AIDS. Susie was aware that Marshall had abused intravenous drugs in his past and had assumed that Marshall was aware of his risk of contracting AIDS and would tell her of any illness. She felt their relationship was built on love and trust.

Susie learned of Marshall's illness during his last hospitalization shortly before his death. She felt betrayed and angered that Marshall had deliberately made love to her knowing that he had AIDS that could be transferred to her.

Susie now lives with deep depression stemming from her worry that she will contract AIDS. Upon her doctor's advice, she regularly submits to blood tests and other physical examinations. So far these tests have come back negative but Susie continues to worry and is unable to work or enter any intimate relationships. What is the most appropriate tort doctrine upon which Susie may base her suit?

Library Resources

Handbook of the Law of Torts (Prosser on Torts), William L. Prosser, West Publishing Company, 1941. The "granddaddy" of tort texts. Advanced discussions on the application and theory of tort law.

Torts in a Nutshell, Edward J. Kionka, West Group, 1999. Part of the Nutshell series, this text provides a comprehensive yet accessible discussion of tort law.

Restatement on the Law of Torts, 2nd Edition, The American Law Institute. 1990 Scholarly discussions and reframing of tort doctrine.

Torts: Cases, Problems and Exercises, Russell L. Weaver, and John T. Cross., Anderson Publishing, 2002. Excellent in-depth text with explanations and case studies.

Online Resources

Jurist, http://www.jurist.law.pitt.edu
Good resource guide for locating relevant texts; also contains relevant articles on tort law.

Hieros Gamos, http://www.hg.org/torts.html
Good general-resource tort site.

Mega Law, http://www.megalaw.com/top/tort.php
Nice listing of related Web sites.

CHAPTER 3

Contracts

INTRODUCTION

Corporate law, real estate law, and general practice are just a few of the areas of legal practice in which a firm grasp of the theory of contract law is necessary. Paralegals may be involved in all aspects of contract law, from negotiations and drafting of contracts to breach of contract litigation. This chapter provides an overview of contract law theory.

THE ELEMENTS OF A VALID CONTRACT

contract: A legally enforceable agreement between two or more individuals or entities. The symbol of a lower case **"k"** is often used by lawyers and paralegals as an abbreviation for contract.

The most elementary definition of a **contract** is a legally enforceable agreement between two or more individuals or entities.

A number of elements must be satisfied in order for an agreement to be considered legally enforceable. In order for a contract to be legally enforceable, the following elements must be in place.

offer: The act that initiates the contract.

acceptance: The intent by the acceptor to be bound by the terms and conditions of the offer.

intent: A "meeting of the minds"; all parties to the contract share the same understanding regarding the terms and conditions of the contract they are entering.

consideration: Anything of value.

capacity: The legal qualification to engage in or perform an act that has legal consequences.

object: The goal or purpose of the contract.

- The contract must contain an **offer**.
- The offer must be **accepted**.
- All parties to the contract must manifest their **intent** to enter into the contract.
- **Consideration** must be provided.
- All parties to the contract must possess the **capacity** to enter into such an agreement.
- The **object** of the contract must be lawful.

Valid Contract Checklist

- ☑ offer
- ☑ acceptance
- ☑ meeting of the minds
- ☑ consideration
- ☑ capacity of parties
- ☑ lawfulobject

Exhibit 3-1 Valid Contract Checklist

1. Offer

The offer is the act that initiates the contract. The offer may be made orally or in written form. An offer may be simple: "I'll give you ten bucks for that lamp" or complex: a five-page written real estate contract. The party making the offer must intend to make an offer that may lead to a legally binding contract if the other elements are satisfied. The offer must be specific regarding to whom the offer is being made and the terms of the contract must be clear and unambiguous.

Practice Alert:

The Uniform Commercial Code (UCC), which applies to commercial contracts, imposes some additional requirements and has been adopted by most states. For example, under the UCC all commercial contracts must be written. In this chapter, we discuss the broad theory of contract law. Consult the UCC as adopted in your jurisdiction when dealing with commercial contracts.

The following are examples of valid and invalid offers:

- A valid offer: "I will pay you $50 to wash my car." (A specific, unambiguous offer to another party to do a certain act.)
- An invalid offer: "How much for the lamp?" (This is a non-specific inquiry; not an offer to purchase.)

Offers are generally revocable at will by the offeror at any time prior to acceptance, unless the terms of the offer state otherwise.

Advertisements are not considered valid offers because they contain non-specific offers to large groups of people. Advertisements are generally viewed as invitations to potential customers to come and make an offer, not as an offer itself. For example, an advertisement stating "Come to Super Electronics this Saturday only—iPods for $20.00" does not constitute an offer. (Although, if intentionally misleading, it may be subject to consumer protection laws.) The potential shopper is presumed to understand that the advertised goods may or may not be available at the time they are ready to purchase.

2. Acceptance

The second required element of a valid contract is acceptance. Acceptance is the intent by the acceptor to be bound by the terms and conditions set by the offer. A conditional acceptance of an offer does not constitute acceptance and a valid contract; it is a **counter-offer**.

counter-offer: A conditional acceptance of an offer in which the terms and conditions of the offer are changed.

During the course of negotiating a valid contract, many offers and counter-offers may be given back and forth before an enforceable contract is reached.

Consider the experience of buying a car. The salesperson approaches and says "She's a real beauty, huh? I can get you a great deal—only $15,000." (This constitutes an offer.) You reply "Okay, but throw in four-wheel drive and anti-lock brakes." (This constitutes a counter offer.) This process may continue until an agreement is reached and the essential elements of a valid contract are met or the negotiations are ended without an agreement and no valid contract is created.

3. Intent/Assent

All parties to a contract must manifest their intent to satisfy all essential terms of the contract. It is essential that all parties have a "meeting of the minds." In other words, the parties must share the same understanding regarding the terms and conditions of the contract they are entering. That is why it is vital that all terms of a contract be unambiguous.

Manifestation of the parties' intent can come in different forms. A party can manifest their intent to make an offer by pointing to an object and displaying the amount of money they wish to pay for it. This would constitute a valid offer because the party manifested his intent to offer through physical gestures.

Similarly, acceptance may be manifested by physical gesture, through written or oral communication. A common manifestation of intent to accept is the commencement of fulfilling the terms of the offer.

EXAMPLE Rita places a note in Anna's mailbox that states "If you will wash my windows, I will pay you $50." Anna reads the note, goes to Rita's house, and begins washing windows.

Intent has been demonstrated by each party in the following ways:

- Rita manifested her intent to make the offer and enter into the valid contract by writing the note and placing it in Anna's mailbox.
- Anna manifested her intent to accept Rita's offer by actually washing the windows.

Conflict and subsequent litigation on intent can arise in a number of different ways. What if one party to a contract manifests intent and a meeting of the minds at the time of signing the contract but later asserts that it was all meant as a "joke." In *Lucy v. Zehmer* (196 Va. 493, 84 S.E.2d 516 (1954)), the defendant claimed he was drunk and kidding when he offered to sell the plaintiff his farm for the fair market price of $50,000. The defendant claimed that the plaintiff should have known he was kidding even though the contract's terms were clear and unambiguous and the parties' mutual promises were enforceable.

The court found in favor of the plaintiff stating that the defendant's actions including writing the contract himself and asking his wife to sign all manifested his intent. "An agreement or mutual assent is of course essential to a valid contract but the law imputes to a person an intention corresponding to the reasonable meaning of his words and acts. If his words and acts, judged by a reasonable standard, manifest an intention to agree, it is immaterial what may be the real but unexpressed state of his mind."

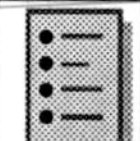

Discussion Point

Applying the standard stated in *Lucy v. Zehmer,* discuss scenarios in which an offeror's behavior would and would not manifest an intention to agree.

4. Consideration

Another essential element of a valid contract is consideration. Consideration is anything of value. It can be money, goods, services, and even a promise to not do something. Without consideration, an enforceable contract cannot be formed. That is why the promise of a gift is generally not considered an enforceable contract.

As with all essential elements of a contract, the parties must indicate that they mutually understand what the consideration is and assent to it. Accidental benefit does not constitute consideration, nor does something that a party would be obligated to do anyway. An example is "If you mow my lawn, I will let you drive my convertible to the baseball game." The consideration is the use of the convertible, which has no monetary value, but is still valuable. "If you paint my house, I will go to work today." In this example, the party is already obligated to go to work and therefore the act of going to work is not consideration.

5. Capacity of the Parties

It is generally assumed that parties entering into a contract have the capacity to do so. Instances in which a party may be deemed to lack legal capacity may include mental disability, such as those under the influence of drugs or alcohol, and minors. The determination of capacity is made on a case-by-case basis and is raised by the party claiming incapacity. If a party to a contract is found to lack capacity, the contract is considered invalid and legally unenforceable because no meeting of the minds regarding the contract is possible without capacity of all parties.

6. Object Must be Lawful

Finally, a contract is not enforceable if its object is illegal. This is a matter of public policy—it would not be in society's best interest to legally enforce contracts that involve illegal actions. Even though all the essential elements are satisfied and the agreement is otherwise a valid contract, if the object is illegal, it is not enforceable. For example, a contract to steal a car cannot be legally enforced as a matter of public policy.

TYPES OF CONTRACT

Once a valid contract has been established, it may be distinguished by its type. It is helpful to determine the type of contract in order to fully understand the roles of the parties and the agreement.

1. Unilateral Contract

A **unilateral contract** is a contract in which only one party makes a promise. The consideration in a unilateral contract is not a return promise but the completion of an act by one party.

unilateral contract: A contract in which only one party makes a promise.

EXAMPLE Elizabeth offers a reward of $100 for the return of her lost bracelet. David finds the bracelet and returns it to Elizabeth. Elizabeth is contractually obligated to give David $100. Only Elizabeth has made a promise—to pay $100 to whoever finds her bracelet.

2. Bilateral Contract

A **bilateral contract** is a contract in which promises are made on both sides. The consideration here is the promises to each other. The completion of the contract depends upon both parties keeping their promises.

bilateral contract: A contract in which promises are made by both parties.

EXAMPLE Grandma Jones is ill and fears she has only a short time to live. She calls her granddaughter, to whom she has always been close and says "Promise to come live with me and I promise to leave you all my money in my will." If the granddaughter accepts, the contract is unilateral because both sides have made promises to each other. (See *Davis v. Jacoby,* 1 Cal.2d 370, 34 P.2d 1026 (1934).)

3. Express Contract

express contract: A contract that is expressed in words, either orally or in written form.

An **express contract** is a contract that is expressed in words, either orally or in written form. All parties have reduced the essential elements of their contract into oral or written form. An example of an express contract is an insurance policy.

It should be noted that a provision included in the UCC and adopted by most states requires that a contract be made in written form under certain circumstances. This rule is called the **Statute of Frauds**.

Statute of Frauds: Doctrine requiring certain contracts to be in writing and adopted through the UCC in most states.

Those circumstances required by the UCC include: any contract that cannot be completely performed within one year of its commencement; any contract involving the sale or purchase of real estate; any contract to answer for the debt of another person; and any contract involving the sale of goods for a price in excess of $500. Different states may have additional or different requirements, so always consult your local jurisdiction's statutes.

4. Implied Contract

implied contract: A contract in which the essential elements of the contract are expressed through conduct of the parties.

An **implied contract** is a contact in which the essential elements of the contract are expressed through conduct of the parties.

EXAMPLE Norm goes to a self-serve gas station to fill his car's gas tank. He begins filling it. This action "implies" that Norm acknowledges his obligation to pay for the gas after filling the tank, even though there is no written or oral word exchange.

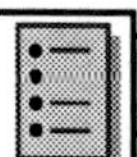

Discussion Point

Provide examples from your own experience of each type of contract discussed above: unilateral, bilateral, express, and implied.

BREACH OF CONTRACT

breach of contract: When a party to a contract fails to perform as promised in the contract, without legal justification.

A **breach of contract** occurs when a party fails to perform as promised in the contract, without legal justification. When a breach occurs, litigation often follows. It should be noted that the aggrieved party is always obligated to mitigate any damages that may occur as a result of the breach by the other party. In other words, the aggrieved party must make sure that no further damages result that may be prevented after the breach occurs.

Litigation for breach of contract may be based on different theories of the breach: simple, immaterial or partial, and material or total.

simple breach: One or more parties to a contract fails to fulfill one or more of the terms and conditions of the valid contract.

Simple breach of contract occurs when one of the parties fails to fulfill one or more of the terms and conditions of the agreed upon valid contract. For example, I agree to pay you $20 if you give me your textbook. You give me the textbook and I do not pay you.

immaterial breach: A breach of minor terms or provisions of the contract that does not materially change the nature or value of that contract.

Immaterial or partial breach is a breach of minor terms or provisions of the contract that does not materially change the nature or value of the contract. An aggrieved party may be entitled to some damages or other remedy as a result of the minor breach but is not entitled to cancel the contract.

The concept is well illustrated by a famous case written by Judge Cardozo for the New York Court of Appeals in 1921 (*Jacob & Youngs Inc. v. Kent*, 230 N.Y. 239, 129 N.E. 889 (1921)). In the case, the plaintiff had been hired to build a large country home for $77,000—a substantial fee in 1921. The contract called for a specific brand of plumbing pipe, Reading brand, to be installed. About a year after the defendant moved in, he found out that a different brand of pipe, Cohoes, had been installed. The defendant demanded that the walls be ripped down, the Cohoes pipes removed and Reading pipes installed. The plaintiff refused. The defendant, in turn, refused to pay the final payment and the plaintiff sued.

Cardozo found for the plaintiff stating that the mistake had been inadvertent and the pipes were substantially the same quality and therefore "the measure of allowance is not the cost of reconstruction." In other words, the difference from the agreed upon material was "trivial" and not a material change that would require the plaintiff to completely remedy.

Material or total breach is a breach of the major and material terms and conditions of the contract. Such a breach materially changes the nature and value of the contract, rendering it void. The aggrieved party is entitled to damages and to end the contract while also being relieved of any obligations under that contract.

material breach: A breach of major and material terms and conditions of the contract.

In *Jacob & Youngs,* if the default had involved a more visible item, such as using granite to face the front of the house instead of brick, the default may be considered material because it materially changes the nature and value of the building the parties had agreed upon.

REMEDIES

If the aggrieved party decides to sue for **damages**, there are different types of damages that may be applicable to compensate for the injury suffered as a result of the breach.

damages: The plaintiff's request for a sum of money to be paid by the defendant for civil wrongs committed by the defendant.

The following section describes some of the possible types of damages for breach of contract.

Compensatory Damages are awarded to compensate for the loss of benefits the plaintiff would have received had the defendant performed in conformance with the contract.

Compensatory Damages: Damages awarded to compensate for the loss of benefits the plaintiff would have received had the defendant performed in conformance with the contract.

The formation of a contract creates an expectancy by the parties that benefits will be obtained by the performance of the other party pursuant to the contract. When a breach occurs, damages are awarded in an attempt to place the victim as nearly as possible to their position if the contract had been performed. These damages may include actual financial loss suffered, such as the cost of hiring someone else to mitigate your damages. For example, Ariana hires Margot to paint her living room walls. Margot finishes half the room and leaves. Ariana could sue for the cost of hiring another painter to finish the job as compensatory damages.

Consequential Damages are expenses or losses beyond those compensatory damages that the plaintiff never would have incurred without the breach.

Consequential Damages: Damages awarded to compensate for expenses or other losses besides compensatory damages that occur as a result of the breach of contract.

For example, if a breach involves the installation of a faulty gas furnace that explodes, the compensatory damages would include repairing the building and replacing the furnace. The consequential damages would include the medical expenses and pain and suffering expenses incurred.

Specific performance is a situation in which the plaintiff is not suing for money damages, but for the actual performance called for in the contract. This remedy is based in equity and is used when money is not a satisfactory substitute because the subject of the contract is unique, such as real property or fine art.

specific performance: When the plaintiff sues to recover for the actual performance called for in the contract.

EXAMPLE A museum contracts to purchase a Matisse from a dealer. The dealer breaches the contract by refusing to give up the painting. The museum could sue for specific performance, asking the court to order the dealer to hand over the painting. The museum doesn't want money, only the Matisse to finish its collection.

rescission: A remedy in which the court cancels the contract and relieves the defendant of any economic benefit he derived as a result of his breach because such a result would be unjust.

Rescission is a remedy that asks the court to cancel the contract and restore the parties to their original state prior to the establishment of the contract. Specifically, the plaintiff asks the court to relieve the defendant of any economic gain he retained as a result of the breach. This remedy is generally sought when the breach is a result of mutual mistake or fraud where it would be unjust for the defendant to retain any economic benefit as a result of his breach.

EXAMPLE Anna agrees to sell her house to Sam and Sam provides a deposit. Sam asks Anna and her real estate agent if the home has termites; they answer it does not. An inspection reveals that the house is heavily infested with termites. The contract may be rescinded and Sam's deposit refunded. (See *Halpert v. Rosenthal,* 107 R.I. 406, 267 A.2d 730 (1970)).

Key Terms

acceptance
bilateral contract
breach of contract
capacity
Compensatory Damages
Consequential Damages
consideration
contract
counter-offer
damages
express contract
immaterial or partial breach
implied contract
intent
material or total breach
object
offer
rescission
simple breach of contract
specific performance
Statute of Frauds
unilateral contract

Exercises

For each of the following fact patterns, determine the following:

- whether a valid contract exists and is enforceable
- what type of contract
- whether a breach of contract exists, the basis for that breach
- if a breach exists, what type of remedy to pursue

1. Eileen, Kara, and Holly were having lunch together. Eileen said "I'd really love to get one of those new Dell notebooks—I'd pay at least $1500 for one." The next day Kara comes to Eileen's dorm room, hands her a new Dell notebook with a bill for $1500. Eileen refuses the notebook and refuses to pay Kara anything.

2. Don and his friend Pete run a small after-hours club in their apartment on the weekends as a way to make extra money selling liquor at an inflated price. They have a deal with Sandra to accept two cases of vodka every Thursday afternoon at $50 a case and two cases of club soda at $15 a case. One week Don and Pete accept Sandra's usual delivery but fail to make payment.

3. Karen is very fond of her niece Darla. Karen owns a piece of property in Martha's Vineyard and wishes to give the property to Darla in a few years and wants Darla to know she can count on having it. After doing some research on the Internet, Karen learns that a gratuitous promise is not binding so she writes up the following note and sends it to Darla: "I, Karen, hereby promise to sell my property located in Martha's Vineyard to my niece Darla for the sum of $1.00." Darla writes back to her aunt, with an enclosure of $1.00 "Thank you, Aunt Karen. I accept your offer."

4. Meg comes to work complaining about the new car she has just purchased. She states to a number of her co-workers "I'd love to unload that car." A co-worker, Dwayne, responds "I'll take it off your hands." Dwayne then wrote an agreement to purchase the car for the Kelly Blue Book price and Meg signed it and handed him the keys. Sam is aware that Meg has a substance abuse problem and was aware that ~~Sandra~~ Meg had ingested some drugs prior to signing. The next day, Meg tells Dwayne she wants her car back and that she never meant to sell the car to him; she thought he was joking.

5. Carter regularly sells and buys item on eBay, specializing in antique musical instruments. He posted a picture of a recent find along with this description: "Available: Rare and beautiful 1756 Stradavary violin." He immediately received many bids and a winning bid of $5, 600 was reached five days later. He duly shipped the item to the winning bidder, Sanford. Sanford received the violin and quickly recognized it as a 1756 Jacomo Stradavary violin whose work is considered by collectors to be inferior to the works of his brother, Mario Stradavary. The Jacomo violin's worth is estimated to be only $1,000 whereas a Mario violin would be worth $6,000. Sanford asks for his money back and Carter refuses.

6. Luke works at a small manufacturing company. For the past three years he and three co-workers have contributed $10 a piece to purchase lottery tickets whenever the jackpot reached $8 million or above. Luke would inform the other three co-workers when the pot reached $8 million, collect their contribution, and purchase the tickets. One week the pot reached $8 million and Luke informed two of the group but neglected to find Nick. Luke purchased the tickets without Nick's contribution. One of the tickets purchased contained the winning numbers and was worth $35 million. Nick approached Luke and asked for his share of the winnings. Luke and the other two co-workers declined to share.

A valid contract exists – all elements of a legally enforceable agreement exist: offer, acceptance, intent/assent, consideration, capacity of parties and object is lawful. It's a bilateral contract btw Luke and his 3 co-workers. There's a breach (simple) when Luke fails to tell Nick that the pot has reached 8 million and needs to contribute his $10. The remedy to pursue is compensatory damages, Nick's share of the $35 million.

Library Resources

Contracts in a Nutshell, Claude D. Rohwer, West Group, 2006.
This is an excellent and comprehensive discussion of all aspects of contract law.

Concepts and Case Analysis in the Law of Contracts 3d Edition, Marvin A. Chirelstein, Foundation Press, 2006.
A valuable overview of contracts.

Online Resources

Legal Information Institute, http://www.law.cornell.edu/topics/contracts.html
Always an excellent source. The discussion on contract law contains a nice overview as well as valuable case references.

Legal Database, http://www.legal-database.com/contractlaw.htm
Quick overview of key points, including Statute of Frauds.

CHAPTER 4

Criminal Law

INTRODUCTION

This chapter provides an overview of theory and application of criminal law. Paralegals practicing criminal law are either employed by the government prosecuting criminal violations or employed by attorneys defending criminal defendants. Exercises are included that are designed to illustrate the important elements of criminal law.

THEORY OF CRIMINAL LAW

Criminal law is distinguished from civil law by its punishment. A criminal defendant found guilty of a crime may be sentenced to serve time in prison whereas civil remedies do not include imprisonment. The deprivation of liberty and freedom is the most severe punishment that can be given and therefore the constitutional protections offered are strong.

Constitutional guarantees applicable to the criminal process include those listed in the following section.

The **Fourth Amendment** prohibits "unreasonable search and seizure" and requires a showing of "probable cause" for the issuance of any search warrant or arrest warrant.

The **Fifth Amendment** requires indictment by a grand jury for persons held for "capital" or "otherwise infamous" crime. The Fifth amendment prohibits double jeopardy and requiring a criminal defendant to "be a witness against himself" and provides that no citizen shall "be deprived of life, liberty, or property without due process of law."

The **Eighth Amendment** states that "Excessive bail shall not be required, nor excessive fines imposed, nor cruel and unusual punishments inflicted."

The **Fourteenth Amendment** prohibits the states from making or enforcing any law that abridges the "privileges or immunities" of citizens of the United States and further holds that no state shall "deprive any person of life, liberty, or property, without due process of law; nor deny to any person within its jurisdiction the equal protection of the laws."

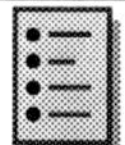

Discussion Point

Think of current criminal cases you have read about in the news. Which constitutional issues have been discussed? Discuss how these constitutional guarantees play a role in every citizen's life.

In criminal prosecutions, the state bears the burden of proof. This means that the state must prove that the defendant is guilty of the crime beyond a reasonable doubt. This standard is intended to give the criminal defendant the benefit of any reasonable doubt. If jurors believe the defendant is only probably guilty of a crime, or they have a reasonable belief of a possibility of innocence, they must acquit. However, a passing or imaginary doubt is not reasonable doubt. The rationale is that it is better that 20 guilty people are set free than one innocent person imprisoned.

A criminal defendant is not required to present any evidence; the burden of proof rests entirely upon the prosecution. However, in practice most criminal defendants do mount a defense.

mens rea: The state of mind that makes the performance of a particular act a crime.

perpetrator: One who commits a crime.

Another substantial difference between criminal law and civil law is the concept of **mens rea**. Mens rea translates from Latin as "guilty mind" and is the state of mind that makes the performance of a particular act a crime. (Random House dictionary)

This essential element requires that in order for an act to be criminal in nature, the **perpetrator** of the act must have certain intentions. Some crimes require a high level of intent whereas others require less. This idea of required mens rea is consistent with the idea that harsher criminal sanctions are appropriate for those who intend to cause harm, not those who cause harm without intent to do so.

EXAMPLE The statutes of the State of South Carolina provide: "'Murder' is the killing of any person with malice aforethought, either express or implied." (Sec. 16-3-10) Mens rea is a required element of the crime of murder expressed through the phrase "malice aforethought." In order to be found guilty of the crime of murder in the South Carolina, the jury must find that the defendant intended to kill the victim.

"With regard to the crime of involuntary manslaughter, criminal negligence is defined as the reckless disregard of the safety of others." (Sec. 16-3-60) Mens rea is not a required element of the crime of involuntary manslaughter in South Carolina. The "reckless disregard of the safety of others" requires only that the defendant acted in reckless disregard, not that he intended to cause harm. This reckless disregard is a level of recklessness higher than the civil standard for negligence (i.e., the defendant's lack of regard for the safety of others was so blatant that criminal sanctions are appropriate) but the act was not premeditated with the mens rea to cause harm and therefore the criminal sanctions will be less than that for murder.

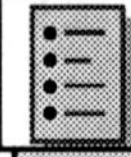

Discussion Point

Provide examples within criminal law of the varying degrees of mens rea required for different crimes.

Criminal law is generally encoded in statutes. The elements of each individual crime are included within the statute. Each element of the crime must be satisfied in order for a defendant to be found guilty of a crime. The state alone prosecutes criminal offenses. Unlike civil cases in which one individual can initiate an action against another individual, in criminal cases only the state has the authority, through the police and judicial systems, to prosecute and ultimately punish defendants.

Practice Alert

Each state has its own code of criminal procedure as does the federal court system. Consult your jurisdiction's rules of procedure.

Specific Crimes

Most crimes can be divided into three basic categories: (1) Crimes against the person; (2) Crimes against property; and (3) Inchoate crimes. It is not possible to discuss every type of crime here but a good representation of the three types of crimes are discussed.

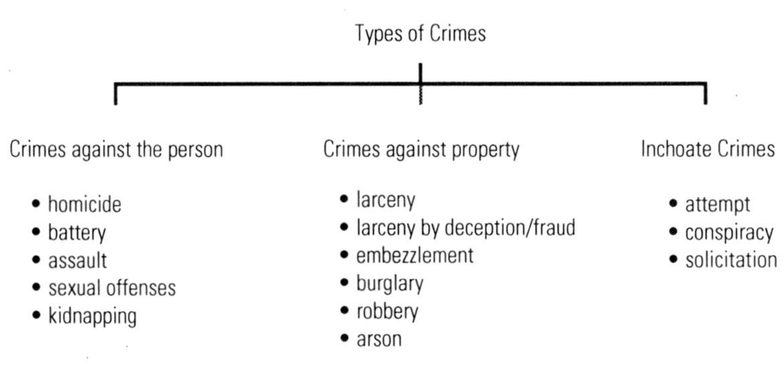

Exhibit 4-1 Types of Crimes

1. Crimes Against the Person

a. Homicide

Homicide is an act or omission resulting in the death of another person. Homicide can be further classified into degrees depending upon the intent and acts of the perpetrator.

Practice Alert

Each state legislates its own criminal homicide statutes and classifies the degrees of murder according to those statutes. Please consult your jurisdiction's statutes for the specific classification.

There are several types of homicide, as described in the following section.

- **Malice aforethought homicide** is a type of homicide that includes the most heinous acts and carries the most severe penalties.
- Intentional killings are killings that are premeditated by the perpetrator. For example, Lee is angry that Samantha stole money from him. Lee gets a gun, follows Samantha home, and shoots her dead.
- Another type of homicide is the killing resulting from outrageously reckless behavior. For example, Nancy throws a brick off an overpass to a busy highway, striking a vehicle and causing its driver to crash and die.
- Killings can also result from the perpetrator's intent to inflict serious bodily harm on the victim. For example, Kevin is angry that

Joe stole money from him. Kevin beats Joe with a baseball bat, intending to injure him. Joe dies as a result of his injuries.

- **Felony murder** is a statutory offense that provides that any death resulting from a dangerous felony is murder

EXAMPLE Reuben and Zach are robbing a bank. While fleeing after the robbery the security guard attempts to stop Zach. Zach fires his gun and kills the guard. Both Zach and Reuben would be liable for the guard's homicide under the felony murder rule. Vermont provides a good example of a detailed homicide statute that classifies murder into degrees:

Vermont Sec. 13 V.S.A. 2301: Murder committed by means of poison, or by lying in wait, or by willful, deliberate and premeditated killing, or committed in perpetrating or attempting to perpetrate arson, sexual assault, aggravated sexual assault, robbery or burglary, shall be murder in the first degree. All other kinds shall be murder in the second degree.

- **Manslaughter**: The crime of causing the death of another person under circumstances falling short of murder. There are two types of manslaughter, voluntary and involuntary. Voluntary manslaughter includes killings that would be considered murder except for certain extenuating circumstances. The classic example of voluntary manslaughter is the "crime of passion." A woman kills her husband in a fit of rage after finding him in bed with another woman. Her inflamed passion is the extenuating circumstance that makes the killing manslaughter and not murder. Involuntary manslaughter includes killings through recklessness or what is known in some states as criminal negligence. Involuntary manslaughter may also result when the killing is unintentional but caused by the defendant while perpetrating a crime other than a felony. For example, a motorist driving 100 mph down a highway collides with another vehicle causing the death of a passenger. The recklessness of driving at such an excessive speed was the cause of the death and is involuntary manslaughter.

Discussion Point

Provide three facts patterns to support prosecution for malice aforethought homicide. Provide two facts patterns to support prosecution for voluntary manslaughter. Provide two facts patterns to support prosecution for crime involuntary manslaughter.

b. Battery

Battery is intentional bodily injury or offensive touching of another. Generally grouped with assault (see next), battery is a criminal offense to the person's body. Physical contact must be made in order for the crime of battery to occur. For example, punching someone in a bar fight constitutes battery.

c. Assault

Assault is the intentional infliction of the fear of bodily injury or offensive touching (battery). Note that no bodily contact is required for the crime of assault. For example, Meghan waves a knife at Samantha ordering her to give up all her money or she will "cut her up." Assault and battery are crimes that are often committed at the same time and therefore are often grouped together statutorily. Assault and battery are also often divided by statute according to severity of the physical injury and whether a weapon was used during the commission of the crime.

d. Sexual Offenses

A **sexual offense** is the intentional touching of another person in a sexual way without that person's consent, or when that person lacks the capacity to legally give effective consent. Sexual offenses can range from rape (forcible sexual intercourse) to fondling in a sexual manner (sometimes called sexual assault). Each state has its own statutory definitions and classifications of sexual offenses. For example, in most states it is a crime for an adult to have sexual relations with a child under the age of 16. Children are considered incapable of legally consenting to sexual relations and therefore the act is a crime often called statutory rape.

e. Kidnapping

Kidnapping is the forcible removal of a person against their will for ransom, use as a hostage, or harming or terrorizing that person or others. Once again, each state has its own statute for kidnapping and federal law applies to kidnappings that cross state lines.

2. Crimes Against Property

a. Larceny

Larceny is the wrongful taking of personal property of another with the intent to convert it to one's own use. Simply put, larceny is stealing someone else's property with the intent to keep it permanently. Many states categorize larceny by the value of the property stolen, using terms like grand larceny and petty larceny. For example, if your car is stolen from the mall parking lot by a thief who sells it in the next state to a chop shop.

b. Larceny by Fraud and Deception

The criminal counterpart to the tort of intentional misrepresentation, **larceny by deception and fraud** can include a variety of offenses like forgery, mail fraud, and larceny by trick. The essential elements to the crime are knowingly making a false representation about a material fact, generally pecuniary in nature, with the intent that the victim rely on it to their detriment. For example, a car dealer tells you a car you are considering "has only 40,000 miles and has never been in an accident." You purchase the car based on that representation. Two months later, the car needs $2,000 in repairs and you discover that it actually has 120,000 miles and has been involved in three front-end collisions.

c. Embezzlement

Embezzlement is the unlawful conversion of the personal property of another by one who has lawful possession of the property. The distinguishing element of embezzlement is the requirement that the conversion is made by one who has lawful possession of the property. For example, a bookkeeper for a law firm takes $10,000 from a client security fund and uses it to gamble at a local casino. As a bookkeeper, he had lawful "possession" of the funds but is guilty of the crime of embezzlement once he converts those funds to his own use.

d. Burglary

Breaking and entering into the dwelling of another with the intent to commit a crime therein is called **burglary**. The elements of burglary have been interpreted differently in various jurisdictions and in many ways expanded past this traditional definition. For example, shops and cars are often included in modern burglary statutes along with the traditional "dwelling."

e. Robbery

The taking of someone's money or other personal property from the victim's person or in the victim's presence by force or threat of imminent harm is called **robbery**. The element of robbery that distinguishes it from larceny and burglary, is the direct, physical involvement of the victim with the added factor of personal danger. Most states categorize robbery into armed robbery, involving the use of a dangerous weapon, and unarmed robbery. For example, while withdrawing money from an ATM a masked person confronts you with a gun and orders you to hand over all your money. This would constitute armed robbery. A mugger who snatches a purse commits unarmed robbery.

f. Arson

Arson is the act of intentionally causing a dangerous fire or explosion, especially for the purpose of destroying a building of another.

3. Inchoate Crimes

inchoate crimes: "Attempt-type" crimes.

Inchoate crimes are "attempt-type" crimes in which the planning and intent are elements of the crime.

attempt: a serious and substantial but unsuccessful effort to commit a particular crime.

The two most common types of inchoate crimes are attempt and solicitation. **Attempt** is a serious and substantial but unsuccessful effort to commit a particular crime. The rationale for attempt as a criminal charge is that it is necessary to punish those who try to commit a crime but for some reason are unsuccessful in doing so. The prosecution must prove that the actions of the defendant satisfies all required elements of the attempted crime and that only the intended outcome did not take place.

EXAMPLE Daphne is charged with attempted burglary in the second degree in Arizona. She was found inside her ex-boyfriend's apartment holding a crow bar next to a broken window. When questioned by police officers she told them she had broken the window, climbed into the apartment intending to steal his collection of Barry Manilow records but had changed her mind and was about to climb back out the window without the records when the police arrived. Daphne is charged with attempted Burglary in the second degree, which provides:

Sec. 13-1507; (A) A person commits burglary in the second degree by entering or remaining unlawfully in or on a residential structure with the intent to commit any theft or felony therein.

Daphne's acts fulfill all elements of the crime of burglary, in that she entered the apartment unlawfully by breaking the window and she intended to steal the records. The fact that she did not actually steal the records makes her crime an attempted burglary in the second degree.

b. Conspiracy

Conspiracy is an agreement between two or more individuals to commit an unlawful act or a lawful act in an unlawful manner. As discussed earlier, merely thinking about committing a crime (mens rea) is not a crime, the mens rea must be coupled with the act of committing a crime (**actus reus**). In the crime of conspiracy, the agreement to commit an unlawful act constitutes the actus reus and the intent to commit the unlawful act constitutes the mens rea. Conspiracy requires that two or more individuals agree to commit a crime. A single person cannot commit the crime of conspiracy; without the act of agreeing with another person, only the mens rea would exist and hence no crime would be committed.

Conspiracy: The agreement between two or more individuals to commit an unlawful act or a lawful act in an unlawful manner.

EXAMPLE Velma lives above a bank. She devises a plan to rob the bank by drilling through her bedroom floor into the vault. Realizing she needs some brute strength, Velma calls her pal Fred and tells him of her plan. Fred agrees that Velma has a terrific idea and tells her he will purchase the drilling equipment the next day. Velma and Fred are arrested that night and charged with conspiracy.

Velma and Fred's acts fulfill all elements of the crime of conspiracy, in that they agreed to rob the bank together and made plans to do so (actus rea), they intended to rob the bank together (mens rea), and robbing a bank is an unlawful act.

Key Terms

actus reus
arson
assault
attempt
battery
burglary
conspiracy
Eighth Amendment
embezzlement
felony murder
Fifth Amendment
Fourteenth Amendment
Fourth Amendment
homicide
inchoate crimes
kidnapping
larceny
larceny by fraud and deception
malice aforethought
manslaughter (voluntary and involuntary)
mens rea
perpetrator
robbery
sexual offenses

Exercises

Complete the following exercises. Be sure to look at the accompanying statutes that are provided at the end of the questions. Use these statutes to determine culpability. You may also discuss any applicable criminal charges you can think of that are not listed in the included statutes.

1. Monica and Rachel are long-time best friends. Rachel is diagnosed with a neurological disorder that doctors predict will cause her to become paralyzed within six months and die within 12 months. Rachel confides to Monica that she does not want to die this way and would much rather "be put out of her misery." Monica goes to Rachel's hospital bed the next day and suffocates Rachel with a pillow. What crime(s) should Monica be charged with and why?

2. Bobby is a bookkeeper for a large grocery store chain. One of his duties is to count and bag all cash receipts each afternoon and bring them to the bank for deposit. For the past year, Bobby has taken at least $50 from the cash deposits and used the money to fund his gambling habit. One day his coworker Marcia hides a small video recorder in his cubicle because she is suspicious that he has been taking coffee from the communal pot without leaving a contribution. Viewing the tape later that day, Marcia sees Bobby taking cash from the bag and placing it in his wallet. She confronts him the next day and says she will not turn him in if he promises to give her $50 a day. Bobby agrees and begins to take $100 from the cash deposit each day. Six months later an internal audit reveals that the money is missing. Discuss who, if anyone, may be charged with which, if any, crime(s)? Explain your reasoning.

3. Ross lives with his wife Emily in a small subdivision. The homes in the subdivision are similar in size and style. One evening Emily returns home with the news that she has just been named supervising paralegal at the law firm where she is employed. In celebration of this news, Ross breaks open a bottle of fine merlot he has been saving for such an occasion. At 9:00 p.m., after the pair consumed two bottles of the fine wine, Ross receives a phone call from the insurance company where he works, asking him to come in to help with an emerging computer crisis. Emily, disappointed but sleepy, has a nightcap and goes to bed.

Meanwhile, next door to Ross and Emily, their neighbors Joey and Phoebe are having an argument. Newly wed, Joey is certain Phoebe is having an affair and after their argument drives to a local pub. After drinking five shots of whiskey in two hours, Joey drives home and tries to enter his front door but finds it locked. Joey believes that Phoebe has changed the locks but he has actually mistaken Ross and Emily's home for his own. Joey breaks open a basement window and makes his way to the stairs, ready to confront Phoebe. He stumbles over a space heater, hits his head becomes unconscious. When Joey awakes a minute later, he sees that the space heater has caused a fire and that he is not in his own basement. He leaves through the broken window and drives to his mother's house. He does not call the fire department, figuring that someone will see the fire and call. He then goes to sleep on the couch.

Emily, in a deep sleep, does not hear the smoke alarm. Ross returns home an hour after the fire has started and noticing the flames, calls the fire department. Unfortunately, it is too late to save Emily and she dies.

You are a paralegal assisting the state's attorney. She has asked to you write a memorandum telling her whom (if anyone) she should prosecute, for what crime(s). Be sure to include your reasoning.

Applicable Laws

Sec. 19-42 Murder

Murder committed by means of poison, or by lying in wait, or by willful, deliberate and premeditated killing, or committed in perpetrating or attempting to perpetrate arson, sexual assault, aggravated sexual assault, robbery or burglary, shall be murder in the first degree. All other kinds shall be manslaughter.

Sec. 19-43 Manslaughter

(1) A person is guilty of manslaughter when:
  (a) a killing is committed recklessly; or
  (b) a killing which would otherwise be murder is committed under the influence of extreme mental or emotional disturbance.

Sec. 20-56 Burglary

A person is guilty of burglary if he unlawfully enters a building or occupied structure, with the purpose of committing a crime therein.

Sec. 20-60 Arson

A person is guilty of arson if he starts a fire or causes an explosion with the purpose of:
  (a) destroying a building or occupied structure of another; or
  (b) destroying or damaging any property, whether his own or another's, to collect insurance for such loss.

Sec. 20-58 Assault

A person is guilty of assault if he:

(a) attempts to cause or purposely, knowingly, or recklessly causes bodily injury to another; or

(b) negligently causes bodily injury to another with a deadly weapon; or

(c) attempts by physical menace to put another in fear of imminent serious bodily harm.

Sec. 5-78 Criminal Conspiracy

(1) Definition of conspiracy. A person is guilty of conspiracy with another person or persons to commit a crime if with the purpose of promoting or facilitating commission he:

(a) agrees with such other person or persons that they or one or more of them will engage in conduct which constitutes such a crime or an attempt to commit such crime; or

(b) agrees to aid such other person or persons in the planning or commission of such crime or of an attempt or solicitation to commit such crime.

Sec. 7-3 Criminal Embezzlement

A person is guilty of embezzlement if he unlawfully converts funds over which he has a fiduciary duty to his own use.

Library Resources

Criminal Law: Examples and Explanations 3rd Edition, Richard G. Singer & John Q. LaFond, Aspen Publishers, 2004.
Good criminal law overview and resource.

Gilbert Law Summaries: Criminal Law (17th Ed), George E. Dix, Harcourt Legal and Professional, 2001.
One of the primary law school summaries—a supplement to the law school course.

Online Resources

Legal Information Institute at Cornell, http://www.law.cornell.edu/topics/criminal.html
As always, a terrific overview of the substantive law topic.

Nolo Law Center, http://www.nolo.com/resource
Provides articles on specific criminal law topics.

Jurist, http://jurist.law.pitt.edu/sg_crim.htm
Provides good links and listing of criminal law periodicals and articles.

PART 2

THE LITIGATION PROCESS

CHAPTER 5

Legal Interviewing and Investigation for the Paralegal

INTRODUCTION

An important skill of the legal profession is the ability to communicate with and extract information from our clients. As a paralegal, you will often interact directly with clients and other individuals and need to be able to make them feel comfortable with you while professionally obtaining relevant information.

THE ART OF LEGAL INTERVIEWING

client counseling: The act of giving advice to a client that only an attorney may do.

legal interviewing: The process of obtaining relevant information from an individual for a specific case.

intake interview: The initial interview the client has when hiring a firm.

Paralegals do not counsel clients. **Client counseling** involves giving legal advice to clients that ethically only attorneys may do. (See Chapter 10 for a detailed ethics discussion.)

However, paralegals regularly interview clients and other persons. **Legal interviewing** is the process of obtaining relevant information from an individual for a specific case.

Paralegals may conduct legal interviews in many different contexts. Here are just a few examples:

- A paralegal in a small medical malpractice plaintiff's firm is asked to conduct an **intake interview** for a new client. In this interview, the paralegal obtains basic biographical information and the facts surrounding the clients' injury.
- A paralegal in the trust and estates division of a large firm is asked to call a number of banks and insurance companies to find out what accounts may be included in an estate. The paralegal must know what questions to ask to elicit the information he needs.
- A paralegal in a mid-sized personal injury plaintiff's firm accompanies the firm's investigator into the field to conduct interviews of witnesses to their client's motor vehicle accident.

Discussion Point

What other examples of legal interviewing and investigation can you think of?

Preparation is vital in conducting effective legal interviews and investigations. Before beginning any type of legal interview, you must learn as much as you can about the person you will be interviewing as well as the law guiding the interview. For example, if you are interviewing a witness to a motor vehicle accident that your client was involved in, you should know as much biographical information about the witness as possible (name, employment, etc.) and also have a good understanding of the theory of negligence that your client's case is based upon.

Many firms have prepared checklists used in interviews to ensure that all relevant information is gathered. This is often true of firms that specialize in an area of law, such as medical malpractice or personal injury. These checklists allow the paralegal to avoid "re-inventing the wheel" every time she interviews someone with the same type of claim. It is important to remember, however, that as valuable as checklists can be, you must be flexible enough to veer from them when necessary to obtain important information not mentioned in the checklist.

Fillmore & Harding, P.C.
100 President's Avenue
Suite 805-B
Washington, D.C.

Medical Malpractice
Client Interview Checklist

- ❑ Full name and address ______________________
- ❑ Date of incident(s) ______________
- ❑ Client phone ( )-________
- ❑ Client email ____________
- ❑ Preferred method of contact
- ❑ Insurance
  - Company ________ Contact ________
  - phone________ email________
- ❑ Medical (doctors)
  - Firm / hospital ________
  - Contact ______
  - phone________ email ____________
- ❑ Current medical condition
  ____
  ____
  ____

Exhibit 5-1 Interview Checklist

Many interviews will be conducted by more than one person, such as a paralegal and attorney, a paralegal and legal investigator, two paralegals, and so on. A **legal investigator** is an employee dedicated to conducting investigations. This person generally has some understanding of the law but is not trained as a paralegal. Their expertise lies in leading investigations. Not all firms hire legal investigators; often paralegals and attorneys in the office will conduct all investigations.

legal investigator: An employee dedicated to conducting investigations.

A bit of psychology and common sense are helpful in performing an effective interview. The following is an **interview checklist**, which will be helpful to follow during the interview process.

HELPFUL TIPS FOR CONDUCTING LEGAL INTERVIEWS

Develop trust.

Extend your hand for a shake first and always start with a smile. Most people entering a legal office or meeting with an attorney or paralegal are nervous and unsure. It is your job as a paralegal to put them at ease. Realize that the vast majority of people who walk into a law office are there because they have a problem they want fixed.

Project a professional image.

Be aware of how you are dressed; be sure you project a professional image. Your office or conference area should be tidy, organized, and private. Be sure to introduce yourself as a paralegal.

Be empathetic.

A person is more likely to be forthcoming with information if they feel they are being understood. By displaying empathy you demonstrate to the witness they you understand their problem. Responses such as "I understand that must have been difficult for you" can go a long way in developing an empathetic relationship.

Don't get defensive.

Avoid questions that appear judgmental or harsh. This type of question can make the interviewee defensive and hostile. Similarly, you should strive to maintain a pleasant demeanor during difficult interviews.

Be flexible in your questioning.

Sometimes you need to follow the lead of the person you are interviewing. If your conversation takes you to an area you had not considered, it is often worthwhile to follow through.

Be able to take a rambling statement and put the interview back on track. Derive the facts.

As important as it is to be flexible, it is equally important to keep the interview in focus. An outline or checklist prepared prior to the start of the interview is helpful with this point.

Consider your demeanor and body language.

Slouching, lack of eye contact, and crossed arms all indicate a lack of interest. This type of negative body language should be avoided by the interviewer.

Do not rush and minimize office distractions.

Allow ample time for the interview. It is important that the meeting does not feel rushed or unimportant. Keep office distractions down to a minimum by turning down your phone ringer and closing the door.

Always ask permission before taking notes.

It can be distracting and intimidating to speak with someone as they write down every word you say. Always ask if it is all right to take notes. Most people will say yes. Be sure to maintain eye contact as you take any notes.

Be able to communicate what you've learned to your supervisor. Include candid observations.

Most attorneys will ask you to prepare a memorandum summarizing the interview. (See the sample that follows.) Follow the format used by your office. Most will ask for your candid observations so be sure to include them in a respectful and professional manner.

Look for inconsistencies and gaps.

As you conduct the interview, be conscious of any factual inconsistencies or gaps. You can then ask follow-up questions to clarify.

Ask the interviewee for their help.

Studies have shown that people are more open to honestly sharing information if they are asked for their help. See: *Legal Interviewing and Counseling in a Nutshell* for more tips on this aspect of interviewing. Using phrases such as "Your information is very important and we really appreciate your assistance" conveys a sense of importance and collegiality to the interviewee.

Write a summary of the interview as soon as possible.

Write your summary of the interview while it is still fresh in your mind. Waiting too long after the interview has taken place risks forgetting small but possibly important details.

If asked for advice, refer to an attorney. Make your status as a paralegal clear.

As previously discussed, paralegals may not give legal advice. Refer any legal questions to your attorney and be sure that the person you are interviewing is clear from the start that you are a paralegal, not an attorney.

Phrase your questions intelligently.

How you phrase your questions will determine the type of response you will receive. Open-ended questions such as "Tell me what happened that day" employ a "storytelling" method that may generate a lot of information but may be too generalized or rambling. Mixing open-ended questions with more specific questions such as "While you were stopped at the red light, what other cars did you see?" can often garner the most valuable information efficiently.

Apply listening versus hearing.

One of the skills of a good interviewer is the ability to listen, not just hear, what the person is saying. When you listen, you take in what the person is saying and try to understand it without making judgments or conclusions.

THE EFFECTIVE INTERVIEW

The effective interview incorporates all of these skills and techniques. Consider the following illustration.

Ineffective interview:

Client: I'm not sure what you can do for me. My wife made me come see you.
Paralegal: Okay, why don't you tell me what is happening.
C Okay, I will tell you what is happening—those jerks down at work have fired me!
P Why?
C Aw, I don't know...
P Did you do something wrong?
C NO! Do you think I'm a criminal or something? I was a great employee—the best they had!!

In this example of an ineffective interview the paralegal:

- Asks specific questions that do not allow the client room to respond fully.
- Fails to display any empathy by using empathic responses.
- Places the client on the defensive by asking the judgmental question "Did you do something wrong?"

EFFECTIVE INTERVIEW:

C I'm not sure what you can do for me. My wife made me come see you.

P It's understandable to be hesitant. Take your time and when you are ready tell me what happened to bring you here today.

C I was fired for no reason! They gave me this new dumb boss and he hates me. I did nothing wrong and he gave me the axe!

P You obviously feel you did a good job and it was wrong that you were fired—that is upsetting.

C You can say that again. I did good work for them. I like what I do, or did, I guess.

P I understand. It is hard to know a boss's expectations.

C Exactly. That stupid boss said he fired me because I caused too much trouble on the floor. I could run that place—I know more about that factory than anyone! It just burns me up!

P Is that why you are so angry or are there other reasons too?

C Well, yeah but I'm also worried I'm never going to get another job. This is a pretty small town you know.

P Well, we're going to talk about your concerns for your future and what happened on the job. Let's start by going through your story from the beginning. When did you begin work at the factory...

In this example of an effective interview because the paralegal:

- Uses empathy to gain the trust of the client.
- Employs the storytelling method to elicit facts.
- Avoids judgmental questions.

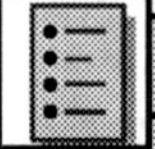

Discussion Point

Consider some of your own experiences in being interviewed (school, jobs, etc.). What made them positive/negative experiences?

SUMMARIZING THE INTERVIEW

Soon after the conclusion of the interview, a summary must be written. The **interview summary** includes all relevant facts gathered from the interview as well as observations and recommendations. Some firms prefer to have this summary written in an interoffice memorandum form, others have specific forms.

Harrison, Grant & Polk, LLC.
100 President's Avenue
Suite 806-E
Washington, D.C.

To: Attorney Angus
From: Pete Paralegal
Re: Initial interview of David Richard, File No. 070261

A. Biographical Information

Mr. Richard is a 54 year old, white male who is considering a civil suit against his former employer based on a claim of age discrimination.

I met with Mr. Richard on _________. He provided the following facts:

- Mr. Richard had been employed by Acme Mechanical for thirty two years.
- His most current position was senior mechanic...
- He had a red 1968 Chevy

Exhibit 5–2 Sample Interview Summary

Key Terms

Client counseling	Intake interview	Interview checklist
Legal interviewing	Legal investigator	Interview summary

Exercises

In this role-playing exercise, you will work with a partner. One student will play the role of the client, the other of the paralegal interviewer. The interviewer will have 10 minutes to prepare questions and 25 minutes to conduct the interview—use the *entire* 25 minutes!

At the end of the interview, the client should complete the evaluation form found at the end of this exercise and then review with the interviewer. You will then switch roles using Scenario 2 on the following pages and follow the same evaluation process.

Look only at the portion of this exercise that pertains to the role you are playing—no cheating! Have fun!

Scenario 1. To Client:

You are a 65-year-old woman/man meeting for the first time with a paralegal from the law firm you have just retained to handle a medical malpractice claim. Feel free to make up any details (name, address, etc.) but stick to the basic facts provided. Do not volunteer information. Try to play the role!

Six months ago, you underwent a procedure called liposuction in an effort to regain your girlish/boyish figure. While recovering in the hospital, you overheard one nurse state to another nurse, "Dr. Shakes did it again. This time he left in a sponge." You confronted Dr. Shakes who in turn admitted he had left in a "small sponge" in your abdominal cavity, but assured you that it would have no effect on your health. Subsequent X-rays have confirmed that you do indeed have a small sponge in your abdominal region.

Since then, you have suffered from frequent pains in your side, insomnia, and a phobia of sponges, all of which affect your daily life and have prevented you from embarking on a long-planned vacation to Graceland.

Miscellaneous Facts:

You've been married three times and you've sued two other doctors for malpractice, both over 20 years ago.

Scenario 1. To Interviewer:

Conduct an initial interview with this client. All you know about the case thus far is that your office has agreed to represent this client and that he/she has a medical malpractice claim.

Gather all relevant facts and information to provide the basis for investigation and settlement negotiations. Start by introducing yourself and stating the purpose of the interview. Take notes after requesting the client's permission. If time permits, you will write an intake memo from these notes in class.

Scenario 2. To Witness:

You are a 22-year-old man/woman who has been charged with criminal assault and battery. You are meeting for the first time to tell your story to a paralegal in the law office you have retained to represent you. Feel free to make up details (name, address, friend's names, etc.) but stick to the basic facts. Do not volunteer information. Try to play the role!

You are a member of a semi-famous (i.e., one-hit wonder) rock band. While on tour two weeks ago, you and your bandmates stopped at a local pub after your gig opening for a famous rock band at the local arena. After quaffing three pints of beer in quick succession, you decided to give karoake a go. While belting out a spirited rendition of "Stand By Your Man" a member of the audience began heckling you. Outraged, (you are famous, right?) you lunged at the heckler, yelling "I'm an artist—I'll get you for this!" and smacked him in the head with the karoake microphone. The local police were summoned and you were arrested and booked for assault and battery. The heckler suffered lacerations to his head but was released from the hospital the same evening.

Miscellaneous Facts:

You are a large contributor to many charities as well as the president's last campaign and you have a sealed juvenile record for dealing drugs at 15.

Scenario 2. To Interviewer:

Please conduct an initial interview with this client. All you know about the case thus far is that he/she has been charged with criminal assault and battery and has retained your firm to represent him/her. Gather all relevant facts and information to provide a basis for investigation and initial meetings with prosecutors. Start by introducing yourself and stating the purpose of your interview. Take notes with the client's permission. If time permits, you will write an intake memo based on these notes.

Legal Interviewing Evaluation Form Score all questions (1 = not at all, 3 = somewhat, 5= mostly, 7 = absolutely) and make additional comments.

Did the interviewer gain your trust?

____

____

____

____

____

____

Did the interviewer project a professional image and demeanor?

Did the interviewer demonstrate empathy in her questioning?

Did the interviewer appear flexible in her questioning?

Did the interviewer direct the questioning effectively?

Did the interviewer derive all relevant information?

What information did the interviewer fail to elicit?

Did the interviewer listen effectively?

Does the written summary accurately and clearly represent the interview?

____

____

____

____

____

____

Library Resources

Legal Interviewing and Counseling in a Nutshell (3rd ed.), Thomas L. Shaffer & James R. Elkins, West Group, 1997.

101 Ways to Improve Your Communication Skills Instantly (4th Ed)., Jo Cardrill, Goalminds, Inc., 2005.

Effective Client Communications Handbook: A lawyer's handbook for interviewing and counseling, Paul M. Lisnek, West Publishing Co., 1992.

Online Resources

Mindtools, http://www.mindtools.com
Includes helpful articles on active listening and other communications skills.

U.S. Air Force, http://www.au.af.mil/au/awc/awcgate/awc-comm.htm#general
U.S. Air Force site with good articles on developing effective communication skills.

CHAPTER 6

Civil Procedure

INTRODUCTION

In order for a lawsuit to be formally initiated, certain rules of court must be observed. Each jurisdiction has its own rules of court, generally known as **rules of practice** or **rules of civil procedure**. These rules ensure that all documents submitted to the court conform to standards set by the court.

Practice Alert

Note that this is a discussion of civil procedure. Criminal proceedings have a separate and distinct set of procedural rules. Consult your local jurisdiction's rules of criminal procedure.

THE COMPLAINT

The documents that initiate the lawsuit are called pleadings. Pleadings are the legal documents in which parties to a civil case formally state their case or respond to a claim or defense. The first pleading document to be submitted to the court is the complaint. The complaint is filed by the plaintiff stating their intention to sue the defendant and includes the plaintiff's legal basis for suing. The complaint is also called a petition in some jurisdictions. The complaint serves two main purposes: (1) to notify the defendant that a suit is being commenced, and (2) to notify the court that a suit is being commenced against the defendant.

The complaint in all jurisdictions must contain certain information and follow specific format rules contained in that jurisdiction's rules of practice. In general, complaints must include the following information

- a caption heads the complaint setting forth the names of the parties, venue, and identifying dates or numbers
- jurisdictional statement that informs the court that it has jurisdiction to hear the case
- a legal basis for the suit
- facts that if true, would support the legal basis for suing
- a **request for damages** (prayer for relief, wherefore clause, ad damnum clause)

Discussion Point

What is the title of your state's rules of court? What other rules does the text include (rules of professional responsibility, rules of criminal procedure)?

Consider the following fact pattern. This model case synopsis will be the basis of the pleadings and other examples used in this book.

MEMORANDUM

To: R. Dahl, Paralegal
From: C. Bucket, Esq.
Re: Salt Case, File # 1234

Our firm has been retained by Veruca Salt to advise her regarding injuries she suffered as a result of an accident in her home. Ms. Salt wishes to know what remedies are available to her under the law to provide compensation for the injuries she has suffered.

I have detailed the facts of the case, as related by Ms. Salt, below. Please review the facts carefully and determine what cause(s) of action, if any, Ms. Salt may pursue. Also, please indicate what further investigative action should be taken.

FACTS

Ms. Salt is a long-time client of the firm. We have advised her on estate planning and contract issues. She is a 37-year-old actress with an annual income of approximately $320,000. This income is derived primarily through Ms. Salt's work in television commercials and guest appearances on various television programs.

On the morning of August 1, 2004, Ms. Salt was at her home in Hartford, preparing for an audition for a major motion picture scheduled later in the day. After washing her hair, she began drying it with a hair dryer she had purchased approximately four months earlier from Wonka's World of Beauty, a retail beauty supply shop located in Hartford. Ms. Salt has purchased her beauty products from Wonka's for the past 20 years.

She states that in her line of work, beauty products are vitally important and she had always been satisfied with Wonka's quality until recently. In fact, she had been so satisfied that she has acted in commercials for Wonka's two years ago commending their quality. Six months prior to this incident, Willy Wonka, the founder of the business retired and passed control of the store to his son, Willy, Jr. Ms. Salt reports that she felt customer service has degraded since the takeover, and she was considering buying her beauty products elsewhere.

On the morning of August 1, Ms. Salt plugged the hair dryer into the outlet in her dressing room, where she customarily dried her hair. After approximately one minute of use, Ms. Salt noticed an acrid odor and then pain on the left side of her scalp. Looking toward the mirror, Ms. Salt was horrified to see her hair on the left side of her head was on fire. Thinking fast, Ms. Salt doused her head in a waiting pedicure bath and extinguished the fire. Ms. Salt called for her housekeeper to summon an ambulance and promptly fainted.

Ms. Salt was transferred by ambulance to Hartford Hospital where she was treated for third-degree burns to her scalp and emotional collapse. She was kept overnight and released. One week later, she underwent surgery to apply skin grafts to the burned areas. The skin grafts healed the burn but no hair has regrown in that area. Despite the graft, visible scars exist on Ms. Salt's scalp and are not expected to improve. Her medical bills currently exceed $25,000.

Ms. Salt's hair before the incident was shoulder length and blond. She is now forced to wear a wig, which irritates the healing area and may contribute to the failure of hair re-growth. Doctors have urged her to allow circulating air to reach the area but due to her profession and personal embarrassment, she feels it is necessary to wear a wig at all times.

As a result of this disfigurement, Ms. Salt has not worked as an actress since the incident. She has been told by her agent that her use of a wig is detrimental to her career. She has an audition for the next PixAir animated movie but feels this is a "step down" in her career.

Ms. Salt has been extremely depressed since the incident and has been under the care of a psychiatrist. Ms. Salt has spent over $10,000 for psychiatric care and medically necessary drugs. She has spent over $12,000 for various wigs, healing creams, and alternative medicine therapies.

Ms. Salt says she feels Willy Jr. has been cutting corners and she blames him for her injuries. She wants to know how she can recover some of her out of pocket costs and loss of income.

RETURN DATE: JUNE 19, 2005	:	SUPERIOR COURT
VERUCA SALT	:	J.D. OF HARTFORD
V.	:	AT HARTFORD
WONKA'S WORLD OF BEAUTY, INC	:	JUNE 4, 2005

COMPLAINT

1. Plaintiff Veruca Salt is a person residing in Hartford, Connecticut who brings this action pursuant to the Connecticut Product Liability Act, as set forth in Connecticut General Statutes, Sections 52-572m to 52-572r (hereinafter referred to as "the Act").
2. Defendant Wonka's World of Beauty, Inc. is a Connecticut corporation that operates a retail store at 0 Girard Street in Hartford, Connecticut.
3. At all relevant times, the defendant was engaged in the business of marketing, selling, or distributing beauty products and equipment to the retail consumer market in the State of Connecticut.
4. The defendant is a product seller within the meaning of the Act.
5. On April 1, 2004, the plaintiff purchased a Lovely Time hair dryer, model 098-LEMON, from the defendant.
6. The plaintiff subsequently used the hair dryer in her home in the customary manner and did not modify, misuse, or alter the hair dryer in any way.
7. On August 1, 2004, while the plaintiff was drying her hair with the Lovely Time hair dryer purchased from the defendant, the hair dryer began to emit sparks and excessive heat causing the plaintiff to sustain various painful personal injuries and emotional distress.
8. At the time the defendant sold the hair dryer to the plaintiff it was defective and unreasonably dangerous in that:
   a. it was inadequately designed;
   b. it was sold without proper warnings;
   c. it was inadequately tested.
9. The defective hair dryer proximately caused the plaintiff to sustain the following serious, permanent and painful injuries:
   a. a first-degree burn to her scalp resulting in permanent scarring;
   b. a permanent loss of hair on the left side of her scalp;
   c. pain, suffering, and distress.
10. As a further result of her injuries, the plaintiff has been unemployable in her chosen profession as an actress and her earning capacity has been greatly impaired, all to her further financial loss.

11. As a further result of her injuries, the plaintiff incurred substantial expenses for diagnostic testing and medical care including plastic surgery and hair plug therapy.

WHEREFORE, the plaintiff demands:

1. Money damages;
2. Punitive damages pursuant to Connecticut General Statutes, Section 52-240b;
3. Such other relief as this Court deems fair, equitable, and just.

THE PLAINTIFF,
VERUCA SALT
By:________________
Charlie Bucket, Esq.
Bucket and Bucket, LLC.
Her Attorneys
11 Chocolate Way
Hartford, CT 06110
(860)651-0000
Juris No.: 000000

summons: a court-issued document accompanying the complaint which informs the defendant that he is being sued and when and where to respond.

The complaint is generally accompanied by a **summons**, which is a court-issued document that informs the defendant that he is being sued and where and when to respond.

NOTE: Use spacebar to check boxes. Right click any blank area to bring up menu for print, zoom, page and date options.

For case type list, see electronic form JD-CV-1c.

SUMMONS - CIVIL
(Except Family Actions)
JD-CV-1 Rev. 1-2000
C.G.S. § 51-346, 51-347, 51-349, 51-350, 52-45a, 52-48, 52-259, P.B. Secs 3-1 thru 3-21, 8-1

STATE OF CONNECTICUT
SUPERIOR COURT
www.jud.state.ct.us

"X" ONE OF THE FOLLOWING: *Amount, legal interest or property in demand, exclusive of interest and costs is:*
- less than $2,500
- $2,500 through $14,999.99
- $15,000 or more

("X" if applicable)
- *Claiming other relief in addition to or in lieu of money or damages.*

INSTRUCTIONS

1. *Type or print legibly: sign original summons and conform all copies of the summons.*
2. *Prepare or photocopy conformed summons for each defendant.*
3. *Attach the original summons to the original complaint, and attach a copy of the summons to each copy of the complaint. Also, if there are more than 2 plaintiffs or 4 defendants prepare form JD-CV-2 and attach it to the original and all copies of the complaint.*
4. *After service has been made by a proper officer, file original papers and officer's return with the clerk of court.*
5. *The party recognized to pay costs must appear personally before the authority taking the recognizance.*
6. *Do not use this form for actions in which an attachment, garnishment or replevy is being sought. See Practice Book Section 8-1 for other exceptions.*

TO: Any proper officer; BY AUTHORITY OF THE STATE OF CONNECTICUT, you are hereby commanded to make due and legal service of this Summons and attached Complaint.

RETURN DATE (Mo., day, yr.) (Must be a Tuesday)

JUDICIAL DISTRICT / HOUSING SESSION / G.A. NO.	AT (Town in which writ is returnable) (C.G.S. 51-346, 51-349)	CASE TYPE (*See JD-CV-1c*) Major / Minor

ADDRESS OF COURT CLERK WHERE WRIT AND OTHER PAPERS SHALL BE FILED (No., street, town and zip code) (C.G.S. 51-346, 51-350)	TELEPHONE NO. (w/area code)

PARTIES	NAME AND ADDRESS OF EACH PARTY *(No., street, town and zip code)* *NOTE: Individuals' Names: Last, First, Middle Initial*	Form JD-CV-2 attached	PTY NO.
FIRST NAMED PLAINTIFF			01
Additional Plaintiff			02
FIRST NAMED DEFENDANT			50
Additional Defendant			51
Additional Defendant			52
Additional Defendant			53

NOTICE TO EACH DEFENDANT

1. **YOU ARE BEING SUED.**
2. This paper is a Summons in a lawsuit.
3. The Complaint attached to these papers states the claims that each Plaintiff is making against you in this lawsuit.
4. To respond to this Summons, or to be informed of further proceedings, you or your attorney must file a form called an "Appearance" with the Clerk of the above-named Court at the above Court address on or before the second day after the above Return Date.
5. If you or your attorney do not file a written "Appearance" form on time, a judgment may be entered against you by default.
6. The "Appearance" form may be obtained at the above Court address.
7. If you believe that you have insurance that may cover the claim that is being made against you in this lawsuit, you should immediately take the Summons and Complaint to your insurance representative.
8. If you have questions about the Summons and Complaint, you should consult an attorney promptly. **The Clerk of Court is not permitted to give advice on legal questions.**

DATE	SIGNED *(Sign and "X" proper box)*	Comm. of Superior Court / Assistant Clerk	TYPE IN NAME OF PERSON SIGNING AT LEFT

FOR THE PLAINTIFF(S) PLEASE ENTER THE APPEARANCE OF:

NAME AND ADDRESS OF ATTORNEY, LAW FIRM OR PLAINTIFF IF PRO SE (No., street, town and zip code)	TELEPHONE NUMBER	JURIS NO. (if atty. or law firm)

NAME AND ADDRESS OF PERSON RECOGNIZED TO PROSECUTE IN THE AMOUNT OF $250 (No., street, town and zip code)	SIGNATURE OF PLAINTIFF IF PRO SE

# PLFS.	# DEFS.	# CNTS.	SIGNED *(Official taking recognizance; "X" proper box)*	Comm. of Superior Court / Assistant Clerk	*For Court Use Only* FILE DATE

IF THIS SUMMONS IS SIGNED BY A CLERK:
a. The signing has been done so that the Plaintiff(s) will not be denied access to the courts.
b. It is the responsibility of the Plaintiff(s) to see that service is made in the manner provided by law.
c. The Clerk is not permitted to give any legal advice in connection with any law suit.
d. The Clerk signing this Summons at the request of the Plaintiff(s) is not responsible in any way for any errors or omissions in the Summons, any allegations contained in the Complaint, or the service thereof.

I hereby certify I have read and understand the above:	SIGNED *(Pro Se Plaintiff)*	DATE SIGNED	DOCKET NO.

Exhibit 6-1 Sample Summons

In addition to submitting the complaint to the court to initiate the lawsuit, the plaintiff must also ensure that the complaint and summons are served in the proper manner. Most jurisdictions require that the complaint and summons be served, or delivered, to the defendant

- by an **indifferent person**; usually a marshal or sheriff.
- by personal service; generally required that the complaint and summons be served to the person themselves or at their last known address to someone present there.

Practice Alert

Note that some jurisdictions, including federal courts, now permit service by mail in order to save the expense of personal service. (See Federal Rules of Civil Procedure Rule 4(d)(2)) Consult your local rules.

- within a certain time period prescribed by local rules.

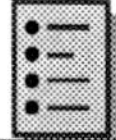

Discussion Point

Why do you think personal service is required in many jurisdictions? What other types of service are you aware of? What are the pros and cons of each type of service?

DEFENDANT'S RESPONSES TO THE COMPLAINT

Once the defendant has been served with the complaint and summons, he may consider what type of response to make. The defendant's responses may include those listed in the following section.

Motion to Dismiss

The defendant may file a **Motion to Dismiss** the plaintiff's complaint for a number reasons, including lack of subject matter jurisdiction, lack of personal jurisdiction, improper venue, and insufficiency of service of process. The judge will consider the motion and either grant the motion or deny it. If the judge grants the motion, he may then dismiss the plaintiff's complaint but allow the plaintiff to re-submit an amended complaint.

The Answer

The answer is a pleading filed by the defendant with the court, and sent to the plaintiff, responding to allegations contained in the complaint. In the answer, the defendant admits or denies the allegations made by the plaintiff in his complaint. If the defendant feels he can neither admit nor deny an allegation, he may state that he is without knowledge or information sufficient to form a belief as to the truth of the allegation.

The defendant may also include defenses, sometimes known as special or affirmative defenses, in his complaint. The most of commonly used of these defenses is that of comparative negligence in which the defendant asserts that the plaintiff contributed to his injuries through his own negligence. Any defenses asserted in the answer must arise from facts and allegations contained in the complaint.

DOCKET NO. CV 03-0444444 S	:	SUPERIOR COURT
VERUCA SALT	:	JUDICIAL DISTRICT
	:	OF HARTFORD
V	:	AT HARTFORD
WONKA'S WORLD OF BEAUTY, INC.	:	JULY 14, 2005

ANSWER

1. Paragraphs 1 through 3, inclusive, of the Plaintiff's Complaint, are hereby admitted.
2. With respect to Paragraph 4 of the Plaintiff's Complaint, the Defendant has insufficient knowledge or information upon which to form a belief and therefore leaves the Plaintiff to her proof.
3. Paragraph 5 is admitted.
4. With respect to Paragraphs 6 and 7 of the Plaintiff's Complaint, the Defendant has insufficient knowledge or information upon which to form a belief and therefore leaves the Plaintiff to her proof.
5. The Defendant denies Paragraphs 8 and 9 of the Plaintiff's Complaint.
6. With respect to Paragraphs 10 and 11 of the Plaintiff's Complaint, the Defendant has insufficient knowledge or information upon which to form a belief and therefore leaves the Plaintiff to her proof.

DEFENDANT'S SPECIAL DEFENSES

FIRST SPECIAL DEFENSE

1. Any injuries, losses, or damages sustained by the Plaintiff were caused by her own negligence and/or carelessness in one or more of the following ways:
   a. She neglected to use reasonable care in operating the hair dryer;
   b. She voluntarily consumed alcoholic beverages to the extent that she was impaired and unable to operate the hair dryer safely.

SECOND SPECIAL DEFENSE

1. The Plaintiff was contributorily negligent in causing any injuries she claims in that she:
   a. Failed to operate her hair dryer using reasonable care;
   b. Voluntarily consumed alcoholic beverages to the extent that she was impaired and unable to operate the hair dryer safely.

THE DEFENDANT

By ____________________

Oliver Slugworth, Esq.
Slugworth & Hershey. P.C.
31 Weasel Way
Hartford, CT 06119
860-561-2333
Juris No. 202020

Counterclaim

A counterclaim is made by the defendant against the plaintiff regarding the same cause of action. In this case, the defendant has claims of his own against the plaintiff arising from the same transaction or occurrence and can essentially initiate an action against the plaintiff for damages within the original suit.

EXAMPLE Veruca has sued Wonka's World of Beauty for injuries suffered from use of the faulty hairdryer. Wonka, the defendant, could file a counterclaim against Salt for defamation, claiming that her statements regarding the hairdryer were libelous.

Crossclaim

A crossclaim is made by the defendant against a co-defendant included in the plaintiff's complaint. In a crossclaim, one defendant sues a co-defendant on claims arising from the same transaction or occurrence of the subject matter of the original suit.

EXAMPLE In her original suit, Veruca sued Wonka's World of Beauty and the Lovely Time Hair Dryer Company as co-defendants in her original action. Wonka may choose to file a crossclaim against Lovely Time, asserting that the company provided faulty merchandise to them.

Third-Party Complaint

A third-party complaint is a claim made by the defendant against a person not originally a party to the case. A defendant essentially brings another party into the litigation by initiating a separate complaint against the third party. The third-party complaint is generally tried with the original case because the facts are shared.

EXAMPLE Veruca has named Wonka's World of Beauty and Lovely Time Hair Dryer Company as co-defendants in her original action. Lovely Time may choose to file a third-party complaint against Curly's Coil Company alleging that Curly's provided them with faulty heating coils.

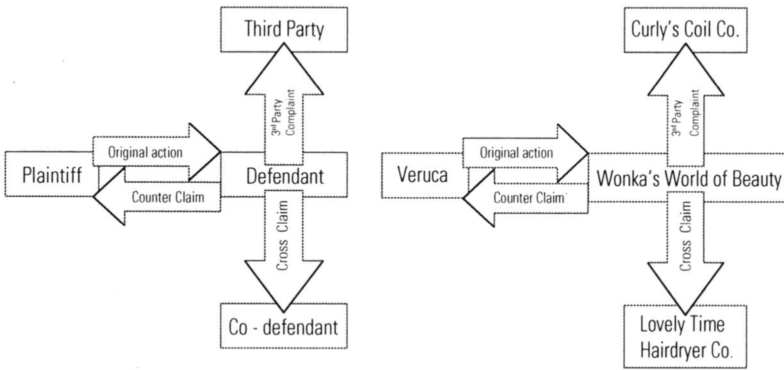

Exhibit 6-2 Counterclaims, Cross Claims, Third Party Complaints

Key Terms

indifferent person

motion to dismiss

request for damages (wherefore, prayer for relief, ad damnum)

rules of civil procedure

rules of practice

Exercises

1. For these exercises, you will need to consult your local rules of practice. Using the index, locate, and cite the applicable provision(s) for each of the following:

   Complaint

   Answer

   Counterclaim

   Crossclaim

   Third-Party Complaint

   Subpoena duces tecum

Notice of Deposition

Interrogatories

2. Using the facts of the model case synopsis in this chapter, *Salt v. Wonka's World of Beauty*, draft a third-party complaint by Wonka against the Lovely Time Hair Dryer Company. Follow the rules of practice of your jurisdiction.

Library Resources

Federal Rules of Civil Procedure: Pretrial Litigation in a Nutshell (3rd ed.), R. Lawrence Dessem, West Publishing Co., 2001.
The Nutshell series is always valuable for concise and accessible information.

Moot Court Casebook, all volumes, New York University School of Law Moot Court Board, 1998.
This book contains good case materials and examples.

Online Resources

Law Information Institute at Cornell, http://www.law.cornell.edu/rules/frcp/overview.htm
This site provides overview of civil procedure with links to primary and secondary sources.

Megalaw, http://www.megalaw.com/top/civpro.php
This site includes federal rules of court and links to all states' civil procedure statutes.

Federal Judicial Center, http://www.fjc.gov
The Web site for educational and research agency for the federal courts.

CHAPTER 7

Discovery

INTRODUCTION

Discovery is an important part of the pre-litigation and litigation process. Paralegals often play vital roles in the discovery process by preparing and organizing discovery documents as they are received. Paralegals must be familiar with the use and application of all discovery tools. This chapter introduces the student to those tools.

DISCOVERY TOOLS

discovery: The formal process of fact gathering prior to commencement of trial.

Discovery is the formal process of fact gathering prior to commencement of trial.

Practice Alert

Discovery rules are generally encoded in the rules of practice of each jurisdiction. Please consult your state's rules of practice for specific rules of your jurisdiction.

The discovery process begins after pleadings have been filed and generally ends at the start of trial. Discovery rules differ by jurisdiction but most are very liberal and allow vast amounts of information to be discoverable. The rationale for this liberal allowance of information between parties to an action includes:

- to allow both parties to learn as much as possible before the start of trial
- to facilitate settlements prior to trial by exposing the strengths and weaknesses of each side's case
- to speed the process of trial once it begins by eliminating surprise evidence
- to help the parties frame the legal issues that will be most relevant to prevailing in the action

Although court rules allow a wide degree of discretion in discovery, requests must relate to the subject matter of the pending action and/or assist the parties to prove their case or defend themselves. Discovery is optional and often very expensive; however, most actions include some degree of discovery.

Discussion Point

Do you think liberal discovery rules are a good idea? Why or why not? Do you think some information should be protected from discovery? Explain.

Formal discovery documents are used to request specific information. Although these documents follow court rules as to form, they are not generally filed with the court. The discovery documents are served to each of the parties to the action and are then used by the parties as they prepare for trial. If a party fails to comply with a discovery request within the time specified by that jurisdiction's rules of practice, the requesting party may file a **Motion to Compel** with the court, which requests that the judge compel the other party to comply with discovery requests.

motion to compel: A motion requesting that the judge require the other party to comply with discovery requests.

If the court determines that the discovery request is valid, the judge may then order the non-complying party to fulfill the discovery request or face sanctions.

Formal discovery documents include Interrogatories, Requests for Production, Request for Admissions, Request for Physical or Mental Exam, and Depositions. Each discovery document is discussed individually below.

Interrogatories

Interrogatories are written questions answered, in writing, under oath.

interrogatories: Written questions answered, in writing, under oath.

The interrogatories will include written questions directed to the responding party with space provided for each written answer. Interrogatories are generally the first discovery tool to be implemented and in most jurisdictions may only be directed to the plaintiff or defendant in the action.

Some jurisdictions require that standardized interrogatories be used in certain cases, usually personal injury cases. Most firms will maintain copies of interrogatories used in previous cases to be used in subsequent, similar cases. Sample interrogatories may also be found in practice books and form books on discovery at the law library.

Interrogatories are ideal as a starting point in the discovery process because

- they are inexpensive. Interrogatories are drafted in the law office and mailed to the opposing counsel's office. More than one set of interrogatories may be drafted and sent throughout the discovery process.
- they can be comprehensive. Because they may be drafted and redrafted at the discretion of the requesting party, the advantage of time allows for well-crafted and thought-out questions to be issued.

- they provide the foundation for determining the path of future discovery requests. Well-drafted interrogatories can elicit responses that will lead to obtaining additional, important information. A response to an interrogatory may lead to uncovering documents relevant to the case.

As valuable as interrogatories may be, there are some drawbacks. Just as the requesting party has time to draft the questions, the responding party has time to answer them. In most jurisdictions, responses must be provided within 30 days. Because the answers can be so well planned and drafted, the responding party will attempt to give as little "away" as possible. Interrogatories offer little insight into the responding party's personality, biases, or effectiveness as a potential witness.

Requests for Production

requests for production: Written requests to inspect or copy documents and other tangible items under the opposing party's control.

Requests for Production are written requests to inspect or copy documents and other tangible items under the opposing party's control.

Like an Interrogatory, the Request for Production seeks information from the opposing party. Tangible items commonly requested include photographs, written reports and correspondence (including email), computer hard drives, statements, charts, and graphs. Requests for Production are commonly served with Interrogatories because questions often will make references to specific documents or other tangible items.

Requests for Admissions

requests for admissions: Written statements sent to the opposing party that must be admitted or denied.

Requests for Admissions are written statements sent to the opposing party that must be admitted or denied.

Unlike Interrogatories, Requests for Admissions are not phrased as a question but as a statement of fact. Their purpose is to pinpoint areas of agreement between the two opposing parties that can then be the basis for stipulation, to highlight contested issues, and attempt to compel the Defendant to admit liability. For example, in a contract case, a Request for Admission may look like this:

On February 23, 2003, the Defendant agreed to provide 1000 blue widgets to the business place of the Plaintiff located on 40 Acorn Street, Hayville NY, on the following day, February 24, 2004, no later than 4:00pm.

RESPONSE: (The Defendant would insert his response here.)

Space for a response is provided in the Request immediately following the statement.

Request for Physical or Mental Examination

request for physical or mental examination: A written request to allow a physician to conduct an examination of the opposing party.

Request for Physical or Mental Examination is a written request to allow a physician to conduct an examination of the opposing party.

This discovery tool is used when a party's physical or mental health is at issue. This request is most commonly used in personal injury cases and medical malpractice cases. If the plaintiff has raised the issue of his physical or mental health, then he must submit to an examination by the physician chosen by the defendant. This examination is commonly referred to as an **IME**, or independent medical examination and allows the defendant the opportunity to independently verify or dispute the physical or mental injuries claimed by the plaintiff.

IME: Abbreviation for Independent Medical Examination.

The defendant may make this request only if he can demonstrate to the court that he has good cause for such an examination. In other words, as liberal as discovery is, it does not allow examinations of the plaintiff by a physician as a "fishing expedition."

Discussion Point

In what type of cases do you think an IME would be appropriate? Explain.

DEPOSITIONS

Depositions are an oral questioning under oath.

Unlike the previously discussed discovery tools, depositions may be directed to parties to the action and to non-parties who may potentially testify at trial and have information relevant to the case. Depositions are transcribed by a stenographer and often videotaped.

Advantages of employing depositions as a discovery tool include:

- they may be directed toward non-parties, which makes them very useful for collecting information not obtainable through other forms of discovery.
- because depositions involve live questioning, a sense of the deponent's strengths and weaknesses as a potential witness at trial may be assessed.
- depositions preserve evidence in the event a party or non-party is unavailable when the case reaches trial.

There are some disadvantages to using depositions, including the fact that depositions are generally the most expensive form of discovery. They require the expense of a stenographer/videographer and are time consuming. Depositions are also admissible at trial but only for limited purposes.

depositions: Oral questioning under oath.

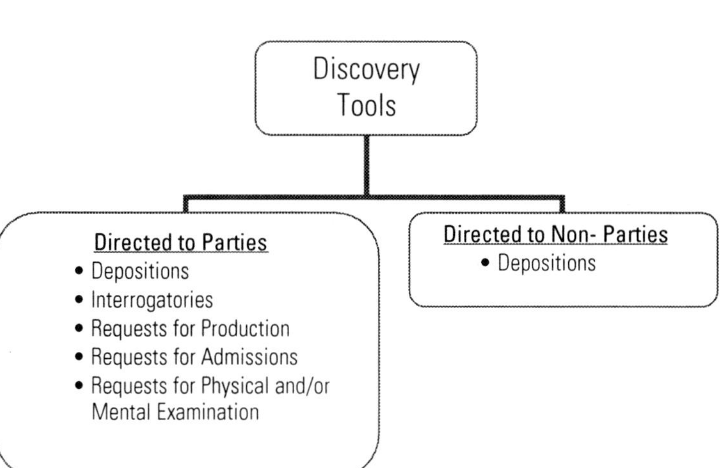

Exhibit 7-1 Discovery Tools

DIGESTING DEPOSITIONS

digesting depositions: The process of summarizing the content of a deposition in order to make the information contained therein easy to access.

A common task completed by paralegals is **digesting depositions**, which is the process of summarizing the content of a deposition in order to make the information contained therein easy to access.

A paralegal reads the transcript of the deposition and provides summaries of it. Your supervising attorney will instruct you as to the particular information she wishes you to summarize from the deposition. For example, a deposition of an expert witness in a professional malpractice case may extend to over 500 pages. Your attorney may ask you to prepare a digest of that deposition, which provides summaries of the expert's deposition in chronological order. Or, your attorney may ask you to summarize the deposition by subject matter.

Your digest will then be included in the case file and used to quickly access information regarding that particular witness. Therefore, it must be accurate and include all relevant information. The digest should be concise without excluding any pertinent information. The digest is usually placed in an interoffice memorandum format. In concise, numbered paragraphs, the paralegal provides a brief summary of the statements made by the deponent. Generally, the line number from the deposition transcript will be included to direct the reader to the actual line in the deposition for reference purposes. There are many excellent software packages available that make the task of digesting depositions considerably easier.

EXAMPLE Example of a chronological deposition digest (excerpt):

Dr. Brant received his undergraduate degree, B.S. in Biology, from St. Lawrence University in Canton N.Y. in 1980. He received his medical degree from the University of Connecticut in 1984. (line 3)

He is board certified in obstetrics and has been in private practice for the past 18 years. (line 4)

He maintains medical offices in Hartford and Simsbury Connecticut. (line 4)

He maintains hospital privileges at General Hospital. (line 5)

On September 24, 2002, he accepted Susan Jones as an obstetrical patient and examined her that day in his Hartford offices. (lines 6 & 7)

Key Terms

depositions
digesting depositions
discovery
IME
interrogatories
motion to compel
requests for admissions
requests for physical or mental examination
requests for production

Exercises

1. Using the Salt case facts and pleadings in Chapter 5, draft the documents listed below. In this exercise, you will be a paralegal for Charles Bucket, plaintiff Salt's attorney. Be sure to follow all relevant practice book procedures and formats for your jurisdiction and to cite the proper sections within your documents.
   a. Draft a set of 10 interrogatories directed to the defendant, Willy Wonka, Jr.
   b. Draft a set of 10 requests for production directed to the defendant, Willy Wonka, Jr.

c. Draft a set of 10 requests to admit directed to the defendant, Willy Wonka, Jr.
d. Draft a notice of deposition directed to the defendant, Willy Wonka, Jr.
e. Draft a demand letter directed to the defendant, Willy Wonka, Jr. offering to compromise Salt's claim for $100,000 and an apology.
f. Draft a status letter directed to your client, Veruca Salt for the signature of your supervising attorney Charles Bucket. The letter should inform your client of the current status of her case after the completion of the foregoing discovery activities.
g. Draft a third-party complaint on behalf of your client, directed at the Lovely Time Hairdryer Corporation as the third-party defendant. Your third-party complaint should be based in negligence as a cause of action.

2. The following is an example of an actual assignment you may receive from your attorney. Please provide a digest of this deposition, providing summaries in chronological order.

To: Paralegal
From: Supervising Attorney
Re: File No. 1234; Deposition of Veruca Salt; Digest
Date: November 5, 2004

We conducted a deposition regarding the above referenced case on October 31, 2004. Attached please find the transcript of that deposition of Augustus Gloop, an employee of the defendant, Wonka's World of Beauty. Please provide a digest of this deposition, providing summaries in chronological order.

DOCKET NO. CV-03-0444444S:	SUPERIOR COURT
VERUCA SALT:	JUDICIAL DISTRICT OF HARTFORD
V:	AT HARTFORD
WONKA'S WORLD OF BEAUTY:	OCTOBER 31, 2004

DEPOSITION OF AUGUSTUS ADOLPH GLOOP

This deposition was conducted at the offices of Charles Bucket, Esq., 11 Chocolate Way, Hartford, CT beginning at 11:03am and ending at 12:08pm.

Appearances:

For the Plaintiff:	Charles Bucket Bucket & Bucket, LLC 11 Chocolate Way Hartford, CT 06110
For the Defendant:	Oliver Slugworth Slugworth & Hershey 31 Weasel Way Hartford, CT 06119

BY MR. BUCKET:

Q: Would you state your full name for the record?
A: Augustus Adolph Gloop.

Q: Where are you currently employed, Mr. Gloop?
A: At Wonka's World of Beauty.

Q: And in what capacity are you employed at Wonka's?
A: I am day manager of retail sales.

Q: How long have you held that position?
A: 2 years.

Q: What is your employment history prior to that?
A: Well, I worked as a sales clerk for Wonka's three years
before I was promoted to manager. Before that, I was in high
school and worked at a drycleaner's on weekends.

Q: How old are you, Mr. Gloop?
A: I'm 24, 25 next month.

Q: Okay, let's get back to your work at Wonka's. What are your responsibilities as day manager?
A: Um, I open up in the morning-

Q: What time is that?
A: 8:30am Tuesday through Sunday. We're closed on Mondays, which works well since most beauty salons are closed then, too.

Q: Alright then, what else do you do there?
A: I make sure all the clerks are there for their shift—usually 20 there are two clerks are with me on the day shift from 9am-5pm. Then I unlock the cash registers, make sure there is change. Then I review stock lists and assist customers as necessary. I usually assist customers only when there's some sort of problem.

Q: What sort of problems?
A: Well, if someone wants their money back or wants to return something. You know, just troubleshooting.

Q: Do you need to "troubleshoot" very often?
A: (Laugh) You'd be surprised. Yeah, I'd say I have to deal with a customer at least once a day. It's part of being a Manager. We usually can make them happy.

Q: How do you "make them happy?"
A: Well, we can give them a discount or credit towards future purchases, that works well. We try to avoid giving refunds, since most of our products can't be re-sold due to health codes and stuff.

Q: Can hairdryers be resold?
A: They shouldn't be. The health inspector has included them on the list of banned resale items.

Q: How are you aware of this list?
A: It's posted on the stockroom door at work.

Q: On the stockroom door at Wonka's World of Beauty, in clear view? Is that right?
A: Yes.

Q: Were you working on March 27, 2003 at approximately 1:30pm?
A: Yes.

Q: Do you know the plaintiff, Ms. Salt?
A: Well, I know her through the store. She was a very good customer of ours and used to be in a lot—until all of this.

Q: Did Ms. Salt come into Wonka's World of Beauty retail store on March 27, 2003 at approximately 1:30pm?
A: Yes, she did.

Q: Please tell us what happened after Ms. Salt entered the store on that date.
A: Umm, well I think she came first to me. She usually would request to deal with the manager only. She was pretty demanding, often rude.

Q: What did she say?
A: She told me she wanted a new hairdryer. She said she had to have our best, most expensive model. I think she said something about having an important photo shoot that week. So, I recommended the Lovely Time model. I told her it was our top of the line model and that many of our best customers used it and loved it.

Q: Was that true? That your best customers used and loved this model?
A: Pretty much. I mean, I have to use some selling techniques, but yeah it's a good seller.

Q: How many of those hairdryers did you sell during the year of 2003? And how many in the month of March 2003?
A: According to my records, we sold 154 Lovely Time hairdryers in 2003 and 17 in March.

Q: I'll take those copies under our Request for Production. Thanks.

Q: Okay, back to March 27th. Did Ms. Salt purchase the hairdryer based on your recommendation.
A: Wait a minute, it wasn't just my recommendation. She checked it out before she bought it.

Q: Checked it out?
A: She picked up the box and looked at it. She said it looked European, and she liked that.

Q: Did she open the box and handle the actual hairdryer?
A: No. I didn't see her do that.

Q: Then what happened?
A: She paid, by credit card I think, and then she left. Oh, and she asked me to leave a message for Junior to call her.

Q: "Junior"—is that Willy Wonka Jr.?
A: Yeah.

Q: Have you seen or spoken with Ms. Salt since March 27, 2003?
A: No.

Q: Thank you, Mr. Gloop, I think we're all done here.

(The deposition concluded at 11:15 am on October 31, 2004.)

I, Augustus Adolph Gloop, do hereby certify that I have read the foregoing transcript and that it represents a true and complete record of my testimony.

____

Deponent

Subscribed and sworn to me this 2nd day of November, 2004.

My Commission expires____________________

____

Notary Public

Library Resources

Bender's Forms of Discovery, Matthew Bender & Co., Inc., 1997.
This book is the "granddaddy" of discovery forms.

Pretrial Litigation in a Nutshell (3rd Ed.), R. Lawrence Dessum, West Publishing, 2002.
The Nutshell series is always concise and user friendly.

Examples and Explanations: Civil Procedure, (4th Ed.), Joseph W. Glannon, Glannon Publishing, 2001.
This book offers a helpful study aid format.

Online Resources

Discovery Law Update, http://www.techjudge.com/disco1995.htm
This site contains good case references.

CHAPTER 8

Ethics

INTRODUCTION

ethics: A set of rules that provide a standard of conduct and behavior for a certain set of people.

sanctions: Punishment or penalties for failing to conform to the ethical standard.

Contrary to popular belief, **ethics** play a strong role in the legal profession. Because the paralegal profession remains largely unregulated and unlicensed, the code of ethics that applies directly to paralegals is voluntary with no **sanctions** attached to them. Although there are no formal sanctions for violating paralegal ethics, paralegals must be vigilant in maintaining the ethics of the profession.

Although no formal ethics sanctions exist for paralegals, unethical behavior may result in the loss of your job. Attorneys have their own ethics code that does have sanctions and that paralegals must be familiar with because attorneys and law firms are required to follow these regulations. The paralegal's ethics code contains many of the same provisions as the attorney's code of ethics.

Practice Alert

Consult your state's code of professional responsibility for attorney's. You may also consult the American Bar Association's *Model Rules of Professional Conduct.*

ETHICS CODES FOR PARALEGALS

Both the **NFPA (National Federation of Paralegal Associations)** and the **NALA (National Association of Legal Assistants)** have drafted their own model code of ethics and professional responsibility. We will explore some of the primary tenets of these codes in the following section.

Competency

NFPA 1.1 A paralegal shall achieve and maintain a high level of competence.

competency: Using the necessary skills and knowledge to reasonably assist in representing a client.

Competency requires that a paralegal have the necessary skills and knowledge to reasonably assist in representing a client.

To be competent a paralegal has a responsibility to maintain her skill level by partaking in regular continuing education and to be aware when her knowledge and skills do not meet the level required by the client.

Discussion Point

Does your state have a requirement for mandatory continuing education for attorneys? Do you think this is a good practice?

Unauthorized Practice of Law

NALA Canon 3 A legal assistant must not (a) engage in, encourage, or contribute to any act which could constitute the unauthorized practice of law; and (b) establish attorney-client relationships, set fees, give legal opinions or advice or represent a client before a court or agency unless so authorized by that court or agency; and (c) engage in conduct or take any action which would assist or involve the attorney in a violation of professional ethics or give the appearance of professional impropriety.

NALA Canon 5 A legal assistant must disclose his or her status as a legal assistant at the outset of any professional relationship with a client, attorney, or court or administrative agency or personnel thereof, or a member of the general public...

unauthorized practice of law: Practicing law without a license or special authorization. This includes providing legal advice and representing clients before the court and is a criminal offense in most states.

The **unauthorized practice of law** includes giving legal advice and representing clients before a court or agency without a license.

Such behavior is not only unethical, but in most states is a criminal offense. It is important that paralegals always represent themselves as paralegals in order to avoid any mistakes regarding their roles as paralegals. Some tasks completed by paralegals such as drafting legal documents for a client would be considered the unauthorized practice of law if they were completed without the supervision of an attorney but are acceptable under such supervision.

Paralegals may not assist an attorney in violating the attorney's code of ethics. For example, if your supervising attorney asked you to make a representation to court one day in her place, you would be engaging in the unauthorized practice of law and assisting the attorney in violating her code of ethics.

Attorney-Client Privilege

NFPA 1.5 A paralegal shall preserve all confidential information provided by the client or acquired from other sources before, during, and after the course of the professional relationship.

attorney-client privilege: An attorney and his paralegal may not disclose any information regarding the client.

The **attorney-client privilege** extends to the paralegal.

The paralegal has the responsibility to maintain this confidential relationship and may not divulge any information regarding the client. For example, Susie Paralegal is attending a reunion of her paralegal class. During a conversation with Lana Legalassistant, Susie discloses that her firm is representing Tammy Tort and will be filing suit against a client represented by Lana's firm. Susie violated the confidentiality of her client by disclosing her identity and by divulging her intent to sue.

ethical or Chinese wall: A method to isolate a paralegal from any work in a firm that could create a conflict.

A paralegal must preserve a client's confidentiality even when she changes jobs. It is important that a paralegal not disclose confidential information regarding clients from a previous position and firms will create what is called an **ethical or Chinese wall** to isolate that paralegal from any work in the firm that could create a conflict.

The NFPA guidelines describe the ethical wall as "the screening method implemented to protect a client from a conflict of interest. An Ethical Wall generally includes, but is not limited to, the following elements: (1) prohibiting the paralegal from having any connection with the matter; (2) ban any discussions with or the transfer of documents to or from the paralegal; (3) restrict access to files; and (4) educate all members of the firm, corporation, or entity as to the separation of the paralegal (both organizationally and physically) from the pending matter." (*NFPA Model Disciplinary Rules and Ethical Considerations)*

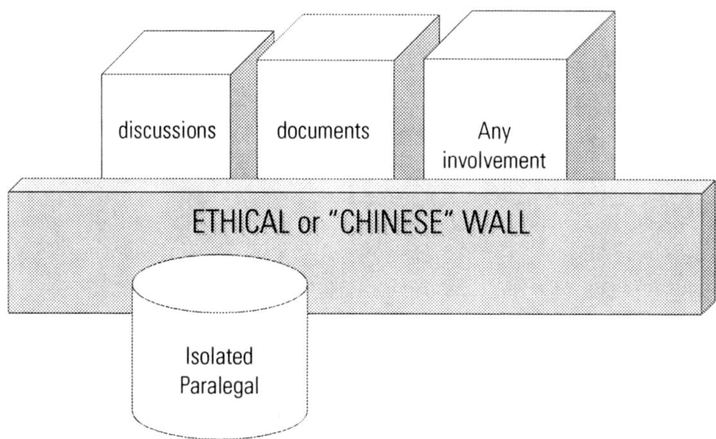

Exhibit 8-1 Ethical Wall

Another protection taken by most firms is the attachment of a disclaimer to all outgoing e-mails and faxes informing the sender that the enclosed material is protected in case of inadvertent or mistaken transmission. Such a disclaimer addresses the problem of mistaken or inadvertent transmission of confidential materials. The following is an example of a disclaimer.

This communication, including attachments, is for the exclusive use of the addressee and may contain proprietary, confidential, and/or privileged information. If you not the intended recipient, any use, copying, disclosure, dissemination or distribution is strictly prohibited. If you are not the intended recipient, please notify the sender immediately by return email, delete this communication, and destroy all copies.

This duty of **confidentiality** extends after the relationship with attorney and paralegal ends, although the client can always consent to disclosure. Such protection of confidentiality allows the client to speak freely and honestly to his counsel and thereby ensure that her attorney and legal team can most effectively represent her interests.

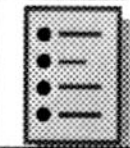

Discussion Point

Have you encountered confidentiality issues in other jobs? Discuss. Why do you think it is so important for paralegals to adhere to strict confidentiality rules?

Conflict of Interest

NFPA 1.6 A paralegal shall avoid conflicts of interest and shall disclose any possible conflict to employers or client, as well as to the prospective employers or clients.

(a) A paralegal shall act within the bounds of the law, solely the benefit of the client, and shall be free of compromising influences and loyalties. Neither the paralegal's personal business interest, nor those of clients or third persons should compromise the paralegal's professional judgment or loyalty to the client.

If a paralegal feels that she has any **conflict of interest** with a client, she is obligated to disclose that conflict initially to her employer. Such conflicts may include competing business interests and personal conflicts.

conflict of interest: The paralegal has competing interests against those of her client that may compromise her ability to provide unbiased judgment and loyalty to that client.

The employer then has the obligation to remove that paralegal from any involvement in the case unless the client is informed of the conflict and consents to the paralegal's continued involvement. For example, Haddas is a paralegal assigned to work on Lynda's contract dispute with Roy's Trash Hauling. Haddas immediately informs her supervising attorney that Roy is her father in law and that she has a personal conflict. Haddas's employer may either isolate her from working on this case or inform Lynda and ask for her consent (if Haddas feels she can conduct herself without bias).

Other Ethical Topics

NFPA 1.2 A paralegal shall maintain a high level of personal and professional integrity.

EC-1.2(d) A paralegal shall not knowingly engage in fraudulent bill practices. Such practices may include, but are not limited to, inflation of hours billed to a client or employer; misrepresentation of the nature of tasks performed; and submission of fraudulent expense and disbursement documentation.

Ethical lapses may result in serious repercussions including criminal prosecution and loss of employment. For example, the submission of fraudulent expense and disbursement documentation could result in criminal prosecution for larceny by fraud.

Billing records must be accurately maintained and a paralegal may not assist an attorney in inflating hours billed to a client. Additionally, paralegals must maintain all financial accounts and funds of a client with accuracy and honesty. In fact, a paralegal has an ethical obligation to report any dishonest or unscrupulous acts by any person, provided that such disclosure does not violate attorney-client privilege:

NFPA EC1.2(f) A paralegal shall advise the proper authority of non-confidential knowledge of any dishonest or fraudulent acts by any person pertaining to the handling of the funds, securities and other assets of a client...Failure to report such knowledge is in itself misconduct and shall be treated as such under these rules.

Key Terms

attorney-client privilege

competency

confidentiality

conflict of interest

ethical or Chinese wall

ethics

National Association of Legal Assistants (NALA)

National Federation of Paralegal Associations (NFPA)

sanctions

unauthorized practice of law

Exercises

1. Which of the following situations violates any code of paralegal ethics discussed in this chapter? Explain and list the appropriate code section.
   a. Fiona received her paralegal certificate 10 years ago. She has practiced exclusively in the area of trust and estates but has never taken a continuing education course.
   b. Same facts as (a) but Fiona's attorney has asked her become managing paralegal on a large worker's compensation case.
   c. Frank has worked as a paralegal in a small firm for over five years. The office is shorthanded when an attorney quits with no notice. Frank's supervising attorney tells Frank to appear for him at a short calendar motion hearing, telling him "You're experienced now, all you need to say is 'Pass.'"
   d. Same facts as (c) but include that Frank went to law school but never passed the bar.

2. Which of the following situations violates any code of paralegal ethics discussed in this chapter? Explain and list the appropriate code section.
   a. Sharene is a paralegal at a mid-sized firm that specializes in personal injury plaintiff's work. Her daily tasks include answering the phone and calling clients to inform them of upcoming deadlines and meetings regarding their case. One client calls and asks to speak with the attorney. Sharene informs the client that the attorney is unavailable but she will leave a message. The client becomes upset and demands to know the date of his scheduled deposition. Sharene tells him.
   b. Same facts as (a) but the client also asks what he should say in his deposition. Sharene proceeds to spend 40 minutes coaching the client on what answers he should supply during the deposition. The client is very pleased and does well at the deposition.

c. Mark is employed as a paralegal at a large corporation in its acquisitions department. During a long and complex negotiation process with another company, Mark has gotten to know an attorney representing the other company, Roz. In the last week of the negotiations, Mark invites Roz to party hosted by one of his old college roommates. At the party, Mark and Roz discuss the case and agree that Mark's company is getting a better deal. At one point later in the evening, Mark regales his college friends with stories about the current negotiations he and Roz are conducting.

d. Same facts as (c) but the negations took place six months prior to the party.

3. Write your own scenario that contains a violation of the following ethical considerations:

- Competency

____

____

____

____

____

____

- Ethical or Chinese Wall

____

____

____

____

____

____

- Unauthorized practice of law

____

____

____

____

____

____

Library Resources

Legal Ethics for Paralegals and the Law Office, Laura Morrison & Gina DeCianci, Thomson Delmar, 1994.
This book offers a comprehensive textbook on paralegal ethics.

Paralegal Ethics, Angela Schneeman, Thomson Delmar, 2000.
A concise guide to paralegal ethics.

Online Resources

National Federation of Paralegal Associations, http://www.paralegals.org
Complete *Model Disciplinary Rules and Ethical Considerations.*

National Association of Legal Assistants, http://www.nala.org
Complete *Code of Ethics and Professional Responsibility* and *Model Standards and Guidelines for Utilization of Legal Assistants.*

American Bar Association, http://www.abaparalegals.org
American Bar Association paralegal information Web site.

CHAPTER 9

Evidence

INTRODUCTION

It is important for the paralegal to have a solid understanding of the rules of evidence. Although paralegals cannot actively participate in court proceedings, their vital role in preparing for litigation requires a firm grasp of the principles of evidence. For example, for effective assistance in preparing discovery documents, a paralegal must know what type of evidence is more likely to be admitted by a judge. This chapter provides a broad overview of the rules of evidence.

evidence: Anything that makes a fact more or less probable.

Evidence is anything that makes a fact more or less probable.

Therefore, in order to prevail in a case, evidence that supports your client's position must be gathered. Evidence is gathered during the investigation phase discussed in Chapter 5. During the investigatory and discovery phases of litigation, all evidence is considered and evaluated. However, once the case goes to trial, formal rules of evidence are introduced and certain types of evidence can be excluded by the presiding judge. These rules are encoded in the **Federal Rules of Evidence** and in each state's code.

Practice Alert

Consult your own jurisdiction for specific rules to your state.

Almost anything can be evidence. Documents, photographs, blood samples, or a murder weapon are tangible evidence, provided they can be touched and felt. Testimony by a witness is also evidence and the jury alone determines which evidence it believes and which is most persuasive.

EVIDENCE IN GENERAL

Consider the types of evidence in steps: admissibility, categories of admissible evidence, and rules of admissibility. These phases will be described in the following section.

Step One: Admissibility

admissible evidence: Evidence that the judge determines may be considered by the jury.

Admissible evidence is evidence that the judge determines may be considered by the jury.

The jury is free to believe or disbelieve admissible evidence. Not all evidence is admissible. In fact, much of the evidence gathered during the discovery and investigatory phases is not admissible.

Step Two: Categories of Admissible Evidence

There are two types of admissible evidence: direct and circumstantial. The first category of admissible evidence is **direct evidence**, which is evidence that is based on personal observation or knowledge, which proves or disproves a fact without the need of inference.

direct evidence: Evidence based on personal observation or knowledge, which proves or disproves a fact without the need of inference.

EXAMPLE Consider the following scenario in which the fact to prove is that a blue sedan hit a pedestrian. George is standing on a street corner facing the street. George watches as a blue sedan hits a pedestrian. George's description of what he saw constitutes direct evidence that the blue sedan hit a pedestrian. George's personal observation of the crash requires no inference to prove that the blue sedan hit the pedestrian, making it direct evidence.

The second category of admissible evidence is **circumstantial evidence**, which must be inferred from another fact and is not based on personal observation or knowledge.

circumstantial evidence: Evidence that must be inferred from another fact and is not based on personal observation or knowledge.

EXAMPLE Consider the following scenario in which the fact to prove is that a blue sedan hit a pedestrian. Abby is standing on a street corner facing a store window, with her back to the street. She hears the squeal of brakes and a thud. Turning, she sees an injured person lying in front of a blue sedan. Based on her reasonable experience, Abby can infer from those facts that the blue sedan hit the pedestrian, making it circumstantial evidence.

Evidence can change categories depending on what it is being used to prove.

The evidence that George saw a blue sedan hit a pedestrian is direct evidence to prove that a blue sedan hit a pedestrian (direct observation). On the other hand, it is circumstantial evidence to prove that the driver was operating the sedan under the influence of alcohol (must make inference).

In the second scenario, the evidence that Abby heard brakes squeal and a thud and saw an injured person on the street is direct evidence to prove that the blue sedan applied its brakes (direct observation). On the other hand, it is circumstantial evidence to prove that the blue sedan was speeding (must make inference).

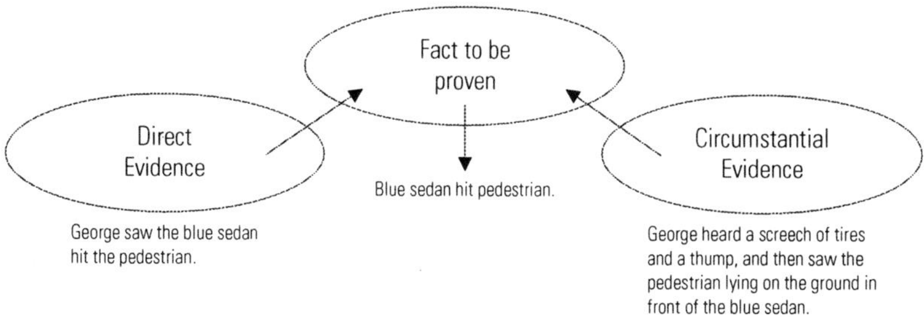

Exhibit 9-1 Direct and Circumstantial Evidence

Direct evidence is not inherently more reliable than circumstantial evidence. Entire cases can be built upon circumstantial evidence (Scott Peterson) and cases lost with direct evidence such as DNA (O.J. Simpson). Observations of the same event can vary wildly between individuals and thereby cast doubt on the reliability of such direct evidence.

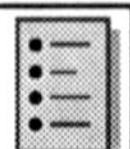

Discussion Point

Consider your own experience. How reliable have you found first-hand observations to be? Think about well-known cases. What type of evidence has been used to prove those cases?

Step Three: Rules of Admissibility

Once evidence has been categorized as direct or circumstantial, the next step is to determine whether it is admissible. In order for evidence to be admissible, it must comply with several requirements. The rules of admissibility are described in the following section.

Relevance

relevant evidence: Any evidence that has a reasonable connection or relationship to the truth or falsity of a fact.

Relevant evidence is any evidence that has a reasonable connection or relationship to the truth or falsity of a fact.

Relevance is not a rigorous standard because a "reasonable connection" is generally not hard to prove. The standard only requires that the evidence *tend* to establish or disprove a fact.

For example, using the same fact scenario as above, the driver of the blue sedan, Thomas, wishes to introduce into evidence at trial the following facts to prove he was not negligent in hitting the pedestrian

- that it was raining at the time of the accident. This is relevant because it tends to prove that it may have been difficult to see or stop the car.
- that he was an altar boy as a child. This is irrelevant because the fact that Thomas is an upstanding citizen has no reasonable connection as to whether he was negligent in operating his motor vehicle.

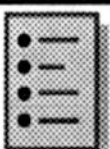

Discussion Point

Determine the relevancy of the following facts, using the same scenario.

- there have been four other accidents at the same intersection in the past six months
- Thomas owns another vehicle, a blue pick-up truck
- the pedestrian had just left a tavern
- the pedestrian was a convicted sex offender

Privilege

privilege: The right to refuse to testify or to prevent someone else from testifying.

A **privilege** is the right to refuse to testify or to prevent someone else from testifying.

There different types of privilege under the rules of evidence, including Fifth Amendment, attorney-client, and other privileges. These privileges are explained in the following section.

Fifth Amendment Under the Fifth Amendment of the U.S. Constitution, a person accused of committing a crime cannot be compelled to testify against himself. This privilege protects against self-incrimination and generally extends to any court proceeding in which an answer may lead to criminal prosecution.

Attorney-Client Privilege Attorneys cannot be compelled to testify regarding any communication made between themselves and a client. This privilege extends to any work product produced as a result of that relationship. (This privilege is more fully discussed in Chapter 10.)

Other Privileges Other privileges, such as doctor-patient, clergy-penitent, and husband-wife privileges exist to protect certain "sacred" relationships.

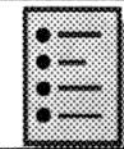

Discussion Point

Do you think any other types of relationships should be protected by privilege? Why or why not?

Competency

In order for a witness to testify, he or she must be deemed competent to provide testimony. No witnesses, including children or mentally disabled, are automatically disqualified. A judge will assess **competency** by applying the following criteria on an individual basis:

- Does the witness understand the duty to tell the truth?
- Does the witness have the ability to communicate his testimony?

Lay Opinion and Expert Testimony

In order for a witness's testimony to be admissible, the witness must have a firsthand or personal knowledge of the matter and must attempt to refrain from offering an opinion.

The Federal Rules of Evidence (FRE) acknowledge that it can be difficult for a witness to convey testimony effectively without giving an opinion, so a certain amount of leeway is granted and lay witnesses are generally allowed to make some opinions when they would be "helpful" provided they are "rationally based" on the witness' "perception." (See FRE Rule 602.)

Opinion is making an inference from fact. For example, I observe that you are flushed, coughing, and feverish. From those facts, I can make the inference, based on my reasonable experience, that you have the flu. This would be a **lay opinion**.

Expert testimony is allowed without the requirements imposed on lay witnesses. Expert witnesses may testify without firsthand knowledge of the matter and may express an opinion on that matter. This exception allows both parties in litigation to present technical and/or specialized information. There is an inexhaustible variety of types of expert witness ranging from medical doctors to experts on tire marks or bugs.

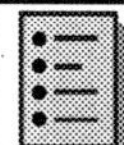

Discussion Point

Think about trials you have studied in class or learned about through the media. What types of experts have testified? What type of expertise did they hold?

In order for an expert witness's testimony to be admissible, the following elements must exist:

- The expert witness must be determined to be an "expert" on the matter about which he is to testify. This is done by questioning the expert witness on the stand to establish his credentials before direct examination can take place.
- The judge determines whether the witness is established as an expert and therefore entitled to make opinions based on secondhand knowledge.

For example, a physician may testify as an expert witness and offer an opinion that you are suffering from the flu based on her evaluation of your chart of symptoms. The physician, as an expert, may make that opinion based on your chart (secondhand knowledge) rather than an examination of you physically (firsthand knowledge).

Impeachment of Witnesses

During cross examination of witnesses, the opposing side will attempt to **impeach** that witness. Impeaching a witness is to question that witness's veracity and credibility. The goal is to make the jury question the credibility of the witness's testimony. The rules of evidence limit the scope of impeachment, generally limiting specific instances of conduct. (FRE 608(a))

Other Routes of Admissibility

There are other ways that evidence is admitted into court. Stipulations, judicial notice, and presumption allow the presenting party to introduce the evidence without having the burden of establishing the fact through witnesses or the introduction of other evidence. These alternate routes or admissibility are described in the following section.

Stipulations A stipulation may be used when both sides agree about a particular matter and that agreement is entered into the record. Generally, the agreement is a mutual acknowledgement of a fact that the opposing party wishes to prove. This stipulation means that neither side needs to provide evidence during trial to prove or disprove the stipulated fact. Judges encourage stipulations made in pretrial proceedings because it streamlines the trial process. For example, both parties stipulate that it was raining the morning of the accident.

Judicial Notice Evidence is admitted under **judicial notice** when it is such a well-accepted fact that the judge will acknowledge it in the record. For example, a judge may take judicial notice of the fact that Thanksgiving is the third Thursday of November.

Presumption A **presumption** is a fact inferred to be true once another fact has been proven. In other words, if I can prove that A is true then you may infer that B is true. Most presumptions in evidence are rebuttable and evidence may be introduced that disproves that evidence. For example, the plaintiff in a trial may introduce evidence that her husband has been missing for over seven years and therefore should be presumed dead, making her eligible for life insurance benefits. This would be a presumption: it is true that the husband has been missing for seven years so we may infer from that fact that he is dead. This would be a rebuttable presumption: The defendant could introduce evidence that the husband is alive, thereby rebutting or disproving the presumption that he is dead.

Other Rules of Evidence

Two other rules of evidence are the best evidence rule and authentication of evidence. These rules are described in the following section.

Best Evidence Rule When introducing a written document into evidence, the document must be the original. An exception to this rule is made when the original document has been destroyed through no fault of the person now attempting to enter it into evidence. This guideline is called the **best evidence rule**.

Authentication Any tangible piece of evidence must be proved to be authentic or genuine. **Authentication** is often achieved by providing testimony by a witness who possesses firsthand knowledge of how the item was obtained and that the item is what it is presented to be. For example, a witness is called to testify that she saw the defendant sign the contract and the same contract is what is now being offered into evidence.

HEARSAY

Hearsay is an out of court statement offered to prove the truth of the matter asserted (FRE 801c). Simply stated, hearsay may be broken down into three essential elements:

- a witness testifies in court, under oath
- about a statement made out of court by another person
- in order to prove the truth of the matter included in the out of court statement

Any testimony that fulfills these three elements is considered hearsay and is thus inadmissible unless one of the exceptions to the hearsay rule applies. The rationale for barring such testimony is that because the statement being offered into evidence was made by an out of court declarant, there is no opportunity for the opposing side to cross examine that person. The importance of preserving the adversarial system requires that both sides be given the opportunity to question and impeach all witnesses.

Hearsay may be in oral, written, or assertive conduct form. For example, Ira testifies that when he asked Robert whether he was drunk, Robert shrugged his shoulders and nodded his head. This "assertive conduct" by Robert, the actions of shrugging and nodding is a substitute for words and can therefore be considered a statement for the purposes of hearsay. (FRE 801(a)) For example, a plaintiff's attorney offers the following testimony to prove George, the defendant was negligent. Abby testifies in court, under oath, "George told me that he fell asleep at the wheel."

Elements of Hearsay

The following list provides the elements of hearsay.

1. Witness testifies in court	Yes: Abby is testifying court
2. About a statement made out of court	Yes: George made the statement to Abby out of court
3. To prove the truth of the matter	Yes: The statement is offered to prove that George included in the out of court statement that he fell asleep at the wheel.

The third element of hearsay is the most complex. If the out of court statement is not offered to prove the truth of the matter of the statement but is instead offered merely to show that the statement was made, then the hearsay rule has no application. However, the testimony may still be ruled inadmissible due to relevancy considerations. Consider the scenario on the previous page. If Plaintiff's counsel offered George's out of court statement merely to show that the words were uttered, it is likely the judge would rule the statement inadmissible because it is irrelevant. The mere fact that George uttered words at that time does not make any other fact more or less probable in that case (the test for relevancy).

Hearsay Exceptions

A number of exceptions to the hearsay rule have been encoded in the rules of evidence (FRE 801 through 804). Most of these **hearsay exceptions** are based on the rationale that circumstance give an inherent credibility to the statement thereby relieving the concern regarding lack of cross examination whether or not the declarant is available for cross examination. Let's consider them separately.

Admissions by party opponents, FRE 801(d)(2)

An admission by a party, when offered by an opponent is admissible. For example, in a medical malpractice case against Dr. Suzie Scalpel, the plaintiff seeks to enter the evidence the following statement by Nurse Carmen: "Immediately after the operation, Dr. Scalpel told me "I really messed that one up." The admission by the party (Dr. Scalpel, the defendant, made the admission) offered by an opponent (the plaintiff is the opponent in the case) is admissible.

Practice Alert

The federal rules and many states now consider admissions by party opponent to be non-hearsay rather than an exception to the hearsay rule. The result is the same; the evidence is admissible.

Present sense impression, FRE 803(1)

A present sense impression is a statement describing or explaining an event made while the declarant was currently observing or experiencing the event, or immediately thereafter. For example, Nurse Carmen testifies that during the operation on the plaintiff Dr. Snooze, the anesthesiologist stated, "Suzie, the patient is bleeding profusely." The declarant (Dr. Snooze) described what he observed while he was observing it ("Bleeding profusely" while observing the bleeding).

Excited utterance, FRE 803(2)

An excited utterance is a statement made by the declarant relating to an exciting event while the declarant was under the stress caused by the exciting event. Unlike present sense impression, the excited utterance must be made *while* the exciting event in question is taking place and the event must be of sufficiently startling quality to produce a spontaneous statement. For example, the State offers this testimony by Marjorie; "I heard Kara scream during the shooting 'Blair has a gun!" The declarant (Kara) while under stress (during the shooting) described what she saw ("Blair has a gun!").

Existing mental, emotional or physical condition, FRE 803(3)

Another hearsay exception is an out of court statement regarding the declarant's then existing mental, emotional, or physical condition. For example, Paul testifies "A moment before he collapsed, Drew said to me 'I feel lightheaded.'" The declarant (Drew) made a statement regarding his then existing physical condition ("I feel lightheaded.")

Business record, FRE 803(6)

This exception includes records that have been kept in the course of regularly conducted business. This includes hospital records, hotel guest ledgers, accounts payable, and so on.

Dying declaration, FRE 804(b)(2)

A dying declaration is an out of court statement made under the reasonable belief of impending, imminent death. For example, Shauna finds Tony in a pool of blood. Shauna testifies that two minutes before he died Tony said to her "Victor shot me." The declarant (Tony) made a statement ("Victor shot me.") under the very reasonable belief that he was dying.

Statement against self-interest, FRE 804(b)(3)

A statement against self-interest is an out of court statement made by a nonparty, that is so contrary to his financial interests that a reasonable person can conclude that the declarant would not have made such a statement unless it was true. The declarant must be unavailable as a witness. For example, Grace testifies that Will told her "I defaulted on three loans yesterday." Will has since left the country. The declarant (Will) made a statement contrary to his financial interests ("I defaulted on three loans.") and is unavailable as a witness.

Key Terms

admissible evidence
authentication
best evidence rule
circumstantial evidence
competency
direct evidence
expert testimony
federal rules of evidence
hearsay
hearsay exceptions
impeach
judicial notice
lay opinion
presumption
privilege
relevant evidence

Exercises

1. After a hard day at work, Antonin stops by the local watering hole, Clarence's Place. While there, Antonin plays four games of darts and engages in one loud political argument with another patron, Ruth. Three hours later, after consuming eight gin and tonics, Antonin gets in his car and proceeds down Route 44 toward his home. He is stopped by local police and arrested for driving under the influence of alcohol after failing a field sobriety test. Which of the following evidence is relevant to the case?
   a. Antonin brews beer in his basement
   b. Antonin is divorced and has five children
   c. Antonin belongs to the Ku Klux Klan
   d. Antonin is mayor of the neighboring town
   e. Antonin was in a different bar earlier in the night

2. Jack is treasurer of the student government at his college. Part of his responsibilities as treasurer include adding weekly receipts received from student-run organizations and making deposits into the student government account. Eight months into his tenure as treasurer, a routine audit reveals that over $25,000 is missing from the account. The college sues Jack for embezzling the funds. Which of the following evidence is relevant to the case?
   a. Jack has 20,000 in student loans
   b. Jack's mother is on board of university
   c. Jack is a member of the Eminem fan club
   d. Jack was arrested for disorderly conduct two years earlier
   e. Jack lost $4,000 gambling at Las Vegas the year before he became treasurer

3. Garrett resides in a small apartment complex. One day in January, Garrett fell down the icy steps leading from his second floor landing. His next-door neighbor Caroline, an elderly retired doctor, rushed to his aid. Garrett's landlord also came to the scene and according to Caroline exclaimed "Oh, that step is so dangerous!" Garrett suffered a broken leg and two bruised ribs. As a result of his injuries, Garrett spent three days in the hospital and missed three weeks of work and classes. Garrett sued his landlord Maggie for negligence. During the trial, Garrett's attorney called Caroline as a witness. Since the accident, Caroline had suffered a stroke, which impaired her speaking ability. Identify any evidence issues Garrett's attorney must consider including relevance, privilege, and competency issues.

4. Louis just got his driver's license. To celebrate, he invited three friends to join him in a car ride to a local lake. The four friends piled into the small car and stopped at a local convenience store to purchase snacks. Pulling out of the store's parking lot, a large dump truck collided with Louis' car. All four friends were seriously injured. Several witnesses are prepared to testify that they heard screams of "Oh no, the truck's going to hit us!" from inside the car just prior to impact. Which of the following evidence would be admissible? Explain why or why not.
   a. Repair and maintenance records of car
   b. Hospital records for victims
   c. The victims' attorney's notes
   d. The police report of the accident
   e. A short story written by one victim recording recovery
   f. Screams heard by witnesses prior to impact

5. Cruella and Omarosa are aging opera stars who have recently agreed to participate in a reality show following their glamorous lives. The two stars meet for dinner during which they discuss their plans for the show and Cruella tells Omarosa she forgives her for stealing her boyfriend years ago. Several hours after dining, Omarosa suddenly exclaims to her housekeeper, Donald, "My feet are going numb—I know Cruella has poisoned me!!" Omarosa then collapses and dies days later. Cruella is charged with Omarosa's murder.
   a. Is Omarosa's statement admissible at trial? Why or why not?
   b. May Cruella testify about what she said to Omarosa during dinner? Why or why not?

6. Russell is a temperamental actor in town to plug his upcoming movie on morning talk shows. His agent reserves him a room at a trendy new hotel often described in gossip magazines. Russell arrives late and attempts to check in. The clerk at the hotel informs Russell that they have no record of his reservation. Russell, upset that he will now have to stay in a lesser hotel, shouts at the clerk "Don't you know who I am? Give me a room or else!!" The clerk refuses and in response Russell takes off his Prada loafer and throws it at the clerk, striking him on the head causing a gash. The clerk sues Russell for medical costs and emotional distress. Which of the following evidence will be admissible at trial? Cite the applicable rule or doctrine.
   a. The clerk's medical records
   b. Records from Russell's therapist
   c. Russell's statement to the clerk
   d. The hotel reservation records
   e. Eyewitness testimony from other guests regarding the altercation

Library Resources

Evidence in a Nutshell: State and Federal Rules (4th Ed), Paul F. Rothstein, Myrna S. Raeder & David Crump, West Publishing Co., 2004.
The Nutshell series always provides concise and readable guides.

Evidence Cases and Problems, Steven I. Friedland, Butterworth Company, 1995.
Provides good examples and cases.

Evidence: Practice Under the Rules (2nd Ed)., Christopher B. Mueller & Laird C. Kirkpatrick, Aspen Law and Business, 1999.
This book is heavy on theory but accessibly written.

Online Resources

Legal Information Institute at Cornell, http://www.law.cornell.edu/topics/evidence.html
This site provides good overall discussions of the law and access to the Federal Rules of Evidence.

Jurist, http://jurist.law.pitt.edu/sg_evid.htm
This site offers good links to relevant sites and access to periodicals and articles on evidence.

PART 3

LEGAL ANALYSIS

CHAPTER 10

Legal Analysis of Statutory Law

INTRODUCTION

Legal analysis is the application of rules to facts. When you represent a client, you must apply the specific facts of your client's case to the rule to determine which rules will guide the outcome. Rules may be statutory or judge created through case law. We will begin by discussing general concepts regarding statutory rules.

STATUTORY RULES

Statutes are created by the legislature: Congress creates federal statutes, state legislatures create that state's statutes, and municipal legislatures create ordinances or local statutes. Administrative agencies create administrative rules or regulations that apply only within that agency's proceedings.

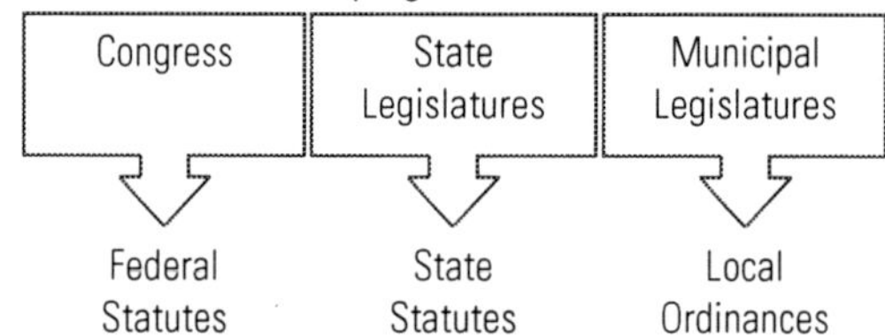

Exhibit 10-1 Creation of Statutes

Each statute has elements and each element must be satisfied in order for a person to violate said statute. Each word is chosen and included by the legislature for a reason; therefore, each word must be considered for its meaning within that statute. Sometimes the legislative history of a statute is researched to determine exactly what the legislators intended as they were creating the law.

Tools of Analysis for Statutory Law

An analysis must be conducted to determine whether a particular statute is applicable to your client's specific set of facts. The best way to understand and apply statutory law is through the technique of **elements analysis**. An elements analysis allows you to apply the individual elements to the particular facts of your case.

elements analysis: Technique that allows you to apply the individual elements of a statute to the particular facts of your case.

The determination can then be made as to whether the statute can be properly applied. The elements are the conditions expressed in the statute that must be satisfied in order for the statute to apply. Every statute may be broken down into elements and in fact, it should become habit to immediately break every statute you read into its elements.

Consider the following statute for burglary:

Sec. 20-56 Burglary

A person is guilty of burglary if he unlawfully enters a building or occupied structure, with the purpose of committing a crime therein.

Break down the elements of the statute

1. a person
2. is guilty of burglary if
3. he unlawfully enters a building
4. or occupied structure
5. with the purpose of committing a crime therein

In breaking down the elements, let common sense be your guide. Each element must make sense on its own. For example "with the purpose of committing" doesn't make sense without the inclusion of "a crime therein." Signposts such as "or" indicate that a separate element should be noted. In the beginning, it is better to break a statute into too many elements than not enough. This technique allows you to be sure you are considering all the essential elements of statute.

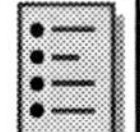

Discussion Point

Using the elements analysis technique, conduct an elements analysis for each of the following statutes:

a. No physician shall dispense narcotics without a prescription.
b. All political advertisements shall display the name of the candidate, the name of the candidate's committee, and the name of the candidate's treasurer.
c. Murder committed by means of poison, or by lying in wait, or by willful, deliberate, and premeditated killing, or committed in perpetrating or attempting to perpetrate arson, sexual assault, aggravated sexual assault, robbery, or burglary, shall be murder in the first degree. All other kinds shall be murder in the second degree.
d. A person is guilty of arson if he starts a fire or causes an explosion with the purpose of: (a) destroying a building or occupied structure of another; or (b) destroying or damaging any property, whether his own or another's, to collect insurance for such loss.

The next step is to apply the facts of your case to the rule to determine what issues exist by creating an **elements chart**. Only by applying your facts to the rule can you determine whether the statute applies to your client and what possible arguments you can make that it does or does not apply. Let us look at the burglary statute again.

1. a person
2. is guilty of burglary if
3. he unlawfully enters a building
4. or occupied structure
5. with the purpose of committing a crime therein

Consider the following scenario. The client's facts are that Roberta is angry with her roommate Anisha for being late with her portion of the rent again. On her way home from quaffing a few pints at a local pub, Roberta passes Anisha's prized Mustang parked in front of the apartment. Roberta decides to take the digital camera Anisha left on the front seat of the car. Roberta opens the unlocked passenger's side door, climbs in, and takes the camera. Unbeknownst to Roberta, Anisha was asleep in the back seat. Roberta is arrested under the burglary statute. The first step is to apply the facts of Roberta's case to the statute, as shown in Exhibit 10–2.

	Elements Analysis Chart **Statutory Elements**	**Facts**	**Issue?**
1	A person	Roberta is a person.	no
2	is guilty of burglary if	-to be determined-	-to be determined-
3	he unlawfully enters a building or	(a) car door was unlocked (b) car is not a building	yes
4	occupied structure	(a) Susan was asleep in the back seat (b) Car is not a structure	yes
5	with the purpose of committing a crime therein.	Roberta intended to steal Susan's digital camera.	no

Exhibit 10-2 Elements Analysis Chart

Now the issues can be determined. From Exhibit 10–2, it is clear that the three issues that arise are (1) whether Roberta "unlawfully" entered the car because the door was unlocked, (2) whether the Mustang may be considered a "building" under the statute, and (3) whether the Mustang may be considered an "occupied structure" under the statute. In reviewing elements for issues, consider the following factors:

- Are any terms or words ambiguous? Ambiguity of terms can be an issue in of itself. For example, what does "occupied" or "structure" mean? Does the fact that Susan was inside the Mustang at the time Roberta broke in make the car "occupied"? Could the car then be considered a "structure" under the statute?
- Look at the specific facts of your case. How do they support or disprove each element? This is how you identify the issues. For example, in considering the element of "unlawfully enters a building," our facts are that Roberta opened an unlocked door to enter the car. These facts tend to disprove the element—is opening an unlocked car "unlawfully entering?" Can a car be considered a building?

The next step is to develop an **issue statement** that identifies the issue in sentence form.

Placing the issue into an issue statement allows you to frame your analysis and prepare the groundwork for the next step in legal analysis: communicating your analysis through writing. Your issue statement should

- be clear and concise. No more than one or two sentences should be necessary.
- always refer back to the rule. "Can a car be considered a 'building' as contemplated by Section 20-56?"
- use the actual language of the statute in your issue statement. Do not paraphrase: use the word "unlawfully" as stated in the statute rather than "illegally."

	Elements Analysis Chart Statutory Elements	Facts	Issue?	Issue Statement
1	A person	Roberta is a person.	no	none
2	is guilty of burglary if	-to be determined-	-to be determined-	none
3	he unlawfully enters a building or	(a) car door was unlocked (b) car is not a building	yes	(a) Does the action of opening an unlocked car door constitute "unlawfully entering" Susan's Car as required by Section 20-56? (b) Can a car be considered a "building" for purposes of Section 20-56?
4	occupied structure	(a) Susan was asleep in the back seat (b) Car is not a structure	yes	(a) Can a car with a sleeping person inside be considered an "occupied structure" for purposes of Section 20-56? (b) Can a car be considered a "structure" for purposes of Section 20-56?
5	with the purpose of committing a crime therein.	Roberta intended to steal Susan's digital camera.	no	none

Exhibit 10-3 Elements Analysis Chart with Issues

Expressing Your Analysis Through Writing

Armed with your elements chart, you may begin communicating your analysis in written form. In this chapter, we will discuss the basic techniques for communicating your analysis. See Chapters 14 and 15 for detailed discussions of legal writing strategies and forms.

Step One

The elements chart has identified the issues you need to analyze and has summarized those issues in issue statements.

1. Does the action of opening an unlocked car door constitute "unlawful" entry of Susan's car as required by Section 20-56?
2. Did Roberta "unlawfully enter a building" in violation of Section 20-56 by opening an unlocked car door and entering that car?
3. Can a car with a person asleep in it be considered an "occupied structure" as contemplated by Section 20-56?

Use these issue statements as the basis for your analysis. Analyze and discuss each issue separately.

Step Two

Good legal analysis conforms to strict guidelines of communication. The most commonly used outline is IRAC: Issue, Rule, Application, and Conclusion. IRAC may be used as a framework for your analysis in individual paragraphs as well as an entire memorandum.

Begin with an Issue. By creating an issue statement in your elements chart, you have already completed this first step: Can a car with a person asleep in it be considered an "occupied structure" as contemplated by Section 20-56?

Next you must introduce the Rule. Section 20-56 provides "A person is guilty of burglary if he unlawfully enters a building or occupied structure with the purpose of committing a crime therein."

The next step is the Application of your facts to the rule. This portion will discuss both sides, providing analysis and counter analysis. In the present case, Roberta entered a parked car that contained a sleeping person in the back seat. A car is a moveable type of machinery, not a permanent housing generally connoted by the term "structure."

The State may argue that the fact that Anisha was asleep in the back seat creates a presumption that the car was some type of resting or dwelling place for her and thereby could be considered a "structure" for purposes of Section 20-56. However, the argument does not ring true because Anisha did not generally use her car for housing evidenced by the fact that she shared an apartment with Roberta.

Now, provide a Conclusion. Therefore, it must be concluded that a car cannot be considered a "structure" for the purposes of Section 20-56.

Placed together, the analysis looks like this: Can a car with a person asleep in it be considered an "occupied structure" as contemplated by Section 20-56? Section 20-56 provides "A person is guilty of burglary if he unlawfully enters a building or occupied structure with the purpose of committing a crime therein."

Note that the individual elements of IRAC are not listed within the paragraph. Use IRAC only as an "invisible" framework for your analysis. Use the IRAC structure for each individual issue. This analysis uses IRAC as a framework over three paragraphs. A new IRAC would begin when discussing the next issue.

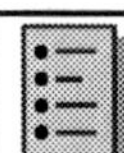

Discussion Point

Use the second issue statement derived from Section 20-56, "unlawfully enters a building," to write an analysis of that issue using the IRAC framework.

IRAC may be used as a framework for any type of written legal analysis. For example, you may use IRAC when writing an analysis of case law. (See Chapter 11.)

Key Terms

elements analysis

elements chart

IRAC framework

issue statement

Exercises

1. Read each of the following statutes. Conduct an elements analysis of each and identify any ambiguities in the language of the statute.
   Sec. 53a-54d: Arson Murder. A person is guilty of murder when, acting either alone or with one or more persons, he commits arson and, in the course of such arson, causes the death of a person.
   Sec. 53a-56: Manslaughter in the 2nd Degree. A person is guilty of this crime when: (1) He recklessly causes the death of another person; or (2) he intentionally causes or aids another person, other than by force, duress or deception, to commit suicide.
   Sec. 53a-102: Burglary in the 2nd Degree. A person is guilty of this crime when such person (1) enters or remains unlawfully in a dwelling at night with the intent to commit a crime therein.

2. Read the following statutes and fact patterns.
   - Conduct an elements analysis of the statute and prepare elements analysis chart.
   - Identify the statutory issues in the accompanying fact patterns. What are the legally relevant facts?
   - Plug those facts into your elements analysis chart and create issue statements.
   - Write a legal analysis of each issue using the IRAC framework.

Statute One:
Consumer Credit Protection Law. It is illegal for any collection agency or employee of a collection agency, in the attempt to collect alleged debt, to harass alleged debtors or to add any additional interest or fees not provided under the law.

Fact Pattern A:
Lily, owner of a clothing boutique, loaned $300 to an employee, Ruby. When Ruby failed to pay the $300 within a week, Lily began leaving threatening messages for her in the employee break room.

Fact Pattern B:
Todd James is the owner of a small collection agency. During a weekend trip to a local casino, Todd loaned his friend Chuck $500 to play the slots after Chuck had gambled his money away. Two weeks later Chuck had failed to repay Todd as they had previously agreed. Todd sent Chuck a note demanding repayment of the $500 and an additional penalty charge of $200.

Statute Two:
Employment Rights Act: If an employee suffers injury to his person arising out of and in the course of his employment, the worker is entitled to recover under this Act.

Facts A:
Spencer runs a small summer tennis camp. Most of his instructors are college students who play for their respective college teams. One morning, the camp was surprised when three world-class players dropped by the camp, accompanied by local news photographers. The players were in town to play in a professional tournament.
Responding to encouragement by Spencer, other instructors and campers, one of the players, Connor, entered one of the courts and began demonstrating his famous serve and volley technique. During the demonstration, Connor pulled a ligament and was unable to play for the rest of the professional season.

Facts B:
Collette was an up and coming advertising executive at a large firm in Los Angeles. As part of a marketing strategy, Collete's supervisor had advised his staff that they should "do what it takes" to keep clients happy with the firm.
During a business trip to Wisconsin to meet with one of the firm's most important clients, Collette was asked to accompany the client on a bungee jumping excursion as part of the client's offsite "trust building" exercises. Collette bungee jumped, plunged to the ground when the bungee snapped and suffered grievous injuries.

Library Resources

Legal Reasoning and Legal Writing: Structure, Strategy and Style (4th Ed.), Richard K. Neumann, Aspen Business and Law, 2001.
This book provides an in-depth text on both reasoning and writing.

Writing and Analysis in the Law (2nd Ed.) Shapo, Marilyn R. Walter & Elizabeth Fajans, Foundation Press, 1991.
Excellent exercises are offered in this book.

Legal Method and Writing (4th Ed.) Charles R. Calleros, Aspen Business and Law, 2001.
This is a comprehensive text often used in law school legal method courses.

Online Resources

Harvard Law School, http://www.law.harvard.edu/library/services/research/guides
This site provides a guide to legal analysis.

University of Connecticut School of Law, http://www.law.uconn.edu/library/clipper/guides
Helpful and concise tips are available at this site.

Cornell University School of Law, http://www.law.cornell.edu
This site offers examples and guides.

CHAPTER 11

Legal Analysis of Case Law

INTRODUCTION

When an appellate judge decides the outcome of a case, that decision is generally written and published as case law. That case law may be then used by subsequent judges to base their decisions upon. Attorneys will conduct legal research to locate case law that supports their position and to persuade a judge to rule in their favor based on rulings made in previous cases. It is necessary to have a clear understanding of how case law is created and how to apply it to your particular facts.

STARE DECISIS AND PRECEDENT

stare decisis: Judges are reluctant to overturn their own rulings.

Two doctrines make this reliance on case law possible. The first is the doctrine of **stare decisis**. Stare decisis holds that judges must be reluctant to overturn their own rulings.

The doctrine of stare decisis is essential because failure to uphold rulings previously made would make it impossible for parties to rely on previous rulings. This lack of reliability undermines the stability of the law. Imagine if the U.S. Supreme Court rules in one session that torture of political prisoners of the government is unconstitutional and then rules in the next that it is constitutional. There would be confusion as to how the government is permitted to act under the law and confusion as to how to decide future similar cases.

opinion: Written document issued by a court that explains their decision in a case.

The judges issue their rulings in a document called an **opinion**.

The opinion explains the court's decision in a case and is written by only one judge. One judge is chosen to write the opinion that the majority of judges agree upon. This is called the **majority opinion**. If a judge agrees with the final outcome of the majority's decision but disagrees with its reasoning supporting that decision, that judge may write her own opinion, called a **concurring opinion**. If a judge or judges disagree with the majority's reasoning and decision, she may write a **dissenting opinion**. Only the majority opinion becomes law and creates precedent.

Although the doctrine of stare decisis is generally upheld, in certain circumstances judges determine that the previous ruling must be overruled based on changing social mores or other conditions. A famous example from the U.S. Supreme Court may be found in the case of *Brown v. Board of Education* (341 US 483 (1954)). In *Brown,* the Court overruled its decision in *Plessy v. Ferguson* (163 US 537 (1886)), which held that "separate but equal" facilities for African Americans was constitutional. Fifty-eight years later, the *Brown* court overruled the separate but equal holding and ruled that such arrangements were unconstitutional.

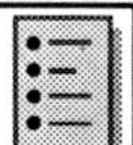

Discussion Point

What other famous U.S. Supreme Court rulings can you think of that overruled a previous decision? Discuss.

This ability to overturn past decisions illustrates the importance of selection of U.S. Supreme Court justices. A change in the justices can alter the court's future decisions, including overruling previous decisions. For example, *Roe v. Wade* (410 US 113 (1973)), is a case decided by the Court in 1973 that extended a constitutional right to privacy to include the right of a woman to legally seek an abortion. Conservatives opposed to that decision have lobbied various presidents to appoint justices to the Court that would vote differently and overrule *Roe*.

A related and equally important doctrine is that of **precedent**. Precedent requires judges to follow rulings made by higher court judges, in the same jurisdiction on a case that is analogous.

precedent: Requirement that judges follow ruling made by higher court judges, in the same jurisdiction on a case that is analogous.

When conducting legal research to locate case law that will assist your client, you are looking for cases that the court will accept as precedent, or, in other words, a case that the judge must follow. (See Chapter 12 for more discussion on precedent.)

UNDERSTANDING CASE LAW

The first step in analyzing case law is to understand it. As you read cases, you will see that some opinions are written clearly and concisely whereas others are more dense and harder to understand. This is because judges with differing writing and analytical skills compose these opinions. It is your job to make sense of the opinion and to take the essential information from that opinion and apply it your specific facts. The best way to make sense of an opinion is to **brief** it. To brief a case means to write a summary of the important elements of the case.

brief: A summary of the important elements of a case.

A brief is meant to be a concise summary that allows you to refer back to it and gain the essentials of the court's reasoning and decision without having to go back and reread the entire opinion. However, it is important to thoroughly read and understand an opinion before attempting to brief it.

A brief should include the title of case and citation and a brief description of the relevant facts of the case in bullet form or short sentences. The following is a list of some important elements to include in a brief.

- Issue(s). List **issues** discussed by the court. Often, there are more than one issue discussed in a case. You must list them all here. Often an opinion will clearly indicate the issues with phrases such as "The first issue to address..." or "There are three issues to be resolved in this case..."
- Rule(s). Identify the **rules** being applied in the case. The rules may include statutes, regulations, and or case law. Often the rule is included with issue, as above.
- Holding. The **holding** is the answer to the issues presented in the case. You may quote directly from the opinion in your brief.
- Reasoning. **Reasoning** explains how the court justifies its holding. This should be the longest part of your brief because it should include a discussion for each of the issues addressed in the

opinion. You will use this portion of the brief to create legal arguments specific to your facts.

- Disposition. **Disposition** describes what the court orders for the case. This can include **affirming** the lower court's decision, **reversing** the lower court's decision, and **remanding** or sending the matter back to the lower court for further proceedings.

When you read a case you plan to brief, it is helpful to make notes as you go along. These notes can be made on the margins of a copy or on a separate page. You may then take those notes and create the written brief.

Eugene J. Wrinn *v.* State of Connecticut ET AL.
(15085)
Borden, Berden, Norcott, Katz and Palmer, Js.

The plaintiff sought to recover damages for personal injuries he sustained when his automobile, which was stopped at a traffic signal, was struck from behind by a motor vehicle owned by the defendant state and operated by a state employee. The trial court refused the plaintiff's request to instruct the jury that the defendant had violated the statue (§ 14-240) that prohibits a driver from following another vehicle too closely. The jury returned a verdict in favor of the defendant and the trial court rendered judgment in accordance with the verdict. Thereafter, the plaintiff appealed to the Appellate Court, which affirmed the judgment of the trial court, and the plaintiff, on the granting of certification, appealed to this court. *Held* that the trial court properly refused to instruct the jury on § 14-240, the plaintiff having presented no evidence that the defendant had breached its duty not to "follow" too closely; the term "follow" as used in § 14-240 implies the movement of two vehicles, there was no evidence that the defendant's vehicle had ever followed the plaintiff's vehicle, and the plaintiff's claim that a rear end collision, regardless of the manner in which the accident occurs, requires an instruction on § 14-240 was unavailing.

Argued May 26—decision released July 25, 1995

Action to recover damages for personal injuries sustained by the plaintiff in a motor vehicle accident allegedly caused by the defendants' negligence, brought to the Superior Court in the judicial district of Stamford-Norwalk, where the court, *Ryan J.*, granted the defendants' motion to strike the complaint as against the defendant Vallerie Tyson; thereafter, the matter was tried to the jury before *Rush, J.*; verdict for the named defendant; subsequently, the court denied the plaintiff's motion to set aside the verdict and rendered judgment in accordance with the verdict, from which the plaintiff appealed to the Appellate Court, *Landau*, *Heiman*, and *Freedman*, *Js.*, which affirmed the judgment of the trial court, and the plaintiff, on the granting of certification, appealed to this court. *Affirmed.*

Karen L. Murdoch, with whom was *Christy Scott*,
for the appellant (plaintiff).

Philip F. von Kuhn, for the appellee (named defendant).

Norcott, J. The dispositive issue in this certified appeal is whether, under the circumstances of this case, the trial court improperly refused to instruct the jury regarding General Statutes § 14-240,[1] which prohibits vehicles from following too closely. The plaintiff, Eugene Wrinn, instituted this action against the defendant, the state of Connecticut,[2] to recover damages for personal injuries sustained when the defendant's vehicle collided with the rear end of the plaintiff's vehicle while it was stopped at a traffic signal at the end of a highway off ramp. The plaintiff alleged that the defendant was negligent in following his vehicle too closely in violation of § 14-240. At trial, the plaintiff requested that the trial court instruct the jury on that allegation. The trial court denied this request. Thereafter, the jury returned a verdict in favor of the defendant and the trial court rendered judgment accordingly. The plaintiff appealed to the Appellate Court, which affirmed the judgment of the trial court. *Wrinn* v. *State*, 35 Conn. App. 464, 646 A.2d 869 (1994). We granted the plaintiff's petition for certification,[3] and now affirm the judgment of the Appellate Court.

As reported in the Appellate Court's opinion, the jury reasonably could have found the following facts. "On May 20, 1986, the plaintiff had been driving south on the Connecticut Turnpike, Interstate 95. He exited the highway in Norwalk at exit sixteen and stopped his vehicle behind another vehicle at a traffic signal at the end of the exit ramp. The weather was rainy and misty, and the road was wet. Vallerie Tyson, an employee of the state department of mental retardation, was operating a motor vehicle owned by the state in the ordinary course of her employment. Tyson entered the turnpike at exit fifteen and proceeded at a speed no greater than forty-five miles per hour between exits fifteen and sixteen. At exit sixteen, Tyson turned onto the exit ramp, and saw two vehicles ahead of her stopped at the traffic signal at the end of the ramp. As she slowed her vehicle it began to slide. Although Tyson attempted to avoid a collision, the vehicle collided with the rear of the plaintiff's vehicle. The tires on Tyson's vehicle were in good condition, the brakes were in good working order, and the vehicle had not skidded at any time prior to the collision." *Wrinn* v. *State*, supra, 35 Conn. App. 465–66.

The plaintiff instituted this negligence action to recover damages for personal injuries sustained as a result of the accident. At trial. "[t]he

---

[1] General Statutes § 14-240 provides: "(a) No driver of a motor vehicle shall follow another vehicle more closely than is reasonable and prudent, having regard for the speed of such vehicles, the traffic upon and the condition of the highway and weather conditions.

"(b) No person shall drive a vehicle in such proximity to another vehicle as to obstruct or impede traffic.

"(c) Motor vehicles being driven upon any highway in a caravan shall be so operated as to allow sufficient space between such vehicles or combination of vehicles to enable any other vehicle to enter and occupy such space without danger. This provision shall not apply to funeral processions or to motor vehicles under official escort or travelling under a special permit.

"(d) Violation of any of the provisions of this section shall be an infraction, provided any person operating a commercial vehicle combination in violation of any such provision shall have committed a violation and shall be fined not less than one hundred dollars nor more than one hundred fifty dollars."

[2] In addition to the state, the plaintiff also named the driver of the state owned vehicle, Vallerie Tyson, a state employee, as a defendant. On October 31, 1988, the court granted the defendants' motion to strike the complaint as to Tyson. We therefore refer to the state of Connecticut as the defendant.

[3] We granted certification to appeal, limited to the following issues: (1) "In the circumstances of this case, should the trial court have instructed the jury in accordance with Connecticut General Statutes § 14-240?" and (2) "If the first question is answered in the affirmative, does the failure to so charge require a new trial?" *Wrinn* v. *State*, 231 Conn. 930, 649 A.2d 255 (1994).

plaintiff filed a written request to charge, in accordance with Practice Book § 318, which included a request as to the applicability of General Statutes §14-240. The trial court refused to charge the jury on this statute stating, 'one of the considerations in application of the statute involves the speed of such vehicles' and ruling, 'there is no evidence that [Tyson] saw the plaintiff's vehicle at any time while it was moving or other than in a stopped condition at the light.'" Id., 468.

Our resolution of the plaintiff's claim hinges on the meaning of § 14-240. Section 14-240 (a) provides in relevant part: "No driver of a motor vehicle shall *follow* another vehicle more closely than is reasonable and prudent . . . ." (Emphasis added.) Neither our statutes nor our case law have defined the phrase "follow another vehicle more closely than is reasonable and prudent." The plaintiff argues that this phrase should be interpreted broadly to mean "going or coming after. The plaintiff asserts that the occurrence of a rear end collision entitles the victim to have the jury instructed on § 14-240, thereby allowing the jury the opportunity to determine whether the defendant is per se negligent if the statute is violated.[4] Therefore, the plaintiff claims that the trial court improperly denied his request to instruct the jury regarding § 14-240. We disagree.

"The objective of statutory construction is to give effect to the legislature. *State* v. *Delafose*, 185 Conn. 517, 521, 441, A.2d 158 (1981). . . .*Forsyth* v. *Rowe*, 226 Conn. 818, 828, 629 A.2d 379 (1993). [Ordinarily, where] the language of the statute is clear and unambiguous, it is assumed that the words themselves express the intent of the legislature and there is no need for statutory construction. . . .*All brand Importers, Inc.* v. *Dept. of Liquor Control*, 213 Conn. 184, 195, 567 A.2d 1156 (1989). . . .*Haesche* v. *Kissner*, 229 Conn. 213, 223, 640 A.2d 89 (1994)." (Internal quotation marks omitted.) *First Bethel Associates* v. *Bethel*, 231 Conn. 731, 739, 651 A.2d 1279 (1995).

"In the construction of the statutes, words and phrases shall be construed according to the commonly approved usage of the language . . . ." General Statutes § 1-1 (a); see *Carpenteri-Waddington, Inc.* v. *Commissioner of Revenue Services*, 231 Conn. 355, 362 650 A.2d 147 (1994); *State* v. *Indrisano*, 228 Conn. 795, 809, 640 A.2d 986 (1994); *State* v. *Jimenez*, 228 Conn. 335, 341, 636 A.2d 782 (1994); *Carr* v. *Bridgewater*, 224 Conn. 44, 56–57, 616 A.2d 257 (1992); *Caldor, Inc.* v. *Heffernan*, 183 Conn. 566, 570, 440 A.2d 767 (1981). In order to ascertain the plain meaning of the word "follow," it is appropriate to look to the dictionary definition. See *State* v. *Indrisano*, supra, 809 (employing dictionary definition); *Aetna Life & Casualty Co.* v. *Bulaong*, 218 Conn. 525, 534-35, 546 A.2d 216 (1988) (same). "Follow" has been defined as: "to move behind in the same path or direction." Webster's New International Dictionary (2d Ed. 1941). More specifically, in the context of a motor vehicle statute, the term "follow" implies movement of two vehicles: a leader and a follower. Thus, § 14-240, read in light of the plain meaning of the word "follow," requires that in order to prove a violation the plaintiff must show that: (1) the rear vehicle "followed" the front vehicle; *and* (2) the distance between the vehicles was closer than is reasonable and prudent under the circumstances. Accordingly, we agree with the Appellate Court's conclusion that "§ 14-240 is applicable to situations in which one motor vehicle is [traveling] behind another in the same lane of traffic, *and* there is evidence that the operator of the rear vehicle failed to maintain a reasonably safe distance between the vehicles, and that failure had a causal

---

[4] Section 14-240 has mitigating elements which raise factual questions for the jury.

connection to a resulting collision." (Emphasis added.) *Wrinn* v. *State*, supra, 35 Conn. App. 473.

Case law from other jurisdictions supports this interpretation of § 14-240. See *Gallacher* v. *Commissioner of Revenue Services*, 221 Conn. 166, 172, 602 A.2d 996 (1992). For example, in interpreting a substantially similar statute,[5] the Wisconsin Supreme Court concluded that the statute was inapplicable in a case where the driver of a tractor trailer, desiring to pass the plaintiff's stopped vehicle, turned his attention to possible traffic behind his vehicle. *Milwaukee & Suburban Transport Corp.* v. *Royal Transit Co.*, 29 Wis. 2d 620, 629-30, 139 N.W.2d 595 (1966). "True, the outcome was a violent meeting that can only be described as *too close* for comfort or safety, but clearly the factor resulting in the impact was failure to keep a proper and reasonably constant lookout. . . . It is perfectly clear that the legislature did not intend the provisions of [the statute] to apply in all rear-end collisions. The statute is directed against the dangerous and pernicious practice of 'tailgating.'" (Emphasis added.) Id., 630; see also *Cosse* v. *Bruley*, 445 So. 2d 41, 42–43 (La. App. 1984); *Houck* v. *Snyder*, 375 Mich. 392, 402–403, 134 N.W.2d 689 (1965); *La Mandri* v. *Carr*, 148 N.J. Super. 566, 571–72, 372 A.2d 1327 (1977).

We reject, therefore, the plaintiff's assertion that a rear end collision, regardless of the manner in which the accident occurs, requires instruction on § 14-240.[6] Such an interpretation would render meaningless the statute's first condition, namely, that the rear vehicle was "following" the front vehicle.

"'The court has a duty to submit the jury no issue upon which the evidence would not reasonably support a finding. . . .'" (Citations omitted.) *Goodmaster* v. *Houser*, 225 Conn. 637, 648, 625 A.2d 1366 (1993). At trial, the plaintiff presented no evidence that the defendant had breached its duty not to "follow" too closely. Indeed, there was no evidence that the two vehicles were simultaneously in motion, one traveling behind the other in the same lane. As discussed above, a rear end collision, in and of itself, is not sufficient evidence that the defendant's vehicle ever "followed" the plaintiff's vehicle, we conclude that the trial court properly refused to instruct the jury with respect to § 14-240.

The judgment is affirmed.

In this opinion the other justices concurred.

[5] Wisconsin Statutes § 346.14 provides in relevant part: "The operator of a motor vehicle shall not follow another vehicle more closely than is reasonable and prudent, having due regard for the speed of such vehicle and the traffic upon and the condition of the highway."

[6] It is clear, however, that § 14-240 sometimes may be applicable in rear end collisions with a stopped vehicle. See, e.g., *State* v. *Tobey*, 2 Conn. Cir. Ct. 485 (1964). Although a rear end collision is not a per se violation of § 14-240, such a collision may be the result of a violation of the statute. For example, if the front vehicle, which previously had been moving, stops and is rear-ended *because* the driver of the rear vehicle was "following" too closely, a jury instruction in accordance with § 14-240 would be proper. In order to reach the issue of causation, however, the plaintiff must first present evidence to show that prior to the collision, the defendant was following too closely.

Exhibit 11-1 *Wrinn v. State* of Connecticut

A sample case of *Wrinn v. State* of Connecticut is provided in Exhibit 11-1. A sample brief of *Wrinn* is provided in the following section.

EXAMPLE *Eugene J. Wrinn v. State of Connecticut, et al.,* 234 Conn. 401 (1995)

Facts: The P had been driving on Interstate 91 on a rainy day and stopped at the end of an exit ramp. The D, an employee of the state, also exited at that ramp and while braking, her vehicle began to slide and struck the back of the P's vehicle. P instituted negligence action against the D. At trial, the P attempted to apply CGS Sec. 14-240, but the trial court refused. P appeals the trial court's decision.

Issue: Does the occurrence of a rear end collision entitle the victim to have the jury instructed on CGS Sec. 14-240, thereby allowing the jury the opportunity to determine whether the defendant is negligent per se if the statute is violated?

Rule: CGS Sec. 14-240 provides: "(a) No driver of a motor vehicle shall follow another vehicle more closely than is reasonable and prudent, having regard for the speed of such vehicles, the traffic upon and the condition of the highway, and weather conditions."

Holding: The court rejects the P's assertion that "a rear end collision, regardless of the manner in which the accident occurs, requires instruction on Sec. 14-240. Such an interpretation would render meaningless the statute's first condition, namely, that the rear vehicle was 'following' the front vehicle."

Rationale: The P failed to provide any evidence at trial that the D had breached her duty to not "follow" too closely. "More specifically, in the context of a motor vehicle statute, the term 'follow' implies movement of two vehicles: a leader and a follower. Thus, Sec. 14-240, read in the light of the plain meaning of the word 'follow,' requires that in order to prove a violation the plaintiff must show that: (1) the near vehicle 'followed' the front vehicle, *and* (2) the distance between the vehicles was closer that is reasonable and prudent under the conditions." The P failed to meet this burden.

Disposition: Affirmed.

APPLYING OPINIONS

As discussed previously, judges decide cases by looking to earlier cases and applying that reasoning to the present case. This is called applying precedent. Therefore, it is the lawyer's job, with the assistance of a good paralegal, to find case law that a judge will apply in the current case. The lawyer must demonstrate to the judge that the earlier cases she is presenting are close enough factually and are analogous in legal principles. This is accomplished by discussing the facts and reasoning of the precedential case and arguing that it should be applied in your case.

Applying the Facts

It is virtually impossible to find a case that is identical factually to yours. Apply cases that closely relate to your facts. For example, a medical malpractice case involving a faulty cardiac monitor is factually similar to a medical malpractice case involving a faulty respirator. After briefing a case, identify all the factual similarities and differences between your facts and the facts of the case you wish to apply.

Your Facts

Your client is the owner of a small coffee shop. He buys all his coffee beans from a distributor located in another state who imports coffee beans from

Brazil. The distributor has made weekly deliveries of 200 pounds of beans for the past 2 years to the coffee shop and for which your client has paid for upon delivery. Last week the distributor failed to make his delivery. When our client called the distributor to complain, he was told that all deliveries are now going to the new Moondollar Coffee Shop down the street. Our client wants to sue for breach of contract. A paralegal finds the following case and thinks it can apply to our client's case.

Facts of Case

In *Ranchero v. Hugeburger* (302 W.V. 234 (2000)) a multinational food retailer, Hugeburger, sued a beef producer Ranchero for providing tainted meat to its franchises in three states. Hugeburger had a standing agreement with Ranchero to deliver 600 pounds per week, per store. Hugeburger alleged that Ranchero knew the meat was tainted but delivered it to the stores anyway because it had recently received a more lucrative contract to provide meat to one of Hugeburger's competitors. The court held that Ranchero had breached its contract with Hugeburger by delivering tainted meat instead of edible meat.

The analogous facts between the cases are that both involve commercial agreements, both our client and Hugeburger are food retailers to the public, and both involve breach of contract issues involving substandard delivery. The factual differences between the cases are that Hugeburger is a large company whereas our client is a small business, the products sold are different (meat vs. coffee), and no delivery at all differs from delivery of a tainted product. Based on this comparison, it may be concluded that the facts are analogous and the opinion may be properly applied.

Exhibit 11-2 Applying Opinions

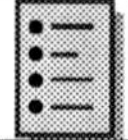

Discussion Point

Read each of the following. Using the strategies discussed in this chapter, determine for each opinion

- factual similarities
- factual differences
- whether the opinion may be properly applied to your facts based on factual analogies
- choose the opinion that is closest factually to your case

Our client's facts: John and Paul own a condo together. Part of the condo agreement provides that all front steps must have an awning over them. Their condo did have an awning when they purchased the unit, but John removed it to allow more sun to reach his prize azaleas. One evening, Paul hosts a Tupperware party at the condo. He invites 15 guests to enjoy wine and cheese and browse the latest Tupperware offerings. As one of his guests, George, is leaving the party, he slips and falls on the front steps that have become wet and slippery from a rainstorm and breaks his hip. George sues John and Paul for his injuries suffered as a result of his fall.

Opinion 1 *Panyard v. Tressy* (306 Colo. 54 (2001)) Facts: D hosted a neighborhood block party in her backyard. Each family paid $30 to the D to pay for the costs of the party. As part of the entertainment for the children, D purchased and erected a trampoline with a safety net. During the party, two children jumping on the trampoline collided and one child suffered head injuries.

Opinion 2 *Ervin v. Melba* (444 Ky. 103 (2002)) Facts: P was employed as a cashier at a convenience store. Part of his daily duties included scrubbing the store's floors, restocking shelves, and bringing trash to a dumpster. One evening, P was bringing the trash outside, when he slipped on wet stairs and suffered a broken collarbone.

Opinion 3 *Cohen v. Birt* (275 Vt. 98 (1999)) Facts: D is a large, hardware supply chain store. P was shopping in her local store with her young child. As they were walking through the aisles looking for a particular type of sink faucet, P's child reached out and grabbed a box on a shelf. This action dislodged boxes located above and a number fell down and two struck P on the head, causing severe head injuries.

Applying the Rule

Apply cases that involve the same rule. A discussion of a court's treatment of the definition of forseeability is not persuasive if your case is dealing with the definition of recklessness.

For example, using the same scenario as above, except the *Ranchero v. Hugeburger* court strictly applied a federal statute to determine breach of contract whereas your case is being tried in state court under a state statute. In this case the rule would not be the same and therefore the case could not be properly applied.

EXAMPLE The courts have never considered breach of contract to be within the scope of the Royal Commission. Furthermore, the exclusive remedy bar does not apply to damages found in contract. *Milton v. Connecticut* (210 Mass. 43, 50, 213 A2d. 250, 256 (1999)). [Issue and Rule] In *Milton*, the plaintiff sued, alleging violation of merit system rules and improper discharge that resulted in physical and mental injuries. The *Milton* court found injuries to be contractual in nature and outside the scope of the Royal Commission. [Application] Therefore, if breach of contract can be established in the *plaintiff's case*, the court will continue its present course and allow him to recover for breach of his contract with the defendant. [Conclusion]

Key Terms

affirm
brief
concurring opinion
disposition
dissenting opinion
holding
issue
majority opinion
opinion
precedent
reasoning
remand
reverse
rule
stare decisis

Exercises

I.

1. Prepare a brief of *Adams v. Williams,* below.
2. Compare the facts of your client's case and *Adams v. Williams.* Are the relevant facts analogous or distinguishable? Explain.
3. List the facts that are relevant to the court's decision and discuss why you think the court felt they were relevant.
4. Determine what, if any, factual gaps between the facts of *Adams v. Williams* and your client's facts exist. Discuss.

Your client's facts: Your client is a twenty-year-old woman. Sondra is a college student pursuing a bachelor's degree in social work. This semester she has been participating in an internship at a local outreach center for recovering heroin addicts. As part of her internship, Sondra regularly interacts with patients at the center. One evening while leaving the center Sondra notices the back window to her car is rolled down. As she starts the car to leave the parking lot, two police officers shout to her "Stop, and put your hands up!" Sondra immediately stops the car and raises her hands. The police officers instruct Sondra to unlock the car door and she complies. The police officers open the back door and remove three bags of a white substance, that later tested positive for heroin, from the back seat of Sondra's car.

Sondra is then frisked and a forged prescription pad is found in her pocket. Sondra is arrested for possession of heroin and possession of fraudulent prescriptions.

The police officers received a tip from one of the doctors from the clinic that Sondra had stolen a prescription pad from the center.

Adams v. Williams, 407 U.S. 143 (1972)

MR. JUSTICE REHNQUIST delivered the opinion of the Court.

Respondent Robert Williams was convicted in a Connecticut state court of illegal possession of a handgun found during a "stop and frisk," as well as of possession of heroin that was found during a full search incident to his weapons arrest....[The Court of Appeals] held that evidence introduced at William's trial had been obtained by an unlawful search of his person and his car, and thus the state court judgments of conviction should be set aside. Since we conclude that the police officer's actions here conformed with the standards this Court laid down in *Terry v. Ohio,* 392 U.S. 1 (1968), we reverse.

Police Sgt. John Connolly was alone early in the morning on car patrol duty in a high-crime area of Bridgeport, Connecticut. At approximately 2:15 a.m. a person known to Sgt. Connolly approached his cruiser and informed him that an individual seated in a nearby vehicle was carrying narcotics and had a gun at his waist.

After calling for assistance on his car radio, Sgt. Connolly approached the vehicle to investigate the informant's report. Connolly tapped on the car window and asked the occupant, Robert Williams, to open the door. When Williams rolled down the window instead, the sergeant reached into the car and removed a fully loaded revolver from Williams' waistband. The gun had not been visible to Connolly from outside the car, but was in precisely the place indicated by the informant. Williams was then arrested by Connolly for unlawful possession of the pistol. A search incident to that arrest was conducted after other officers arrived. They found substantial quantities of heroin on Williams' person and in the car, and they found a machete and a second revolver hidden in the automobile.

Respondent contends that the initial seizure of his pistol, upon which rested the later search and seizure of the other weapons and narcotics, was not justified by the informant's tip to Sgt. Connolly. He claims that absent a more reliable informant, or some corroboration of the tip, the police officer's actions were unreasonable under the standards set forth in *Terry v. Ohio* [392 U.S. 1 (1968)].

In *Terry* this Court recognized that "a police officer may in appropriate circumstances and in an appropriate manner approach a person for purposes of investigating possibly criminal behavior even though here is no probable cause to make an arrest." (citations omitted). The Fourth Amendment does not require a police officer who lacks the precise level of information necessary for probable cause to arrest to simply shrug his shoulders and allow a crime to occur or a criminal to escape. On the contrary, *Terry* recognizes that it may be the essence of good police work to adopt an intermediate response. A brief stop of a suspicious individual, in order to determine his identity or to maintain the status quo momentarily while obtaining more information, may be most reasonable in light of the facts known to the officer at the time...

Applying these principles to the present case, we believe that Sgt. Connolly acted justifiably in responding to the informant's tip. The informant was known to him personally and had provided him with information in the past....In reaching this conclusion, we reject the respondent's argument that reasonable cause for stop and frisk can only be based on the officer's personal observation, rather than on information supplied by another person...

Once Sgt. Connolly had found the gun precisely where the informant had predicted, probable cause existed to arrest Williams for unlawful possession of the weapon…Under the circumstances surrounding Williams' possession of the gun seized by Sgt. Connolly, the arrest on the weapons charge was supported by probable cause, and the search of his person and the car incident to that arrest was lawful…The fruits of the search were therefore properly admitted at Williams' trial, and the Court of Appeals erred in reaching a contrary conclusion.

Reversed.

II.

Using *Adams v. Williams* and Sondra's fact pattern, prepare the following:

1. Make a list of the facts that are relevant to the court's decision in the matter.
2. Using this opinion as the only precedent, identify the issue(s) in both opinion and fact pattern. Discuss.
3. How would you formulate the holding in of the opinion? How could you apply it in the most advantageous manner for your client?
4. In light of the answers to these questions, would this case be helpful to your case? Explain.

Library Resources

Writing and Analysis in the Law (4th Ed.), Helene S. Shapo, Marilyn R. Walters, & Elizabeth Fajans, Foundation Press, 1999.
An excellent, law school level text.

Legal Reasoning and Writing (4th Ed.), Richard K. Neumann, Aspen Law and Business, 2001.
Clearly written and containing valuable exercises.

Legal Analysis and Writing (2nd Ed.), William H. Putnam, Thomson Delmar Learning, 2003.
A good book on legal writing and analysis.

Online Resources

Harvard Law School, http://www.law.harvard.edu/library/services/research/guides
This site provides helpful guide and examples.

University of Connecticut School of Law, http://www.law.uconn.edu/library/clipper/guides
This site offers great guides with quick tips.

PART 4

Legal Research

CHAPTER 12

Finding Statutory Law

INTRODUCTION

statute: A law written by a legislature.

A **statute** is a law written by a legislature, such as federal, the Congress of the United States, or a state legislature.

Statutes are mandatory law only within the jurisdiction of the legislature that created the law. In other words, a statute written by the Wisconsin legislature is not mandatory law in Massachusetts. In this chapter you will learn how a statute is made and strategies to help you locate relevant statutes for your particular issue.

THE CREATION OF A STATUTE

bill: A new piece of proposed legislation.

The evolution of a statute is often a long and complex process. Some statutes may be creating an entirely new law, whereas others are amending existing law or repealing existing law. The process begins with an idea that may be presented to a legislator from a number of different sources, including but not limited to, a constituent, a lobbyist, or the executive branch. That legislator then introduces the idea, now known as a **bill**, into the legislative process. Many bills never become law or are materially changed from their original state as a bill by the time they become law.

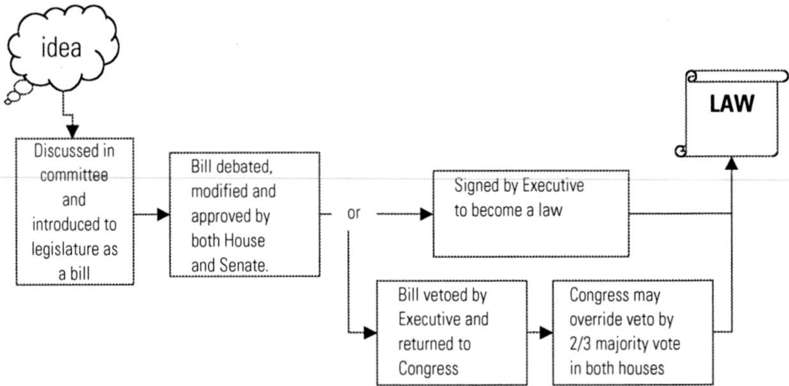

Exhibit 12-1 Creation of a Law

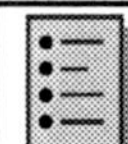

Discussion Point:

Consider your state's legislature. Discuss recent laws that have been passed. Are they entirely new or do they amend existing law?

Once the bill becomes a statute, it is included in the statutory code. Both federal and state statutes are compiled in codes. In order to locate a statute, you must first determine the code it is compiled in. Federal statutes are included in the *United States Code,* or U.S.C. Because the Congress is continually creating and passing laws during its two-year sessions, the code must be continually updated. This is done through a series of publications, each of which publish statutes at different stages. A newly created statute is first printed in a **slip law**, a small pamphlet printed immediately after a law is passed.

slip law: Small pamphlet that contains the text of a statute immediately after it has been passed by the legislature.

At the end of each session of Congress, the slip laws are reviewed, any corrections are made and then cumulated into bound volumes known as **statutes at large**.

statutes at large: Bound volumes containing statutes at the end of a session of Congress.

The statute is finally placed into the *United States Code,* where it appears sorted by subject matter. For example, a criminal statute will be placed in the criminal code section of the *U.S.C.*

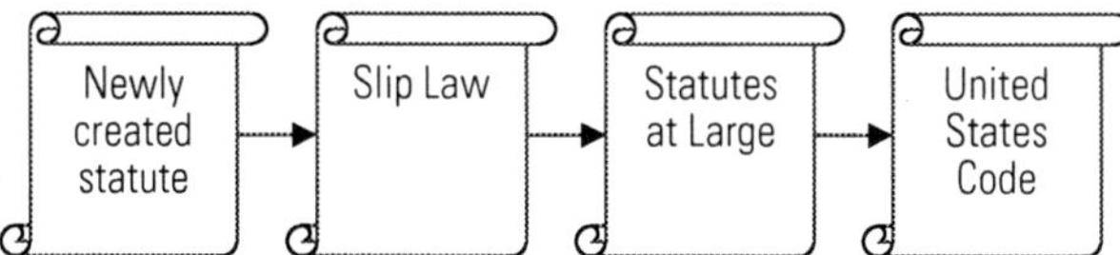

Exhibit 12-2 Federal Law Code

State statutes are also compiled in a code but generally new statutes are included in the bound volume of the state code through a pocket part or soft cover addendum that is periodically integrated into the bound volumes. Both federal and state statutes are printed in an official volume published by the government that includes only the text and short legislative history of the statute. But most state and the federal statutes are also printed in unofficial volumes that include both the actual text of the statute and notes of court decisions that interpret that statute. These annotated versions are helpful in conducting research on a particular statute because they include opinions that interpret that statute as well as relevant secondary materials. Let's look at both types of statutes.

Page 1069 TITLE 18—CRIMES AND CRIMINAL PROCEDURE §1112

tive in terms of physical characteristics or biological descent;

(7) the term "religious group" means a set of individuals whose identity as such is distinctive in terms of common religious creed, beliefs, doctrines, practices, or rituals; and

(8) the term "substantial part" means a part of a group of such numerical significance that the destruction or loss of that part would cause the destruction of the group as a viable entity within the nation of which such group is a part.

(Added Pub. L. 100-606, §2(a), Nov. 4, 1988, 102 Stat. 3046.)

CHAPTER 51—HOMICIDE

Sec.	
1111.	Murder.
1112.	Manslaughter.
1113.	Attempt to commit murder or manslaughter.
1114.	Protection of officers and employees of the United States.
1115.	Misconduct or neglect of ship officers.
1116.	Murder or manslaughter of foreign officials, official guests, or internationally protected persons.
1117.	Conspiracy to murder.
1118.	Murder by a Federal prisoner.
1119.	Foreign murder of United States nationals.
1120.	Murder by escaped prisoners.
1121.	Killing persons aiding Federal investigations or State correctional officers.
1122	Protection against the human immunodeficiency virus.

AMENDMENTS

1996—Pub. L. 104-294, title VI, §601(a)(6), Oct. 11, 1996, 110 Stat. 3498, added item 1122.

1994—Pub. L. 103-322, title VI, §§60005(b), 60009(b)(2), 60012(b), 60015(b), Sept. 13, 1994, 108 Stat. 1970, 1972-1974, added items 1118 to 1121.

1976—Pub. L. 94-467, §3, Oct. 8, 1976, 90 Stat. 1998, substituted "official guests, or internationally protected persons" for "or official guests" in item 1116.

1972—Pub. L. 92-539, title I, §102, Oct. 24, 1972, 86 Stat. 1071, added items 1116 and 1117.

§1111. Murder

(a) Murder is the unlawful killing of a human being with malice aforethought. Every murder perpetrated by poison, lying in wait, or any other kind of willful, deliberate, malicious, and premeditated killing; or committed in the perpetration of, or attempt to perpetrate, any arson, escape, murder, kidnapping, treason, espionage, sabotage, aggravated sexual abuse or sexual abuse, burglary, or robbery; or perpetrated from a premeditated design unlawfully and maliciously to effect the death of any human being other than him who is killed, is murder in the first degree.

Any other murder is murder in the second degree.

(b) Within the special maritime and territorial jurisdiction of the United States,

Whoever is guilty of murder in the first degree shall be punished by death or by imprisonment for life;

Whoever is guilty of murder in the second degree, shall be imprisoned for any term of years or for life.

(June 25, 1948, ch. 645, 62 Stat. 756; Pub. L. 98-473, title II, §1004, Oct. 12, 1984, 98 Stat. 2138; Pub. L. 99-646, §87(c)(4), Nov. 10, 1986, 100 Stat. 3623; Pub. L. 99-654, §3(a)(4), Nov. 14, 1986, 100 Stat. 3663; Pub. L. 100-690, title VII, §7025, Nov. 18, 1988, 102 Stat. 4397; Pub. L. 103-322, title VI, §60003(a)(4), Sept. 13, 1994, 108 Stat. 1969.)

HISTORICAL AND REVISION NOTES

Based on title 18, U.S.C., 1940 ed., §§452, 454, 567 (Mar. 4, 1909, ch. 321, §§273, 275, 330, 35 Stat. 1143, 1152).

Section consolidates the punishment provision of sections 454 and 567 of title 18, U.S.C., 1940 ed., with section 452 of title 18, U.S.C., 1940 ed.

The provision of said section 454 for the death penalty for first degree murder was consolidated with section 567 of said title 18, by adding the words "unless the jury qualifies its verdict by adding thereto 'without capital punishment' in which event he shall be sentenced to imprisonment for life".

The punishment for second degree murder was changed and the phrase "for any term of years or for life" was substituted for the words "not less than ten years and may be imprisoned for life". This change conforms to a uniform policy of omitting the minimum punishment.

Said section 567 was not included in section 2031 of this title since the rewritten punishment provision for rape removes the necessity for a qualified verdict.

The special maritime and territorial jurisdiction provision was added in view of definitive section 7 of this title.

AMENDMENTS

1994—Subsec. (b). Pub. L. 103-322 amended second par. generally. Prior to amendment, second par. read as follows: "Whoever is guilty of murder in the first degree, shall suffer death unless the jury qualifies its verdict by adding thereto 'without capital punishment', in which event he shall be sentenced to imprisonment for life;".

1988—Subsec. (a). Pub. L. 100-690 inserted a comma after "arson".

1986—Subsec. (a). Pub. L. 99-646 and Pub. L. 99-654 amended subsec. (a) identically, substituting "aggravated sexual abuse or sexual abuse" for ", rape".

1984—Subsec. (a). Pub. L. 98-473 inserted "escape, murder, kidnapping, treason, espionage, sabotage," after "arson".

EFFECTIVE DATE OF 1986 AMENDMENTS

Amendments by Pub. L. 99-646 and Pub. L. 99-654 effective respectively 30 days after Nov. 10, 1986, and 30 days after Nov. 14, 1986, see section 87(e) of Pub. L. 99-646 and section 4 of Pub. L. 99-654, set out as an Effective Date note under section 2241 of this title.

SECTION REFERRED TO IN OTHER SECTIONS

This section is referred to in sections 36, 115, 351, 924, 930, 1114, 1116, 1117, 1118, 1119, 1120, 1121, 1503, 1512, 1513, 1751, 1956, 2332, 3559, 5032 of this title; title 7 section 2146; title 15 section 1825; title 21 sections 461, 675, 1041; title 28 section 540B; title 42 sections 671, 2283, 5106a; title 49 section 46506.

§1112. Manslaughter

(a) Manslaughter is the unlawful killing of a human being without malice. It is of two kinds:

Voluntary—Upon a sudden quarrel or heat of passion.

Involuntary—In the commission of an unlawful act not amounting to a felony, or in the commission in an unlawful manner, or without due caution and circumspection, of a lawful act which might produce death.

(b) Within the special maritime and territorial jurisdiction of the United States,

Whoever is guilty of voluntary manslaughter, shall be fined under this title or imprisoned not more than ten years, or both;

Exhibit 12-3 Federal Statute, Courtesy of United States Government

FINDING STATUTES

As a paralegal, you want to locate a statute because it is relevant to the issues faced by your client. Statutes are placed in statutory codes in categories and each statute is given a citation or number for identification purposes and as its "address" to allow it to be easily located. Two major publications provide a guide to how statutes are cited in different states. *The Bluebook: A Uniform System of Citation* is the most commonly used guide to citation but another guide *ALWD Citation Manual, A Professional System of Citation* published by the Association of Legal Writing Directors has gained some acceptance. Consult either of these guides, as used in your office, for questions of citation.

Statutory Code Citation Format, by State, according to *Bluebook* Guidelines

Alabama:	Ala.Code Sec. 46-12-6 (year revised)
Alaska:	Alaska Stat. Sec. 56.12.210 (year revised)
Arizona:	Ariz.Rev.Stat. Sec. 54-1674 (year revised)
Arkansas:	Ark.Code.Ann. Sec. 32-120 (year revised)
California:	Cal.Prob.Code Sec. 645 (year revised)
Colorado:	Colo.Rev.Stat. Sec. 23-6-233 (year revised)

Connecticut:	Conn.Gen.Stat. Sec. 9-333w (year revised)
Delaware:	Del.Code.Ann. tit. 23, Sec. 1456 (year revised)
District of Columbia:	D.C. Code Ann. Sec. 12-4201 (year revised)
Florida:	Fla.Stat. ch. 3.412 (year revised)
Georgia:	Ga.Code Ann. Sec. 210-317 (year revised)
Hawaii:	Haw.Rev.Stat. Sec. 321: 12-34 (year revised)
Idaho:	Idaho Code Sec. 14-2345 (year revised)
Illinois:	4 Ill.Comp.Stat. Sec.101/4-60 (year revised)
Indiana:	Ind.Code Sec. 7-6-1-16 (year revised)
Iowa:	Iowa Code Sec. 344.23 (year revised)
Kansas:	Kan.Stat.Ann. Sec. 23-1234 (year revised)
Kentucky:	Ky.Rev.Stat.Ann. Sec. 534.043 (year revised)
Louisiana:	La.Rev.Stat.Ann. Sec. 40:211 (year revised)
Maine:	Me.Rev.Stat.Ann. tit. 21, Sec. 1976 (year revised)
Maryland:	Md.Code Ann., Sec. 8-201 (year revised)
Massachusetts:	Mass.Gen.Laws ch. 211, Sec. 4-123 (year revised)
Michigan:	Mich.Comp.Laws Sec. 330-2134 (year revised)
Minnesota:	Minn.Stat. Sec. 211.2-101 (year revised)
Mississippi:	Miss.Code Ann. Sec. 12-11-62 (year revised)
Missouri:	Mo.Rev.Stat. Sec. 645.111 (year revised)
Montana:	Mont.Code Ann. Sec. 22-2-424 (year revised)
Nebraska:	Neb.Rev.Stat. Sec. 34-677 (year revised)
Nevada:	Nev.Rev.Stat. Sec. 231.222 (year revised)
New Hampshire:	N.H. Rev. Stat.Ann. Sec. 422:23 (year revised)
New Jersey:	N.J. Rev.Stat. Sec. 32: 54-344 (year revised)
New Mexico:	N.M. Stat.Ann. Sec. 42-5-4 (year revised)
New York:	N.Y. Penal Law Sec. 141.12 (year revised)
North Carolina:	N.C. Gen. Stat. Sec. 14A-5632 (year revised)
North Dakota:	N.D. Cent. Code Sec. 32-11-12 (year revised)
Ohio:	Ohio Rev.Code Ann Sec. 4321.01 (year revised)
Oklahoma:	Okla.Stat. tit. 31, Sec. 211 (year revised)
Oregon:	Or.Rev. Stat. Sec. 340.780 (year revised)
Pennsylvania:	3 Pa.Cons.Stat. Sec. 2112 (year revised)
Rhode Island:	R.I. Gen. Laws Sec. 41-4-5 (year revised)
South Carolina:	S.C. Code Ann. 12-32-11 (year revised)
South Dakota:	S.D. Codified Laws Sec. 12-5-62 (year revised)
Tennessee:	Tenn.Code Ann. Sec. 21-2-403 (year revised)
Texas:	Tex.Penal Code Ann. Sec. 21.02 (year revised)
Utah:	Utah Code Ann. Sec. 23-4-7 (year revised)
Vermont:	Vt.Stat.Ann. tit. 21, Sec. 456 (year revised)
Virginia:	Va. Code Ann. Sec. 14.1-411.1 (year revised)
Washington:	Wash.Rev. Code Sec. 8.32A.111 (year revised)
West Virginia:	W.Va. Code Sec. 12-2-14 (year revised)
Wisconsin:	Wis.Stat. Sec. 32-34 (year revised)
Wyoming:	Wyo.Stat.Ann. Sec. 32-14-211 (year revised)

Statutory code index categories are based on subject matter and are determined by the indexers compiling the statutory code. An index is then created that includes all statutes contained in the code ordered by subject matter using descriptive words. Therefore, in order to efficiently locate statutes, you must begin to think like an indexer of statutory code and determine descriptive words.

Before you begin your search for statutory law, you must organize your search in a way that will allow you to most effectively utilize statutory indexes. Think of the index as a nesting doll. Under each main subject heading, there are many subheadings to be considered before you find the statute you are looking for. You may begin by asking a few basic questions about the issue you are researching.

- What kind of law is involved? Civil or criminal? Substantive or procedural?
- What are the relationships of the parties involved? Parent/child, landlord/tenant?
- What actions are involved? Registering, search and seizure, and so on?

These questions allow you to frame your search and to derive descriptive words that may be used in the index.

For example, your client is 43-year-old college professor. As an investment she purchased a three-family home two blocks from the college campus. She suspects that one of her tenants, a non-tenured, junior faculty member, is having an affair with a student and many of their liaisons take place in her building. She would like to evict the junior professor. Your supervising attorney asks you to locate the relevant statute(s) regarding legal grounds for eviction in your state.

Think like an indexer by beginning with determining the main heading "housing law" [area of law]. Now you must go to the next "doll" or subheading "landlord/tenant" [relationship between parties] to "eviction" [action involved].

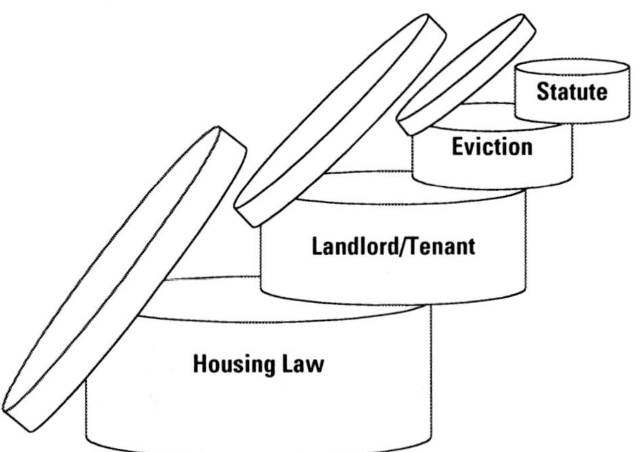

Exhibit 12-4 Index Headings

Another strategy for identifying descriptive words has been developed by William Statsky. The **cartwheel** strategy is a brainstorming exercise that helps you identify many possible descriptive words. You may then take these **descriptive words** and use them to locate the relevant statute.

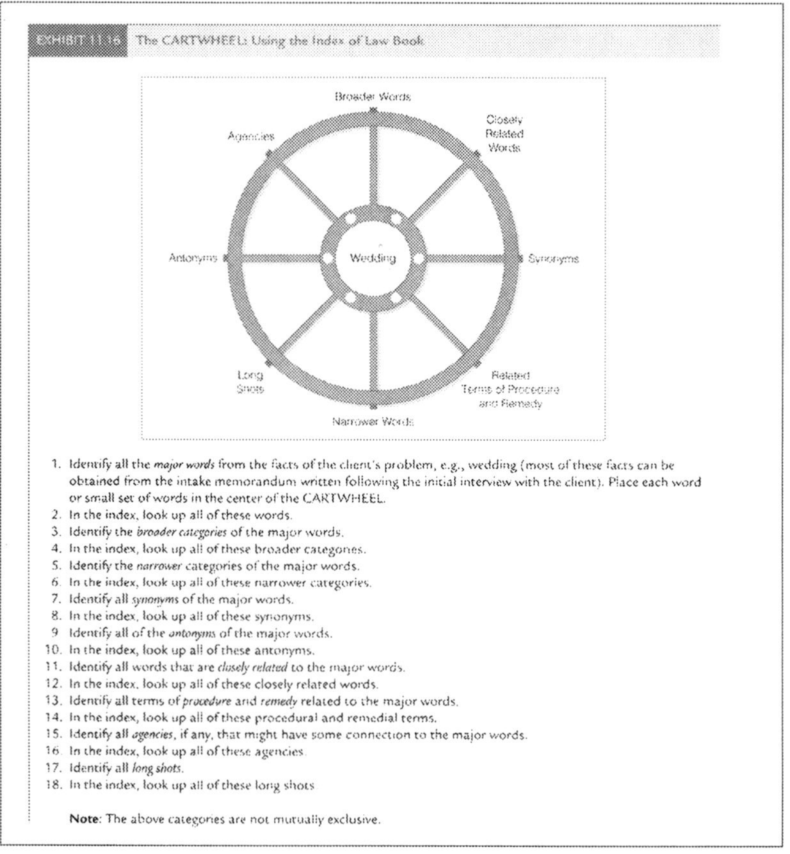

EXHIBIT 11.16 The CARTWHEEL: Using the Index of Law Book

1. Identify all the *major words* from the facts of the client's problem, e.g., wedding (most of these facts can be obtained from the intake memorandum written following the initial interview with the client). Place each word or small set of words in the center of the CARTWHEEL.
2. In the index, look up all of these words.
3. Identify the *broader categories* of the major words.
4. In the index, look up all of these broader categories.
5. Identify the *narrower* categories of the major words.
6. In the index, look up all of these narrower categories.
7. Identify all *synonyms* of the major words.
8. In the index, look up all of these synonyms.
9. Identify all of the *antonyms* of the major words.
10. In the index, look up all of these antonyms.
11. Identify all words that are *closely related* to the major words.
12. In the index, look up all of these closely related words.
13. Identify all terms of *procedure* and *remedy* related to the major words.
14. In the index, look up all of these procedural and remedial terms.
15. Identify all *agencies*, if any, that might have some connection to the major words.
16. In the index, look up all of these agencies.
17. Identify all *long shots*.
18. In the index, look up all of these long shots.

Note: The above categories are not mutually exclusive.

Exhibit 12-5 Cartwheel Strategy; From Introduction to Paralegalism, Perspectives, Problems and Skills, 6E 6th Edition by STATSKY. © 2003. Reprinted with permission of Delmar, Cengage Learning: www.cengage.com/permissions. Fax 800-730-2215.

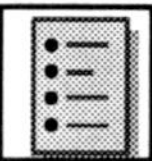

Discussion Point

Identify descriptive words for each of the following: fertility treatments; medical malpractice; student loans; and larceny.

Let's walk through the process. Consider the following scenario. Your client is a 30-year-old man. He recently was laid off from a lucrative job in a high-tech company. Tired of working for someone else, he has decided to create his own software firm, concentrating on video and computer game software. He plans to sell his software through the Internet and by mail order only. He has come to your firm to find out what he needs to do to legally start his business. Your supervising attorney asks you to research the requirements for registering a corporate name in your state of Connecticut.

Step One: Locate the statutory code of the state. It is generally a good idea to start with the annotated statutes. The annotated statutes provide the full text of the statute and citations to opinions that interpret the statute as well as other resource materials.

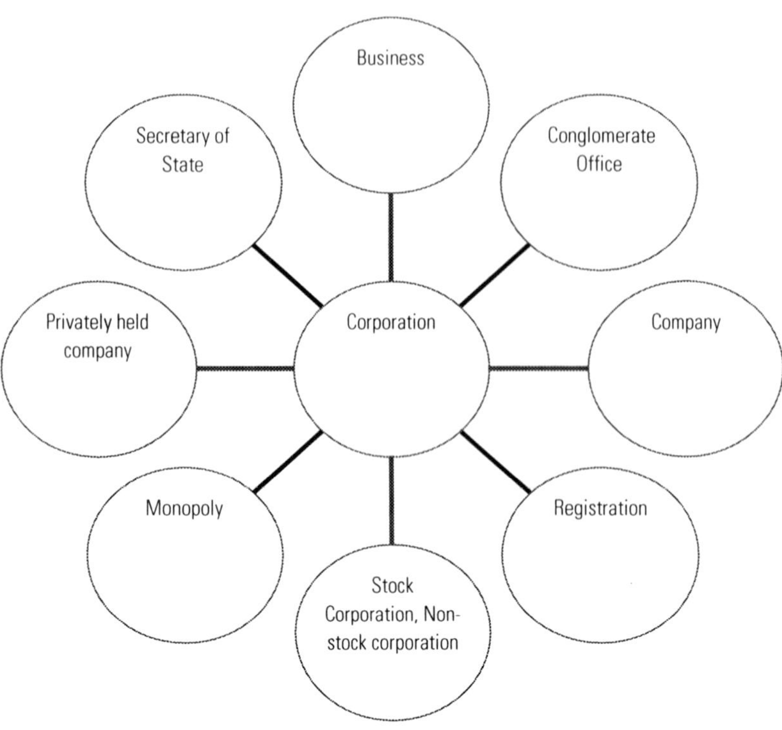

Exhibit 12-6 Cartwheel

Step Two: Identify descriptive words, such as "corporations," "corporate formation," and "corporate name and registration."

INDEX **439**

CORPORATIONS, BUSINESS—Cont'd
Insurance business, authorization to form corporation to transact—
  Certificate, 33-646(a)
  Expenses, 33-646(b)
Interrogatories by secretary of the state, 33-624(a)
  Confidentiality of answers, 33-624(c)
  Failure to answer, 33-624(b)
Investigations—
  Impeding, obstructing or influencing prohibited, 33-1331
    Unfair or deceptive trade practices, 33-1335
Issuance of shares—
  Certificate of incorporation, amendment before, 33-799
Judicial dissolution, 33-896 to 33-900
  Custodianship—
    Appointment, 33-898(a), 33-898(b)
    Compensation, 33-898(e)
    Powers, 33-898(c)
    Redesignation, 33-898(d)
  Mandatory, when, 33-896(b)
  Notice of proceedings to shareholders, 33-897(d)
  Permissive, when, 33-896(a)
  Procedure, 33-897(c)
  Receivership—
    Appointment, 33-898(a), 33-898(b)
    Compensation, 33-898(e)
    Powers, 33-898(c)
    Redesignation, 33-898(d)
  Shareholders need not be parties, 33-897(b)
  Venue, 33-897(a)
Liquidation—See Dissolution, this heading, generally.
Mailing address, designation of, 33-609(c)
Means, defined, 33-602(18)
Meetings—
  Directors—See Directors, this heading, at subheading Meetings.
  Shareholders—See Shareholders, this heading, at subheading Meetings.
Merger, 33-814 to 33-821
  Appraisal rights—See Appraisal rights, this heading.
  Certificate of merger, 33-819(a)
  Definitions, 33-814
  Effect of, 33-820(a)
  Effective, when, 33-819(b)
  Foreign corporations and entities—
    Agent for service of process, 33-820(d)

CORPORATIONS, BUSINESS—Cont'd
Merger—Cont'd
  Foreign corporations and entities—Cont'd
    Dissenters, payments to after, 33-820(d)
    Payments to shareholders, 33-820(d)
    Service of process on after, 33-820(d)
  Parties to merger, 33-815(b)
  Plan of merger, 33-815(a)
    Abandonment, 33-817, 33-821a
    Action by shareholders not required, when, 33-817
    Amendment—
      Provisions, 33-815(e)
    Approval, 33-817
      Separate voting groups, by, 33-817
    Existing corporations, applicability, 33-817
    Mandatory contents, 33-815(c)
    Notice to shareholders, 33-817
    Permissive contents, 33-815(b)
    Submission to shareholders, 33-817
      Conditional, 33-817
    Terms dependent upon facts ascertainable outside plan, 33-815(d)
  Shareholders—
    Liabilities, 33-820(c)
  Subsidiaries, 33-818(a)
    Application of law, 33-818(c)
    Shareholders—
      Notice, 33-818(b)
Mortgage of assets, 33-830
  Shareholder approval not required, 33-830
Names, 33-655 to 33-657 ◄— heading
  Distinguishability, 33-655(b)
    Exceptions, 33-655(c)
  Fictitious names—
    Applicability of act, 33-655(e)
  Foreign corporations—
    Change to improper name, effect, 33-925(e)
    Distinguishability, 33-925(b)
      Exceptions, 33-925(c)
    Registration, 33-657(a) ◄— statute
      Application, 33-657(b)
      Effective, when, 33-657(c)
      Renewal, 33-657(d)
    Required elements, 33-925(a)
    Use of name of other corporation, when, 33-925(d)
  Required elements, 33-655(a)
  Reserved, 33-656(a)
    Termination of, 33-656(c)
    Transfer of reservation, 33-656(b)
  Use of name of other corporation, when, 33-655(d)

Exhibit 12-7 Index; Courtesy of the State of Connecticut

Step Three: Locate statute within the code.

Ch. 601 BUSINESS CORPORATIONS 67

and amended Subsec. (d) to replace "proposed user corporation" with "corporation seeking to use the name", effective January 1, 1997; P.A. 04-240 amended Subsec. (b) by adding Subdiv. (9) re name of other entity carried on records of the Secretary of the State.

Annotations to former section 33-13:

Wrongful appropriation of name of another corporation enjoined. 37 C. 278. Aliter with use of similar name. 72 C. 657. Use of different names. 74 C. 224. Cannot use name likely to mislead public. 83 C. 679. Cited. 109 C. 48, 52. Omission of "The" and abbreviation of "Company" are not fatal defects in an acknowledgment to a contract. 120 C. 52.

Annotation to former section 33-287:

Subsec. (a):

Cited. 208 C. 248, 252.

Sec. 33-656. Reserved name. (a) A person may reserve the exclusive use of a corporate name, including a corporate name of a foreign corporation, with such additional distinctive and distinguishing elements that the corporation agrees to use in this state exclusive of any other name as in the judgment of the Secretary of the State will be sufficient to distinguish its name, by delivering an application to the Secretary of the State for filing. The application shall set forth the name and address of the applicant and the name proposed to be reserved. If the Secretary of the State finds that the corporate name applied for is available, he shall reserve the name for the applicant's exclusive use for a period of one hundred twenty days.

(b) The owner of a reserved corporate name may transfer the reservation to another person by delivering to the Secretary of the State a signed notice of the transfer that states the name and address of the transferee.

(c) Any person for whom a specified corporate name has been reserved pursuant to this section may, during the period for which such name is reserved, terminate such reservation by filing in the office of the Secretary of the State an application for cancellation of reservation of corporate name, together with the applicable fee.

(P.A. 94-186, S. 33, 215; P.A. 96-271, S. 27, 254.)

History: P.A. 94-186 effective January 1, 1997; P.A. 96-271 made a technical change in Subsec. (a) and added Subsec. (c) to authorize a person for whom a specified corporate name has been reserved to terminate such reservation, effective January 1, 1997.

Sec. 33-657. Registered name. (a) A foreign corporation may register its corporate name, or its corporate name with any addition required by section 33-925, if the name is distinguishable upon the records of the Secretary of the State from the names that are not available under subsection (b) of section 33-655.

(b) A foreign corporation registers its corporate name, or its corporate name with any addition required by section 33-925, by delivering to the Secretary of the State for filing an application: (1) Setting forth its corporate name, or its corporate name with any addition required by section 33-925, the state or country and date of its incorporation, and a brief description of the nature of the business in which it is engaged; and (2) accompanied by a certificate of existence, or a document of similar import, from the state or country of incorporation.

(c) The name is registered for the applicant's exclusive use upon the effective date of the application until the close of the calendar year in which the application for registration is filed.

(d) A foreign corporation whose registration is effective may renew it for successive years by delivering to the Secretary of the State for filing a renewal application, which

Exhibit 12-8 Copy of annotated statute

Step Four: Complete an elements analysis (See Chapter _12 to fully understand the requirements of the statute and to apply it to your particular facts.)

Key Terms

bill	descriptive words	statute
cartwheel	slip law	statutes at large

Exercises

Use the statutory code of your state to find the relevant statute for each of the following. Start by developing descriptive words (at least two for each assignment) and looking in the statute index. List the process by which you found the statute as well as the statutory citation itself. Include the title of the statute in your answer as well as the two (at least) descriptive words you used to find that answer.

1. Is it legal to be a spectator at a rooster fight?

____

____

____

____

____

2. What is the governing statute, generally, regarding no-fault motorist insurance in your state?

3. Is there a statute governing the bonding of executors in probate court?

4. Are candidates for elective office required to place a "paid for by" attribution statement on campaign literature?

5. Is there a statute governing damages for actions in libel?

6. Our client was attempting to shoot pigeons in a public city park with a shotgun. What possible statutes did he violate?

7. Our client is starting a business and wants to make sure his corporate name is registered with the state. What statute(s) are relevant?

8. Our client is a partnership. One of its employees fraudulently represented himself to be a partner to clients. What liability does the partnership have regarding the employees actions?

9. Our client is expecting her fourth child. She desires to take a lengthy maternity leave from her job. What statute provides the amount of leave to which she is entitled under the law?

Library Resources

The Process of Legal Research (4th Ed.), Christina L. Kunz, Deborah A. Schmedemann, Matthew P. Downs, & Ann L. Bateson, Aspen Law & Business, 1996.
Clear and detailed discussion of the processes is provided in this book.

Legal Research: A practical guide and self-instructional workbook, Ruth A. McKinney, West Publishing, 1996.
This book offers great exercises.

Legal Research in a Nutshell (7th Ed.), Morris L. Cohen & Kent C. Olson, West Group, 2000.
This book is concise and a good companion with the McKinney workbook.

Online Resources

Harvard Law School, http://www.law.harvard.edu/library/services/research/guides
This site provides helpful guide and examples.

University of Connecticut School of Law, http://www.law.uconn.edu/library/clipper/guides
Great guides with quick tips are available at this site.

CHAPTER 13

Legal Research: Finding Case Law

INTRODUCTION

An important task of the paralegal is to be able to research a legal question and locate legal authority to support your client's position. The process of legal research can be daunting if the researcher is not well prepared before beginning. This chapter explains the foundation of legal research and provides strategies for locating relevant case law.

some statutes deliberately vague e.g. risk of injury to minor
subjective - defined by judge-made law

TYPES OF AUTHORITY

authority: Something a court may rely on in making a decision.

The purpose of legal research is to locate law that will support your client's position. In order for a court to rule in your favor, you must provide the court with law that it must rely on. That law is considered **authority**.

There are different types of authority and it is important to categorize the information you find during your research into basic types of authority:

- **Primary authority** is any law the court can rely on in making its decisions. This includes statutes, constitutions, administrative regulations, and case law.
- **Secondary authority** is any non-law a court may rely on in making its decisions. This includes treatises, legal periodicals, and law review articles.
- **Mandatory authority** is any law the court must rely on in making its decision. Mandatory authority is always primary authority because a court is never required to rely on non-law in making its decisions. Examples of mandatory authority include statutory law being applied in its jurisdiction. (Example: Arizona statute being applied in Arizona.) An opinion is considered mandatory law when the opinion being applied is analogous and the opinion was written by a higher court in the same jurisdiction. This is an example of precedent. (See Chapter 11 for the discussion on precedent.)
- **Persuasive authority** is something a court may rely on but is not required to do so. Secondary authority is always persuasive authority.

Types of Authority

	Mandatory Authority	Persuasive Authority
Primary Authority	YES	YES
Secondary Authority	NO	YES

Exhibit 13-1 Types of Authority

LOCATING AUTHORITY

The next step is to locate the authorities in the law library. Each type of authority is contained in a different text. Some books contain the full text of the law, whereas others help you locate the law.

Kind of Law	Materials That Contain the Full Text of This Kind of Law	Materials That Can Be Used to Locate This Kind of Law	Materials That Can Be Used to Help Understand This Kind of Law	Materials That Can Be Used to Help Determine the Current Validity of This Kind of Law
(a) Opinions	Reports Reporters A.L.R., A.L.R. 2d, A.L.R.3d, A.L.R.4th, A.L.R.5th, A.L.R. Fed. Legal newspapers Loose-leaf services Slip opinions Advance sheets CD-ROM Westlaw LEXIS Loislaw Internet	Digests Annotations in A.L.R. A.L.R.2d, A.L.R.3d, A.L.R.4th, A.L.R.5th, A.L.R. Fed. Shepard's Legal periodicals Legal encyclopedias Legal treatises Loose-leaf services Words and Phrases	Legal periodicals Legal encyclopedias Legal treatises Legal newsletters Annotations in A.L.R., A.L.R.2d, A.L.R.3d, A.L.R.4th, A.L.R.5th, A.L.R. Fed. Loose-leaf services	Shepard's KeyCite GlobalCite Insta-Cite Auto-Cite
(b) Statutes	Statutory Code Statutes at Large Session Laws Compilations Consolidated Laws Slip Laws Acts & Resolves Laws Legislative Services CD-ROM Westlaw LEXIS Loislaw Internet	Index volumes of statutory code Loose-leaf services Footnote references in other materials	Legal periodicals Legal encyclopedias Legal treatises Legal newsletters Annotations in A.L.R., A.L.R. 2d, A.L.R.3d, A.L.R.4th, A.L.R.5th, A.L.R. Fed. Loose-leaf services	Shepard's KeyCite
(c) Constitutions	Statutory Code Separate volumes containing the constitution CD-ROM Westlaw LEXIS Loislaw Internet	Index volumes of statutory code Loose-leaf services Footnote references in other materials	Legal periodicals Legal encyclopedias Legal treatises Legal newsletters Annotations in A.L.R., A.L.R.2d, A.L.R.3d, A.L.R.4th, A.L.R.5th, A.L.R. Fed. Loose-leaf services	Shepard's KeyCite
(d) Administrative Regulations	Administrative Code Separate volumes containing the regulations of certain agencies Loose-leaf services CD-ROM Westlaw LEXIS Loislaw Internet	Index volumes of the administrative code Loose-leaf services Footnote references in other materials	Legal periodicals Legal treatises Legal newsletters Annotations in A.L.R., A.L.R.2d, A.L.R.3d, A.L.R.4th, A.L.R.5th, A.L.R. Fed. Loose-leaf services	Shepard's (for some agencies) List of Sections Affected (for federal agencies) KeyCite (for federal agencies)
(e) Administrative Decisions	Separate volumes of decisions of some agencies Loose-leaf services Westlaw LEXIS Loislaw Internet	Loose-leaf services Index to (or digest volumes for) the decisions Footnote references in other materials	Legal periodicals Legal treatises Legal newsletters Annotations in A.L.R., A.L.R.2d, A.L.R.3d, A.L.R.4th, A.L.R.5th, A.L.R. Fed. Loose-leaf services	Shepard's (for some agencies)
(f) Charters	Separate volumes containing the charter Municipal Code Register Bulletin State session laws Official journal Legal newspaper Internet	Index volumes to the charter or municipal code Footnote references in other materials	Legal periodicals Legal treatises Annotations in A.L.R., A.L.R.2d, A.L.R.3d, A.L.R.4th, A.L.R.5th, A.L.R. Fed.	Shepard's

Kind of Law	Materials That Contain the Full Text of This Kind of Law	Materials That Can Be Used to Locate This Kind of Law	Materials That Can Be Used to Help Understand This Kind of Law	Materials That Can Be Used to Help Determine the Current Validity of This Kind of Law
(g) Ordinances	Municipal code Official journal Legal newspaper Internet	Index volumes of municipal code Footnote references in other materials	Legal periodicals Legal treatises Annotations in A.L.R., A.L.R.2d, A.L.R.3d, A.L.R.4th, A.L.R.5th, A.L.R. Fed.	Shepard's
(h) Rules of Court	Separate rules volumes Statutory code Practice manuals Deskbook CD-ROM Westlaw LEXIS Loislaw Internet	Index to separate rules volumes Index to statutory code Index to practice manuals Index to deskbook Footnote references in other materials	Practice manuals Legal periodicals Legal treatises Legal newsletters Annotations in A.L.R., A.L.R.2d, A.L.R.3d, A.L.R.4th, A.L.R.5th, A.L.R. Fed. Legal encyclopedias Loose-leaf services	Shepard's KeyCite
(i) Executive Orders	Federal Register Code of Federal Regulations Weekly Compilation of Presidential Documents U.S. Code Congressional and Administrative News U.S.C./U.S.C.A./U.S.C.S. Westlaw LEXIS Internet	Index volumes to the sets of books listed in the second column Footnote references in other materials	Legal periodicals Legal treatises Legal newsletters Annotations in A.L.R., A.L.R.2d, A.L.R.3d, A.L.R.4th, A.L.R.5th, A.L.R. Fed. Loose-leaf services	Shepard's
(j) Treaties	Statutes at Large (up to 1949) United States Treaties and Other International Agreements Department of State Bulletin International Legal Materials Westlaw LEXIS Internet	Index within the volumes listed in second column World Treaty Index Current Treaty Index Footnote references in other materials	Legal periodicals Legal treatises Legal newsletters Annotations in A.L.R., A.L.R.2d, A.L.R.3d, A.L.R.4th, A.L.R.5th, A.L.R. Fed. Legal encyclopedias Loose-leaf services	Shepard's
(k) Opinions of the Attorney General	Separate volumes containing these opinions Westlaw LEXIS Internet	Digests Footnote references in other materials		

Exhibit 13-2 Categories of Research Material; From Introduction to Paralegalism, Perspectives, Problems and Skills, 6E 6th Edition by STATSKY. © 2003. Reprinted with permission of Delmar, Cengage Learning: www.cengage.com/permissions. Fax 800-730-2215.

LOCATING AND CITING CASE LAW

Citing Case Law

reporters: Contain full text of court opinions.

headnotes: Brief summaries of key points of an opinion written by private publisher.

Court opinions are published in **reporters**.

Official reporters are published by the government and include only text of the opinion. Unofficial reporters are published by West Publishing, a private publisher, and contain the full text of the opinion as well as brief summaries of key points of the opinion called **headnotes**.

The headnotes are written by editors and are not part of the judge's opinion.

Some states no longer print an official reporter but rely exclusively on the West's reporters. West has divided the country into geographical areas and provides a reporter for each area, called regional reporters:

National Reporter System - Seven Regional Reporters			
Pacific	**North Western**	**North Eastern**	**Atlantic**
Alaska	Iowa	Illinois	Connecticut
California	Michigan	Indiana	Delaware
Colorado	Minnesota	Massachusetts	Maine
Hawaii	Nebraska	New York	Maryland
Idaho	North Dakota	Ohio	New Hampshire
Kansas	South Dakota		New Jersey
Montana	Wisconsin		Pennsylvania
Nevada			Rhode Island
New Mexico			Vermont
Oklahoma			
Oregon	**South Western**	**Southern**	**South Eastern**
Washington	Arkansas	Alabama	Georgia
Wyoming	Kentucky	Florida	North Carolina
Utah	Missouri	Louisiana	South Carolina
Arizona	Tennessee	Mississippi	Virginia
	Texas		West Virginia

Exhibit 13-3 Regional Reporters

The federal appellate courts are reported only in West reporters. U.S. Court of Appeals decisions are reported in the Federal Reporter and U.S. District Court decisions are reported in the Federal Supplement. U.S. Supreme Court decisions are reported in three reporters: the official reporter, published by the U.S. government, United States Reports; West's Supreme Court Reporter; and United States Supreme Court Reports, Lawyer's Edition.

Each opinion reported has a citation, or address. A **citation** is a listing of the location an opinion may be found in a reporter.

citation: Listing of the location an opinion may be found in a reporter.

The rules governing citation require that each citation be uniform so that case law may be easily accessed. The most commonly used guide for citation is *The Bluebook: A Uniform System of Citation*. You may refer to the *Bluebook* whenever you have a question regarding citation. A citation for a court opinion has five main components, as displayed in Exhibit 13-4.

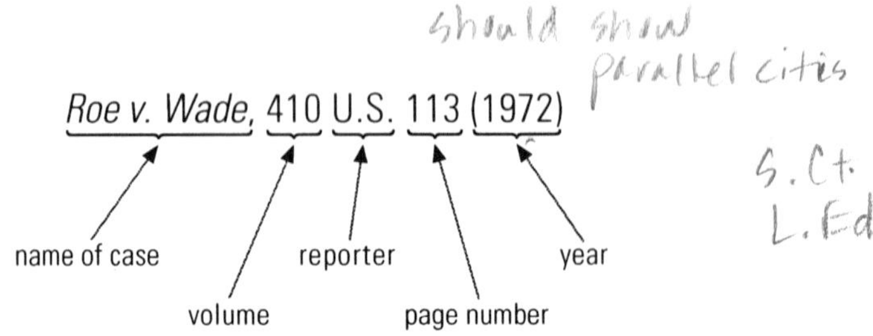

Exhibit 13-4 *Roe v. Wade*

These main components exist in state opinion citations as well, as displayed in Exhibit 13-5. *Woods v. O'Neil,* 54 Mass.App.Ct.768, 767 N.E.2d 1119 (2002):

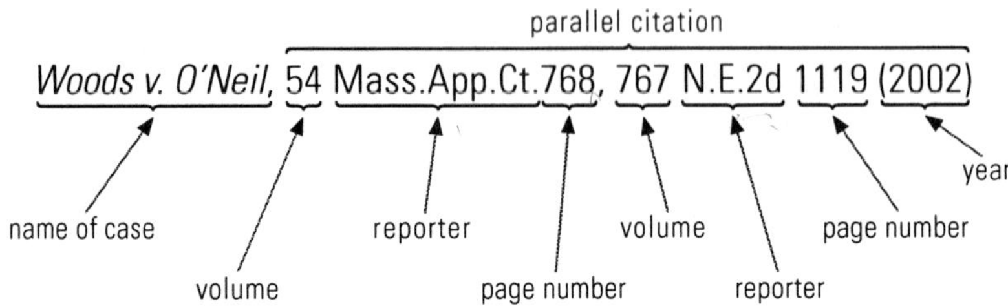

Exhibit 13-5 *Woods v. O'Neil*

Note that when the opinion is reported in more than one reporter, both are generally cited. The official citation always appears first.

EXAMPLE Citations of Selected Reporters:

Federal:	
U.S. Supreme Court	
United States Reports	U.S.
Supreme Court Reporter	S.Ct.
United States Supreme Court Reports, Lawyer's Edition	L.Ed.
Federal Reporter (U.S. Court of Appeals)	F., F.2d, F.3d
Federal Supplement (U.S. District Courts)	F.Supp., F.Supp.2d
Regional Reporters:	
Atlantic Reporter	A., A.2d
North Eastern Reporter	N.E., N.E.2d
North Western Reporter	N.W., N.W.2d
Pacific Reporter	P., P.2d, P.3d
South Eastern Reporter	S.E., S.E.2d
South Western Reporter	S.W., S.W.2d
Southern Reporter	So., So.2d

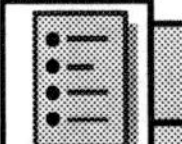

Discussion Point

Which reporter contains your state's opinions? Locate its citation.

Locating Case Law

One of the first places to look when attempting to locate case law is the **West's Digests.** West's Publishing has compiled a digest for each state's judicial opinions. These digests take all opinions issued by that state's appellate courts and assembles them in categories to be accessed by the researcher. Similar to the statutory code index discussed in Chapter 12, the digest assembles the case law by descriptive word. Each digest has a **Descriptive**

Word Index that lists which volume of the digest contains a brief description of the case relating to that descriptive word heading. The digests do not contain the full text of the opinion; instead they provide a brief description of the contents of the opinion and the citation of the case.

The following are steps in using West's Digests:

1. Locate the appropriate digest for the type of case law you are looking for. The digests are usually located directly after the reporter containing that state's case law. For example, if you are looking for a Massachusetts case, you would locate the West's Massachusetts Digest.

WEST'S

MASSACHUSETTS

DIGEST 2d

Volume 3

AUTOMOBILES — BANKRUPTCY ⚷ 2600

ST PAUL, MINN.

WEST GROUP

Exhibit 13-6 Cover of West's Massachusetts Digest; Courtesy of West Publishing Co., a division of Thomson Delmar Learning.

2. Locate the appropriate volume of the Descriptive Word Index. You would base this on descriptive words you created using the cartwheel and descriptive word process. (See Chapter 12 for a detailed discussion.) For example, if you are researching for a case involving a car hitting a pedestrian, you may start by looking up "Automobiles" as the primary topic heading in the descriptive word index. You would then look for topic subheadings under "pedestrian."

WEST'S
MASSACHUSETTS
DIGEST 2d

Volume 26

DESCRIPTIVE - WORD INDEX
A — Cl

Exhibit 13-7 Descriptive Word Digest; Courtesy of West Publishing Co., a division of Thomson Delmar Learning.

3. After you have located the appropriate heading and subheading, make note of the digest volumes listed under those relevant topic headings. For example, under the main heading of "Automobiles" and the subheading "pedestrian" you may find "Generally Key Numbers 160–166." This tells you to locate the volume of the digest that includes "Automobiles" and locate key number 160 under that main heading. Remember, it is very important to make sure you are looking under the correct heading. Key number 160 is something completely different under the heading "Arbitration" when you should be looking under "Automobiles."
4. Look at the outline of the topic heading in the digest. Sometimes this can lead you to other valuable references in the heading that you may have missed in the index.

26 Mass D 2d-317

Heading → **AUTOMOBILE**

Subheading

References are to Digest Topics and Key Numbers

→ **AUTOMOBILE ACCIDENTS**—Cont'd
PASSENGERS—Cont'd
Contributory negligence of—Cont'd

Failure to supervise driver, **Autos ⇔ 224(5)**
Failure to warn driver, **Autos ⇔ 224(5)**
Riding with drunk or impaired driver, **Autos ⇔ 224(8)**
Duty and liability to, **Autos ⇔ 181, 244(20)**
Liability of passengers for injuries to others,
Generally, **Autos ⇔ 198**
Acting in concert, **Autos ⇔ 198(4)**
Failure to warn driver, **Autos ⇔ 198(1)**
Joint enterprise, **Autos ⇔ 198(4)**
Supervision of driver, **Autos ⇔ 198(1)**

PASSING,
Generally, **Autos ⇔ 172, 244(12)**
Care required, **Autos ⇔ 172(8)**
Contributory negligence, **Autos ⇔ 209, 244(44)**
Duties after passing, **Autos ⇔ 172(10)**
Excessive speed, **Autos ⇔ 168(5), 172(8)**
Instructions for jury, **Autos ⇔ 246(11, 48)**
Intersections, **Autos ⇔ 171, 172(11)**
Jury questions, **Autos ⇔ 245(15, 43, 60)**
Parked or standing vehicles, **Autos ⇔ 173(6)**

PEDESTRIANS, ← Subheading
Generally, **Autos ⇔ 160-166, 244(6)-244(9)**
Contributory and comparative negligence,
Generally, **Autos ⇔ 216-223, 244(49)-244(55)**
Crossing road, **Autos ⇔ 217, 244(50)**
Walking along road, **Autos ⇔ 218, 244(51)**
Working on or in road, **Autos ⇔ 219, 244(52)**
Crossing road, **Autos ⇔ 160(4), 162(5)**
Defects in roads, lights, signs or crossings, **Autos ⇔ 160(2), 277**
Intoxicated or impaired pedestrians, **Autos ⇔ 161, 222**
Police officers, **Autos ⇔ 163(4), 219**
Private driveways, **Autos ⇔ 217(8)**
Walking along road, **Autos ⇔ 160(5), 162(6)**
Working on or in road, **Autos ⇔ 163, 244(8)**

PERSONS liable for injuries, **Autos ⇔ 183-200**

PLAN of highway, liability for, **Autos ⇔ 259**

PLEADING
See also heading **PLEADING**, generally.
Generally, **Autos ⇔ 236, 299**

AUTOMOBILE ACCIDENTS—Cont'd
PLEADING—Cont'd

Dismissal for insufficient pleading, **Fed Civ Proc ⇔ 1786**
Judgment on pleadings, **Fed Civ Proc ⇔ 1062**

POLES, telephone. See subheading TELEPHONE equipment, maintenance and construction, under this heading.

POLICE,
Chase. See subheading EMERGENCY vehicles, under this heading.
Injuries to police working or standing in roadway, **Autos ⇔ 163(4), 219**
Negligent driving in general. See subheading EMERGENCY vehicles, under this heading.
Obstructions and hazards on roadway, **Autos ⇔ 252-314**
Traffic control, **Autos ⇔ 277, 290**

PRESUMPTIONS,
Contributory negligence,
Generally, **Autos ⇔ 242(8)**
Defects or obstructions in road, **Autos ⇔ 304(3)**
Ownership of vehicle, **Autos ⇔ 242(5)**
Proximate cause, **Autos ⇔ 242(7)**
Rear-end collision, **Autos ⇔ 242(1-4)**
Res ipsa loquitur, **Autos ⇔ 242(2)**
Scope of employment, **Autos ⇔ 242(6)**
Status of operator, **Autos ⇔ 242(6)**

PRIVATE premises,
Defects or obstructions in, **Autos ⇔ 17**
Entering or leaving, **Autos ⇔ 167**

PROBABLE consequences, **Autos ⇔ 201(6)**

PROCESS,
Generally, **Autos ⇔ 235, 298**
Nonresidents and absentees, **Autos ⇔ 235(3, 4); Fed Civ Proc ⇔ 473**

PRODUCTS liability. See heading **PRODUCTS LIABILITY,** AUTOMOBILES.

PROJECTING articles, **Autos ⇔ 180, 244(18), 245(23)**

PROPERTY adjacent to highway, injury from, **Autos ⇔ 269**

PROXIMATE cause,
Generally, **Autos ⇔ 201, 244(36)**
Act of God, **Autos ⇔ 201(10), 244(40)**
Concurrent causes, **Autos ⇔ 201(8)**
Contributory negligence as, **Autos ⇔ 226(2), 244(58)**

Exhibit 13-8 Digest Index; Courtesy of West Publishing Co., a division of Thomson Delmar Learning.

5. Read all the digest paragraphs under each relevant key number you have located within the topic heading. These provide a short synopsis of individual case holdings and their citations. Based on these summaries, you can determine which cases you wish to read fully.
6. Gather citations of cases you have identified as potentially valuable and locate them in the appropriate reporter.
7. Read each case and determine whether it is valuable for your task.

When reading an opinion printed in a West reporter, it is wise to take advantage of the headnote numbering system. Although it is important to read the entire opinion in order to grasp the full context of what the court is stating, the numbered headnotes can allow you to go directly to the portion of the opinion that addresses the specific area in which you are interested.

🔑144.2(5.1) AUTOMOBILES 3 Mass D 2d—2

772 N.E.2d 53, 55 Mass.App.Ct. 514, review denied 776 N.E.2d 453, 437 Mass. 1110.

🔑144.2(8). Extent of discipline in general; hardship and mitigating circumstances.

Mass. 2004. Defendant charged with second offense operating while under influence of alcohol, who had suffered previous conviction more than ten years ago, and who therefore qualified for disposition under statute providing for probation and rehabilitation of persons convicted of driving under the influence, was subject to loss of license for a maximum of ninety days, despite existence of other statutory provisions calling for more severe penalties for second time offenders. M.G.L.A. c. 90, §§ 24, 24D.—Com. v. Cahill, 810 N.E.2d 1196, 442 Mass. 127.

Mass.App.Ct. 2004. For a lifetime revocation of driver's license, statute does not require two separate accidents, each caused by defendant's intoxicated driving, each resulting in a person's death; statute merely requires two convictions of driving while intoxicated, coupled with a determination by registrar that the second commission of that offense caused a fatal accident. M.G.L.A. c. 90, § 24(1)(c)(4).—Stockman v. Board of Appeal on Motor Vehicle Liability Policies and Bonds, 815 N.E.2d 611, 62 Mass.App.Ct. 159, review denied 818 N.E.2d 1068, 442 Mass. 1114.

Conviction of involuntary manslaughter was a conviction of driving while intoxicated, as required for defendant's license to be revoked for life, where conviction of motor vehicle homicide, which included as an element a finding of driving while intoxicated, had been dismissed for reason that jury also convicted defendant of manslaughter for same offense. M.G.L.A. c. 90, §§ 24(1)(a)(1), (1)(c)(4), 24G(a).—Id.

V. INJURIES FROM OPERATION, OR USE OF HIGHWAY.

(A) NATURE AND GROUNDS OF LIABILITY.

Research Notes

Concepts of proximate cause; contributory negligence generally; duties as to children; duties as to persons in street; duties in particular movements; emergency vehicles; general duties of motorist; negligence as to speed; passengers and occupants, liability to; persons liable, imputed negligence, see Blashfield, Automobile Law and Practice.

Mass.Prac.Series, Automobile Law & Practice, With Forms.

Library references

C.J.S. Motor Vehicles §§ 246 et seq., 564 et seq.

🔑146. Care required and liability in general.

Mass. 2004. There is nothing special about injuries incurred in automobile accidents that sets them apart from other negligently caused injuries.—Kerny v. MacDonald, 801 N.E.2d 260, 440 Mass. 675.

The presence of automobile liability insurance does not create liability where none previously existed.—Id.

🔑154. Right of way.

Mass.App.Ct. 2004. Possession of right of way is factor for jury to take into account when determining whether operator of vehicle performed his duty of due care or was negligent.

M.G.L.A. c. 89, § 8; c. 90, § 14.—Mari v. Delong, 814 N.E.2d 1171, 62 Mass.App.Ct. 87, review denied 818 N.E.2d 1068, 442 Mass. 1114.

🔑160(1). In general.

Mass.App.Ct. 2002. Operator of motor vehicle has duty to exercise a reasonable degree of care to avoid injury to pedestrians.—Woods v. O'Neil, 767 N.E.2d 1119, 54 Mass.App.Ct. 768.

🔑168(1). Care required and liability in general.

Mass.App.Div. 2001. In cases which involve rear-end collisions, questions of fact as to the rate of speed at which the cars were traveling, the distance between the cars and any other relevant circumstances are determinative of whether either operator was negligent.—Yim v. Muszynski, 2001 Mass.App.Div. 243.

🔑168(10). Racing.

See 🔑168(10.1).

🔑168(10.1). —— In general.

Mass.App.Ct. 2004. Speed and a common destination are not enough to establish that the drivers of two vehicles were engaged in racing or a challenge and response.—Picard v. Thomas, 802 N.E.2d 581, 60 Mass.App.Ct. 362, review denied 806 N.E.2d 102, 441 Mass. 1106.

🔑171(4). Right of way.

See 🔑171(4.1).

🔑171(4.1). —— In general.

Mass.App.Ct. 2004. Right of way of driver proceeding straight through intersection does not constitute absolute or unlimited privilege in that driver who possesses right of way at intersection must exercise reasonable care.—Mari v. Delong, 814 N.E.2d 1171, 62 Mass.App.Ct. 87, review denied 818 N.E.2d 1068, 442 Mass. 1114.

Driver intending to turn left in intersection, across path of driver approaching from opposite direction, must yield right of way until such time as turn can be made safely; fact that this does not constitute absolute right or absolve such driver from duty to exercise reasonable care does not mean that driver turning left across path of driver proceeding straight through acquires right of way by entering intersection first. M.G.L.A. c. 89, § 8; M.G.L.A. c. 90, § 14.—Id.

Mass.App.Div. 2001. Until he has complied with the order to stop, one directed to stop by a stop sign may not have the benefit of the general rule governing the right of way at intersections, if the rule grants him the right of way; after stopping, the operator becomes subject to the general rule and may proceed and thereafter exercise the right of way in accordance with that rule. M.G.L.A. c. 89, §§ 8, 9.—Anthony v. Jancsics, 2001 Mass.App.Div. 137.

🔑171(8). Care required in general.

Mass.App.Ct. 2004. Right of way of driver proceeding straight through intersection does not constitute absolute or unlimited privilege in that driver who possesses right of way at intersection must exercise reasonable care.—Mari v. Delong, 814 N.E.2d 1171, 62 Mass.App.Ct. 87, review denied 818 N.E.2d 1068, 442 Mass. 1114.

Mass.App.Div. 2001. Even if an operator has the right of way under the general rule governing the right of way at intersections, that right is subject to the requirement of using due care. M.G.L.A. c. 89, § 8.—Anthony v. Jancsics, 2001 Mass.App.Div. 137.

Possession of the right of way at an intersection is only one factor to be considered in deciding

† This Case was not selected for publication in the National Reporter System

Exhibit 13-9 Summaries; Courtesy of West Publishing Co., a division of Thomson Delmar Learning.

Before the main text of the opinion, the West editors list individual headnotes stating a specific issue discussed within the opinion. The headnotes are numbered and referenced by a key number that can be traced back to the digest. The bracketed headnote numbers are then notated throughout the opinion where that issue is discussed by the court. This allows the reader to easily locate specific issues.

It is important to remember that you should never rely solely on the headnote in conducting legal research. The headnote is not part of the opinion and therefore has no authority or precedential value. Additionally, relying on headnotes alone can allow you to make erroneous conclusions because you do not understand the full context of the opinion.

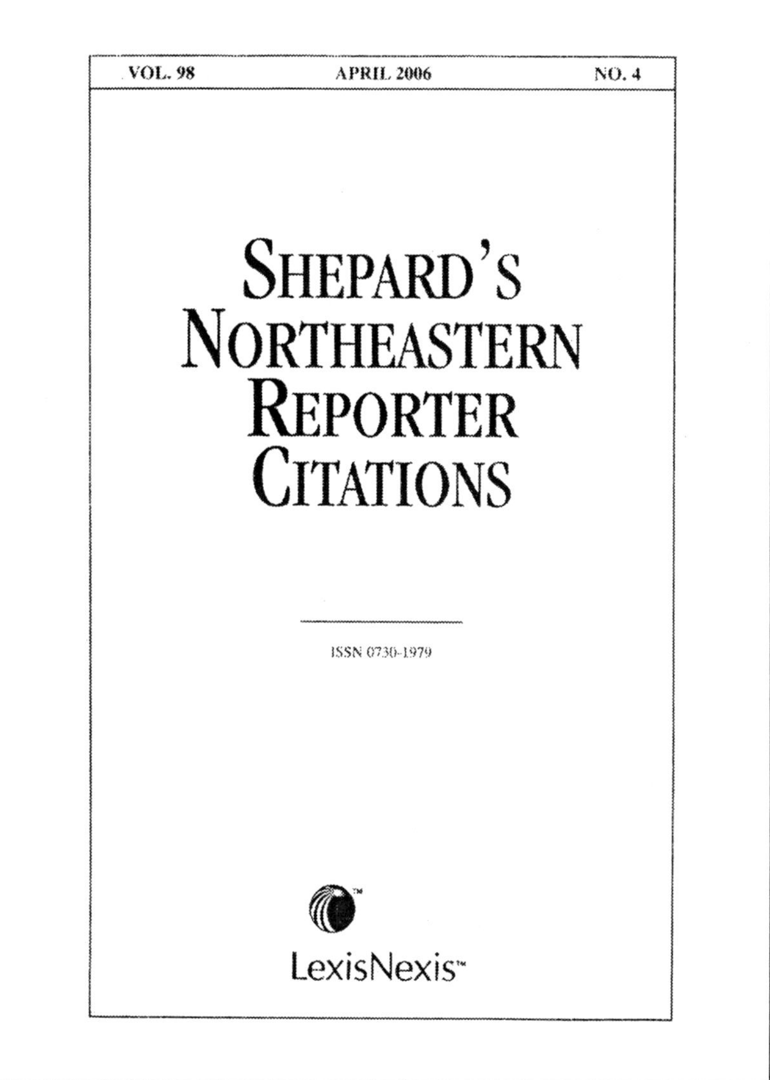
VOL. 98 APRIL 2006 NO. 4

SHEPARD'S NORTHEASTERN REPORTER CITATIONS

ISSN 0730-1979

LexisNexis™

Exhibit 13-10 Massachusetts Shepard's; Courtesy of Shepard's, LexisNexis.

SHEPARDIZING

Shepard's Citations is a valuable resource that allows the researcher to confirm the validity of the law and locate other laws that cite your law in it. Shepard's does not contain the text of the law; it only contains citations to other laws. Some of the things you can **shepardize** include opinions, statutes, constitution, rules of court, and some administrative regulations. The law you are shepardizing is called **cited material**, whereas the law that is provided by Shepard's is called **citing material**.

cited material: The law you are shepardizing.

citing material: The law cited in Shepard's.

Using Shepard's as a Case Locator

In your search of West's Digests for cases involving cars hitting pedestrians, you located *Woods v. O'Neil*. After locating and reading that case, you find that its holding is very helpful. You would like to find other cases that follow the *Woods* holding.

Step One: Find the Shepard's for your cited material, *Woods v. O'Neil*, 767 N.E.2d 1119, in *Shepard's Northeastern Reporter Citations*. Shepard's are generally shelved with the cited material's reporter. Be sure to consult the soft cover supplement that lists the most up-to-date citing material.

NORTHEASTERN REPORTER, 2nd SERIES — Vol. 767

—1118—
2006IllApp LX [4
d 2006IllApp [LX179
h 826NE1130
829NE830
834NE638
841NE1084
Cir. 4
395FS2d407
Cir. 7
2005USDist [LX4588
Ind
f 834NE202
—1132—
f 811NE328
—1136—
q 817NE1043
—1157—
814NE665
841NE561
Cir. 7
2006USDist [LX7261
—1170—
f 2006IndApp [LX164
f 798NE456
f 798NE[1]456
f 820NE126
f 824NE727
828NE906
—1175—
s 811NE415
d 829NE1060
—1190—
797NE321
797NE[3]322
f 797NE323
q 805NE792
823NE1233
—1203—
797NE[8]1184
830NE902
f 839NE258
—1211—
829NE570
829NE940
—1223—
797NE[8]861
839NE175
840NE459
—1240—
825NE837
828NE907
—1247—
2005IndApp [LX1941
817NE615
823NE316

—1258—
834NE150
f 834NE151
—1266—
797NE[1]794
—1288—
819NE578
830NE1044

Vol. 767

—1—
788NE[31]1013
790NE[10]742
797NE[1]465
801NE[25]816
813NE1272
815NE1101
819NE975
824NE851
836NE526
—20—
802NE86
825NE1063
d 831NE356
—29—
807NE241
809NE[9]558
822NE1182
823NE797
—42—
Calif
#j 8CaR3d719
—51—
797NE462
806NE108
824NE852
—66—
829NE1117
—84—
790NE675
—91—
838NE600
—106—
806NE456
d 818NE174
Cir. 1
364FS2d21
—114—
Triplett v Town of Oxford
cc 791NE310
—116—
800NYS2d349
—125—
(97NY393)
(740NYS2d668)
(6A701)
2005NY App [Div LX14769

773NYS2d[3] [642
791NYS2d417
794NYS2d237
796NYS2d[8] [497
796NYS2d[3] [835
799NYS2d[11] [459
800NYS2d343
f 800NYS2d345
804NYS2d208
808NYS2d405
Cir. 2
425F3d133
—132—
808NE339
811NE17
765NYS2d[7] [478
776NYS2d204
778NYS2d755
784NYS2d[11] [405
788NYS2d726
790NYS2d432
791NYS2d720
792NYS2d[11] [641
796NYS2d354
803NYS2d472
805NYS2d871
807NYS2d363
—146—
Meis v ELO Org., LLC
cc 805NYS2d [553
d 821NE534
828NE596
d 788NYS2d [296
791NYS2d869
795NYS2d494
798NYS2d712
—160—
People v Kollar
cc 2005USDist [LX14106
—161—
People v Mills
cc 2005USDist [LX10868
—166—
817NE857
818NE265
819NE234
819NE[9]248
822NE[50]1250
823NE868
f 824NE986
836NE1189
j 836NE1211

f 837NE344
Cir. 6
2006USDist [LX7661
—216—
f 2006Ohio LX [25
818NE[26]250
823NE511
f 826NE283
839NE377
f 840NE151
840NE1053
Cir. 6
2006USDist [LX1507
Conn
844A2d204
—242—
f 827NE806
—268—
802NE657
805NE1127
833NE296
—286—
Haw
j 124P3d983
—314—
j 2005Ill LX [2071
2006Ill LX309
f 2005IllApp LX [1271
2006IllApp LX [20
j 2006IllApp LX [20
2006IllApp LX [129
f 811NE245
813NE325
817NE597
820NE990
821NE1083
821NE1110
821NE1188
f 821NE1190
j 821NE1197
823NE132
f 823NE1052
d 823NE1053
823NE1095
826NE[16]1005
826NE[17]1006
831NE722
836NE780
840NE310
f 841NE1037
—341—
f 2005IllApp LX [22
—357—
Cir. 7
ca 345FS2d922

—366—
832NE277
—376—
f 834NE958
Cir. 7
2003USDist [LX26890
2005USDist [LX13603
2005USDist [LX30260
2006USDist [LX7956
Cir. 9
f 359FS2d1092
—405—
823NE1105
—411—
2006Ill LX11
824NE320
—428—
2005IllApp LX [*337
828NE810
—433—
813NE312
—445—
813NE1069
—452—
826NE577
d 826NE586
—464—
839NE633
—470—
836NE871
Cir. 7
2004USDist [LX22698
—477—
j 2006Ill LX315
818NE750
834NE482
—486—
813NE1147
835NE155
840NE293
—494—
820NE1013
—497—
f 818NE904
—511—
820NE568
—530—
f 2006IndApp [LX164
821NE374
824NE733
829NE524
834NE711
837NE156
837NE1049
839NE725

f 839NE1206
—535—
f 2006IndApp [LX128
2006IndApp [LX249
f 2006IndApp [LX419
d 2006IndApp [LX419
805NE[1]373
806NE19
814NE690
828NE911
831NE839
836NE252
f 841NE238
842NE830
Cir. 7
e 2005USDist [LX29766
f 2005USDist [LX29766
—542—
839NE742
—549—
Mass. Fed'n of Teachers v Bd. of Educ.
798NE[17]960
j 798NE976
802NE113
831NE932
840NE40
—566—
813NE503
827NE700
—578—
f 2006MassApp [LX270
799NE107
f 808NE849
f 808NE[6]849
f 808NE[14]850
—584—
785NE686
—598—
792NE[1]1023
f 792NE1025
792NE[4]1026
—609—
815NE651
—629—
789NE[5]1090
816NE1005
—638—
2006NY App [Div LX538
2006NY App [Div LX1334
2006NY App [Div LX1948
2004NYMisc [LX1553
Continued

621

Exhibit 13-11 Shepard's; Courtesy of Shepard's, LexisNexis.

Step Two: Using the case citation, 767 N.E.2d 1119, look up the volume number, 767, within the Shepard's volume. The volume numbers are shown on the top of the page.

Step Three: Once you have located the volume number, locate the page number of the citation. The page numbers are located within the page under the volume number, in numerical order and boldfaced. The case name is listed below the page number with the **parallel cite** in parentheses.

parallel cite: The citation of the other reporter in which the full text of the cited material may be found.

Step Four: Citing material is listed. These citations are to other cases or materials that mention your case within them. Case law is listed first and is followed by law review article citations, legal periodicals, and legal encyclopedias.

Step Five: Note the abbreviations that are listed in small letters to the left of the citing material. These abbreviations are used to indicate certain things about the cited material. For example, a small "f" means that the cited material's holding follows the holding of the cited material. An abbreviations key is located at the beginning of most Shepard's volumes for easy reference.

This system may be used to shepardize a statute or other materials. Simply substitute the statutory citation and proceed.

CASE ANALYSIS-ABBREVIATIONS

HISTORY OF CASES

a	(affirmed)	On appeal, reconsideration or rehearing, the citing case affirms or adheres to the case you are *Shepardizing*.
cc	(connected case)	The citing case is related to the case you are *Shepardizing*, arising out of the same subject matter or involving the same parties.
D	(dismissed)	The citing case dismisses an appeal from the case you are *Shepardizing*.
De/ Cert den	(denied)	The citing case has denied further appeal in the case you are *Shepardizing*.
Gr	(granted)	The citing case has granted further appeal in the case you are *Shepardizing*.
m	(modified)	On appeal, reconsideration or rehearing, the citing case modifies or changes in some way, including affirmance in part and reversal in part, the case you are *Shepardizing*.
r	(reversed)	On appeal, reconsideration or rehearing, the citing case reverses the case you are *Shepardizing*.
Reh den	(reh./recon. denied)	The citing order denies rehearing or reconsideration in the case you are *Shepardizing*.
Reh gran	(reh./recon. grated)	The citing order grants rehearing or reconsideration in the case you are *Shepardizing*.
s	(same case)	The citing case involves the same litigation as the case you are *Shepardizing*, but at a different stage of the proceedings.
S	(superseded)	On appeal, reconsideration or rehearing, the citing case supersedes or is substituted for the case you are *Shepardizing*.
TD	(transfer denied)	Transfer Denied by the Indiana Supreme Court.
TG	(transfer granted)	Transfer Granted by the Indiana Supreme Court.
US cert den		The citing order by the U. S. Supreme Court denies certiorari in the cases you are *Shepardizing*.
US cert dis		The citing order by the U. S. Supreme Court dismisses certiorari in the case you are *Shepardizing*.
US cert gran		The citing order by the U. S. Supreme Court grants certiorari in the case you are *Shepardizing*.
US reh den		The citing order by the U. S. Supreme Court denies rehearing in the case you are *Shepardizing*.
US reh dis		The citing order by the U. S. Supreme Court dismisses rehearing in the case you are *Shepardizing*.
v	(vacated)	The citing case vacates or withdraws the case you are *Shepardizing*.
W	(withdrawn)	The citing decision or opinion withdraws the decision or order you are *Shepardizing*.

For additional abbreviations on Case and Statutes Analysis, please refer to the Guide to *Shepard's*.

xv

Exhibit 13-12 Abbreviation Table; Courtesy of Shepard's, LexisNexis.

Key Terms

authority
citations
cited material
citing material
descriptive word index
headnotes
mandatory authority
parallel cite
persuasive authority
primary authority
reporters
secondary authority
shepardizing
West's Digests

Exercises

1.

Memorandum
To: Paralegal Extraordinaire
From: Senior Partner
Re: Research Issues/Use of West's Digests

Please locate your state's case law on the following issues:

- Provide the name and citation of the appropriate cases you locate and a one- or two-line answer to the question posed. You may also cite applicable statutes.
- Be sure to shepardize each case that you cite.

1. Locate case law regarding advertising by attorneys, specifically television advertising.
2. Locate case law regarding worker's compensation, specifically the hearing process applicable.
3. Locate your state's case law regarding Fourth Amendment rights of individuals, specifically regarding search and seizure protections.
4. Locate case law regarding the use of an "insanity defense" in criminal cases, specifically locating case law that addresses the "McNaughton (M'Naghton) Rule."

2.

Memorandum
To: Paralegal Class
From: Atty. Dewey Cheatum
Re: Research Assignment

Analyze the following legal questions. Find the answers to the legal questions under your state's law. Write a brief analysis setting forth your answers. In so doing, properly cite your state's statutory code, your state's highest court, appellate courts, and trial court as support for your answers and analysis. Also provide accurate citations to appropriate rules of court. Be sure to shepardize all cases you cite. On a separate page, describe in detail the steps that you took in finding the answers to the legal questions and the sources of law that you consulted in reaching your answers and analysis, if you did not already cite these sources in your memo.

Malek claims that Andre defamed him on January 1, 2005. Malek came to your employer for legal advice on July 19, 2005. The factual investigation reveals that Andre used to work for Malek's interior decorating business and that beginning in the fall of 2002 and continuing through January 1, 2004 (when Andre started his own business), Andre told many of Malek's customers that Malek was a "no good drunken slob" and that he habitually overcharged his customers and used inferior materials. Malek claims that he doesn't know for sure, but he believes that he lost two large accounts because of Andre's statements. It turns out that Malek did have a drinking problem in 1998 and 1999, but that Malek has always used the best quality materials. Your supervising attorney, Rob Reputable, has represented Malek before in real estate transactions. Rob doesn't know much about tort law but has decided to take the case anyway. He wants to sue Andre for defamation per se. Determine the following factors:

1. What elements must Malek prove to recover for defamation per se (include case law)?
2. What statute of limitation applies to the proposed defamation per se claim?
3. Is the proposed defamation per se action time barred by the statute of limitations?
4. What is the burden of proof in a defamation per se action under your state's law (include case law)?
5. What possible defenses (other than statute of limitation) may Andre attempt to raise (include case law)?
6. Can Malek serve process upon Andre himself?
7. Are there any other possible causes of action under your state's law that we could bring?
8. If Malek cannot serve process upon Andre himself, who can serve such process under your state's law?

Library Resources

Learning Legal Research, Charles P. Nemeth & Hope I. Haywood, Pearson Prentice Hall, 2005.
This is a good handbook for legal research.

Nolo's Legal Research (9th Ed.), Stephen Elias & Susan Levinkind, Nolo Publishing, 2004.
This is an excellent step-by-step guide with good exercises.

Advanced Legal Research Exercise Manual, Kathleen A. Portuan Miller, Thomson Delmar Learning, 2001.
Advanced exercises in specialized areas such as bankruptcy, tax law, and environmental law are provided in this book.

Online Resources

http:www.law.cornell.edu
The Legal Information Institute at Cornell provides excellent links and research tutorials.

http:www.nolo.com
Nolo provides user-friendly legal research pointers.

http:www.law.uconn.edu/library
University of Connecticut School of Law site provides helpful library research guides.

CHAPTER 14

Computer Assisted Legal Research

INTRODUCTION

The world of **computer assisted legal research (CALR)** is continually evolving. In the past 20 years, CALR has become an integral part of the legal research process and is a required skill for paralegals. In this chapter, we will review the basic types of online resources and the most useful strategies for accessing information from those resources. This chapter will provide only a broad overview of the vast amount of online resources available. In order to fully take advantage of this chapter, the use of a computer and online access is recommended.

Practice Alert

Due to the constantly changing nature of the Internet, some of the Web site addresses and information provided here may have changed, although all were accurate at the time of publication.

THE BASICS

The vast amount of information made available through the Internet has been both a blessing and a curse for the legal researcher. The advent of CALR has allowed the legal researcher to quickly access information from home or office. However, these advantages do not come without drawbacks. The sheer amount of information available online can be overwhelming and the researcher must employ strategies to eliminate irrelevant information while locating helpful information.

Discussion Point

How do you utilize the Internet in your everyday life? What are the pros and cons of using the Internet to find information?

The most important strategy for any legal research, online or on paper, is preparation. Long before you boot up your computer, you should have an outline in place to guide you through the process. Without an outline, it is too easy to be distracted by irrelevant information. Time spent staring at a computer screen without direction is unproductive time.

Before you start your research, you should determine if a hybrid—that is, using both online and paper research—will be most productive. For example, a general review of a subject online can provide a solid basis to start your research in the library, maximizing your research time.

Three CALR Principles

The following are three CALR principles:

1. Know where to look before you start. Decide which research resource can provide the type of information you need.
2. Know how to use the resource. Most sites have a tutorial that will walk you through the specific applications and rules of that site. It is well worth the five minutes to learn the rules of the site that will enable you to use your time most productively.
3. Be skeptical. You must verify the accuracy of all information you access over the Internet. This is especially true of any treatises, articles, or chat room/discussion board information. Always independently verify information obtained from these sources.

INTERNET RESEARCH RESOURCES

There are three basic types of Internet research resources: directories, search engines, and fee-based services. These resources are described in the following section.

Directories

Directories organize Web sites into logical categories. A group of editors at a Web site determine certain broad subject categories and then break those broad categories into specific subcategories. Similar to the table of contents in a book, the directory lists the title of the "chapter" or broad subject category and beneath it, the specific headings contained in the chapter. Directories may have a general focus that covers a wide variety of topics, or a specialty focus that concentrates on a specific subject matter, such as law or medicine. When using a directory, it is helpful to look for the broad category or concept closest to the issue you are researching and then review each subtopic until you reach the specific information you seek.

Commonly used general directories include http://www. yahoo. com, http://www. excite. com, http://www. lycos. com, and http://www. altavista. com. Commonly used directories with a legal focus include http://www. findLaw.com, http://www. lawGuru.com, and http://www. catalaw.com.

Directories are best used to gain an overview of a subject you are not familiar with and to obtain background information prior to a more specific search (similar to the use of legal encyclopedias in "paper" or library research).

Discussion Point

Have you used directories before? Have you found them helpful in obtaining information? Discuss.

EXAMPLE For example, if you need to get an overview of the crime of embezzlement, perform the following steps.

1. Log onto www.findlaw.com.
2. Scroll down to "Law for People" and click "Criminal Law."
3. Provide your zip code. This allows the site to provide information specific to your jurisdiction.
4. Click "Crimes A–Z."
5. Scroll down and click "Embezzlement."
6. You will find a discussion of the crime and relevant statutory citations.

Search Engines

Search engines search for specific words or phrases you, as the researcher, provide. Using descriptive words, the researcher inputs a command to the engine to search for Web sites that contain those specific words contained in the command. As with directories, search engines may be general or specialized. You may utilize the cartwheeling and descriptive word strategies employed in paper research to develop a CALR search engine command or query. (See Chapter 12.)

Commonly used general search engines include http://www.yahoo.com, http://www. google.com, http://www.excite.com, http://www. lycos.com, and http://www. altavista.com. As discussed before, many of these sites include both directories and search engines. You may access them both, but use them for different purposes. Commonly used legal focus search engines include: http://www. lawguru.com and http://www. findLaw.com.

For example, if you want to read what the U.S. Supreme Court has ruled regarding the insanity defense in criminal cases in the past 10 years, perform the following steps:

1. Log onto http://www.law.cornell.edu, the Legal Information Institute.
2. Click "Court Opinions" located in the left-hand box.
3. Click "U.S. Supreme Court."
4. Go to the search engine box located at the top of the page, type "insanity defense," "decisions since 1991," and "search."
5. You should receive 34 U.S. Supreme Court cases.

Fee-Based Services

Fee-based services charge for use of their extensive databases. The two most widely used fee-based services are LexisNexis and Westlaw. These services are user friendly and contain extensive legal information. It is wise to consult the "How Do I?" tutorial section in each service's Web site to determine the specific guidelines for use. Additionally, LexisNexis and Westlaw regularly send their representatives to conduct training programs for firms and businesses that subscribe to their services. These services utilize a search engine.

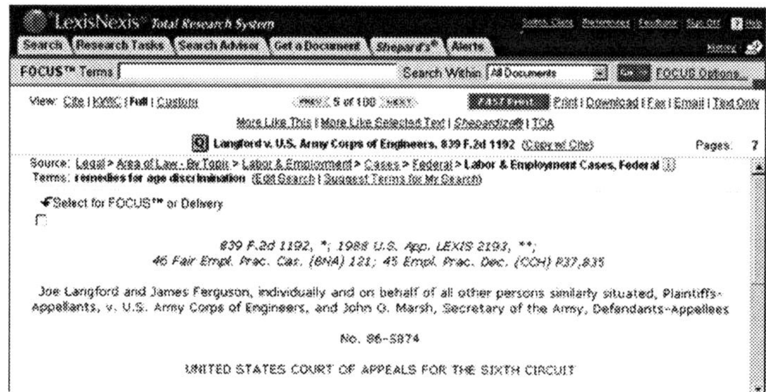

Exhibit 14-1 LexisNexis; Courtesy of LexisNexis

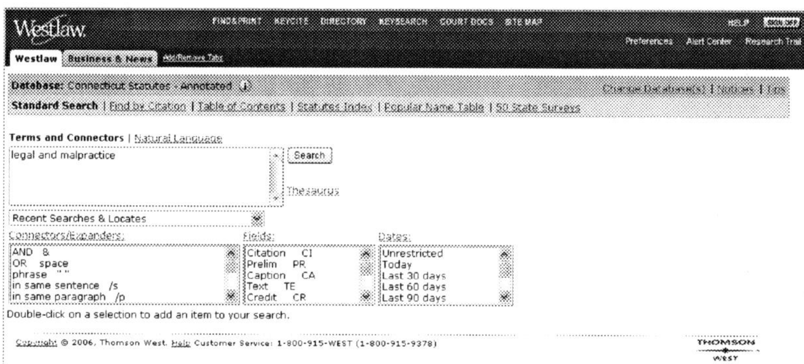

Exhibit 14-2 Westlaw; Courtesy of Westlaw, a division of Delmar, Cengage Learning

Create a Query

In using search engines and fee-based services, you must create a **query** or question on which the service may base its search. This query can be phrased as a "natural word search" or a Boolean language search. In a natural word search you can enter a simple sentence and the search engine will extract keywords and find cases or articles that include those keywords. Natural word searches are easy to use because simple sentences are used. However, natural word searches may result in many responses because the computer can only use the keywords included in the natural word sentence. You must sift through the multiple responses in order to find relevant responses to your search.

With a Boolean search, you use a language the computer understands, called **Boolean language**, to extract specific responses. You use connectors to link search words into sentences. A detailed discussion of Boolean language is provided later in this chapter.

For each issue you research online, ask yourself the following questions:

- What is the general legal concept I am researching?
- What specific rule(s) are at issue?
- What are the important factual circumstances of my case?
- What jurisdiction will my case be under?

Place the answers to these questions in sentence form and derive your **search terms** from those sentences.

EXAMPLE Your client was recently fired from her job as an accountant at a small consulting firm. She tells you she was employed there for 18 months and for that entire period her male supervisor made sexually explicit comments to her in front of other employees. This supervisor also left obscene photographs on her desk at least once month. Your client tells you she went on two dates with the supervisor, but soon after she refused a third date, she was fired. Your supervising attorney asks you to research the elements for filing a sexual harassment suit under federal law. Search using the following four elements:

- General legal concept: sexual harassment in the workplace
- Specific rule: federal laws regarding sexual harassment in the workplace
- Important factual circumstances: Small firm, sexual explicit comments and materials, dating relationship between employer and employee, employee fired
- Jurisdiction: federal

Using these concepts, the following query sentence is developed: What are the federal rules regarding sexual harassment in the workplace when an employee is fired after refusing to date employer?

This query sentence highlights the following search terms: federal rules, sexual harassment, workplace, employer, employee, refusal to date.

BOOLEAN LANGUAGE

With a Boolean search, you use a language the computer understands to extract specific responses. You use **connectors** to link search words into sentences. Use of Boolean language may be used with the fee-based services and non-fee–based services in order to create specific queries and obtain specific responses.

Or

Or is used to connect words or phrases that mean the same thing or to tell the system you want it retrieve all documents that have either of those words in it. This connector expands your number of results. Typing *renter or lessee* retrieves all documents that contain either search term, renter and lessee.

And

And is used to connect words or phrases that you want to appear in the document. By using the *and* connector, you command the system to produce only those documents that contain both of the search words. This connector narrows your number of results. Typing *malpractice and medical* retrieves only those documents that contain both the search terms medical and malpractice.

Practice Alert

Most search engines treat a space between search words to connote the "and" command. Check your service's guidelines.

Quotation marks

Quotation marks are used to group two or more search terms together as a phrase. This command tells the system to retrieve only those documents that contain these search words as a phrase. Typing "medical malpractice" retrieves only those documents that contain the term medical malpractice.

And Not

And Not is used to exclude certain search words from your results. By using this connector you command the system to include one search term with the exclusion of another. Typing *medical malpractice* and not *legal malpractice* retrieves all documents that contain the phrase medical practice but commands that no documents that contain the phrase legal malpractice are retrieved.

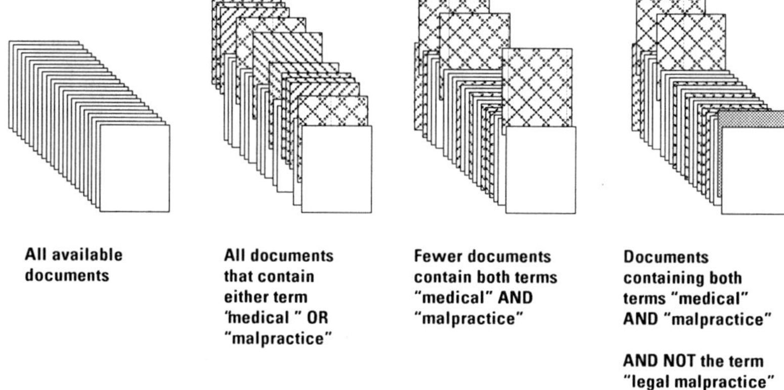
All available documents
All documents that contain either term 'medical " OR "malpractice"
Fewer documents contain both terms "medical" AND "malpractice"
Documents containing both terms "medical" AND "malpractice"
AND NOT the term "legal malpractice"

Exhibit 14-3 Use of "and not"

Root expanders *

Root expanders are used to substitute for all possible roots of a search word. This commands the system to retrieve all documents that contain the search word and all roots. This command expands your number of results without having to type in all variations of a word. Typing *neglig** retrieves all documents that contain the words negligent, negligence, negligently.

Wild Cards ! or ?

Wild Cards ! or ? are used to substitute for a letter in a search word. Some systems use ! and some use ?. Typing *wom!n* retrieves all documents that contain the words woman or women.

Key Terms

Boolean language	connectors	query
computer-assisted legal research (CALR)	directories	search engines
	fee-based services	search terms

Exercises

Using your state as the jurisdiction, research the following questions using one of the fee-based services. Use Boolean connectors to link search terms you have derived using the strategies discussed in this chapter.

1. Your client owns a small coffee shop in Armonk, New York. She has three full-time employees and two part-time employees. She has begun to suspect two of her full-time employees have been taking cash from the register at closing time.

   A friend from the local chamber of commerce group has told your client that he regularly has his employees submit to polygraph tests to ascertain if any have been stealing from his business. Your client wants to know if she can legally make her employees, both full time and part time, submit to a polygraph test. Your attorney believes there are federal provisions that may be relevant. Find these provisions and answer your client's questions.

   ____
   ____
   ____
   ____

2. Your supervising attorney has recently been assisting the Connecticut Bar Association in drafting attorney ethics advisory opinions. She has asked you to find a database containing the last two years of Connecticut ethics opinions.

   ____
   ____
   ____
   ____

3. Your client is a 350-pound, 45-year-old male who recently suffered a major heart attack. He is currently on disability and is unable to work. He claims that he took the prescribed drug Phen Phen 18 months ago for a period of three months. He resides in Fairfax, Virginia. Determine the FDA (Federal Drug Administration) stance on the drug, including whether it is still on the market and what health complications have been associated with this drug; who manufactures the drug; and whether any class action suits are currently pending.

   ____
   ____
   ____
   ____

4. Our client is a candidate running for the statewide office of attorney general. Her campaign is fundraising heavily to make up for her opponent's vast spending. Her opponent is a multi-millionaire who has already spent over $700,000 of her own money on her campaign thus far. Our client's husband's family wholly owns a large manufacturing company and he wishes to make a $50,000 contribution to her campaign from company funds.

   Answer the following two questions for our client, consulting both statutory and case authority:

   - Is there a limit on the amount of personal funds her opponent may spend on her own campaign? Must these expenditures be reported?

     ____
     ____
     ____
     ____

- May our client's husband make a $50,000 contribution from company funds to her campaign?

5. Our client is a wealthy, recent retiree. He owns three homes in three different states and is trying to determine where to maintain his permanent residence in order to gain maximum tax benefits.

   Research the following:

- What criteria does the IRS and your state's tax department consider in determining residency for tax purposes?

- What are the estate tax provisions in your state?

- What is the current status of the federal estate tax?

Use any or all of the following Web sites in your research: http://www.altavista.com, http://www.lawguru.com, http://www.google.com, http://www.findlaw.com, or http://www.law.cornell.edu.

Library Resources

Computer Assisted Legal Research: The Basics, Penny A. Hazelton, West Publishing Co., 1993.
This book provides the basics and is a good resource for general points.

Computer Assisted Legal Research, Susan Coleman, Thomson Delmar Publishing, 2005.
This book offers good exercises and explanations.

Nolo Legal Research (10th Ed.), Stephen Elias & Susan Levinkind, Nolo Publishing, 2002.
This book includes good step-by-step exercises with answers for home study.

Online Resources

Fee-based services, www.lexis.com; www.westlaw.com; www.loislaw.com
Some offer free trial periods to use their service; check the Web site's "Subscriber Options."

SUNY Albany Library, http://www.Internettutorials.net/boolean.html
This site provides clear Boolean tutorial reference.

PART 5

LEGAL WRITING

CHAPTER 15

Legal Writing

INTRODUCTION

Justice Louis Brandeis once noted, "There is no such thing as good writing, only good rewriting." Keep this maxim in mind as you write, for you will find that legal writing requires much preparation and revision. The skill of communicating legal analysis and results of legal research is important. This chapter will discuss the different types of legal writing you will encounter and produce most often as a paralegal. Different styles of writing and points of grammar will also be covered.

TYPES OF LEGAL WRITING

Legal writing takes two forms: objective and persuasive. **Objective writing** discusses the strengths and weaknesses of a position and often includes recommendations for further investigation as well as negotiation strategies. **Persuasive writing** is argumentative. In persuasive writing, the writer presents an argument and authority to sustain that argument. We'll discuss each type in turn in the following section.

Objective writing

The Legal Memorandum

The type of legal writing most commonly produced by a paralegal is the legal memorandum. The legal memorandum often takes the form of an **interoffice memorandum** that is used to discuss the strengths and weaknesses of a particular case and is written specifically for use within the law office only. Often an attorney will request that a paralegal write an interoffice memorandum on a particular issue. The format of the interoffice memorandum varies by office but generally follows the following format.

MEMORANDUM OF LAW

To:
From:
Re:
Date:

Statement of Assignment:
[State what you were asked to analyze in the memorandum. This statement frames the content of the memo.]

Facts:

[State brief summary of the relevant facts of the case. Sometimes the facts portion is omitted when the facts are well known to prospective readers of the memo.]

Issue(s) Presented:

[List the legal issues you will discuss in the Discussion portion of the memo. If you have completed an elements analysis (see Chapter 11) you may use the Issue Statements derived there.]

Discussion:

[This is the "meat" of your memo. Here you will provide legal analysis of the issues presented and you will state the rule of law you are discussing. This portion should generally be the longest part of your memo.]

Conclusion:

[Provide a brief summary of the conclusions made for each of the issues analyzed in the Discussion portion. You may sometimes be asked to include recommendations for further investigation in this portion of the memo.]

Before writing any memorandum, it is important to prepare. You must complete your analysis of the issues as discussed in Chapters 10 and 11. Then you must prepare an outline. The outline should include all relevant information and the product of your analysis.

Consider the following facts. John Adams is a candidate running for municipal office in your state. He called the State Elections Agency two weeks before the election to ask whether he could accept a campaign contribution from his brother in law's beer brewing company.

An inexperienced Agency employee took Adams's call and erroneously informed him that he could accept the contribution. Adams accepted the contribution and his opponent filed a complaint against him with the Agency alleging Adams violated state law by accepting the illegal contribution. Adams wishes to assert estoppel against the Agency, which would prohibit the Agency from holding him liable for relying on the erroneous advice. After completing research and analysis on the issues, an outline for an interoffice memo might look like the following.

OUTLINE

Issues:

1. Can an agent of the State be subject to estoppel?
2. If so, what standard applies?

Discuss:

- General standard for estoppel; *Leycynski* holding
- Specific claims of estoppel invoked against state agencies; *Leycynski, Dupuis,* include three-prong test

The outline would include briefs of the relevant cases, allowing the writer to quickly refer back to relevant language of the case for use in the memo. The completed memo follows.

INTER OFFICE MEMORANDUM OF LAW

To: Benjamin Franklin
State Elections Agency
General Counsel
From: Thomas Jefferson
Paralegal I
Re: Adams Hearing, File No. 1234
Date: June 4, 2005

FACTS PRESENTED:

The Agency Commission is currently considering a claim brought before it by the Respondent, Samuel Adams regarding an alleged violation of Regulation 43-2333. Mr. Adams claims that he was given erroneous advice by an agent of the Agency and by relying on it was injured. He now asserts a claim of estoppel of claim before Agency.

QUESTIONS PRESENTED:

1. Can an agent of the State be subject to estoppel?
2. If so, what standard applies?

DISCUSSION:

Under well-established law in Connecticut, any claim of estoppel must include two essential elements within its offer of proof: "[T]he party against whom estoppel is claimed must do or say something calculated or intended to induce another party to believe that certain facts exist and to act on that belief; and the other party must change its position in reliance on those facts, thereby incurring some injury." *Zoning Commission v. Leycynski,* 188 Conn 724, 731 (1982); *Bozzi v. Bozzi,* 177 Conn 232, 242 (1979); *Dupuis v. Submarine Base Credit Union Inc.,* 170 Conn 344, 353 (1976).

It is also established that estoppel may not generally be invoked against a public agency in the exercise of its governmental functions. *Leycynski,* at 731; *Dupuis,* at 353; *McGowan v. Administrator*, 153 Conn 691, 692 (1966). However, several more recent cases have created an exception when the plaintiff can prove that he would be subjected to a substantial loss if the municipality were permitted to negate the acts of its agents. *Kimberly-Clark Corporation v. Dubno,* 204 Conn 137, 146 (1987); *West Hartford v. Rechel*, 190 Conn 114, 121 (1983).

In deciding those cases, the courts constructed a three prong test that determines that estoppel may be invoked against a public agency (1) only with great caution, (2) only when the resulting violation has been justifiably induced by an agent having authority in such matters, and (3) only when special circumstances make it highly likely inequitable or oppressive to enforce the regulations. All of these circumstances must be met in order for estoppel to be granted. *Kimberly-Clark* at 147; *Rechel* at 123.

It is evident that the Respondent in the current case will be subjected to substantial loss if the Agency is permitted to enforce its statutes against them and are therefore eligible to present a claim of estoppel against the Agency. However, the Respondent must satisfy the standards detailed above in order to be granted estoppel. This memorandum will address the second prong.

The first issue to examine is whether the agent of the Agency had authority to give the advice upon which the

Respondent relied. In *McGowan v. Administrator*, 153 Conn 691 (1966), the court stated "regardless of the action of the administrator [of the Unemployment Compensation Act] in accepting any payments made to him, he cannot waive the rights of the state, nor can he, by any act of his, estop the state from asserting its rights or prevent the performance of his statutory duties." at 146.

State v. Metrusky, 140 Conn 26 (1953), also held that the state could not be estopped from enforcing a statute due to actions of an agent. "Whatever obligation [the plaintiff] had to reimburse the state was not founded in contract between her and the Commissioner of Welfare. It was an obligation imposed by statute...The Commissioner of Welfare has no authority to waive an obligation so imposed by law, and consequently the state cannot be estopped from enforcing it by any conduct on his part." At p. 30 (citations omitted.)

A more recent case decided by the court involving this issue granted estoppel against a public agency. In *Kimberly-Clark v. Dubno,* supra, the Commissioner of Revenue Services issued a declaratory ruling that was then relied upon by the plaintiffs. The court held that because the Commissioner had direct statutory right to give declaratory rulings, that agency may be estopped from asserting its claim against the plaintiffs. 204 Conn at 147.

In *Kimberly-Clark* the court distinguished its decision from *McGowan* and *Metrusky* by stating "in those cases we recognized that the particular state agents had acted outside of their authority." At 148. *McGowan* and *Metrusky* are inopposite to the case at hand. In the current case, "the Commissioner" had express statutory authorization to give the declaratory rulings, which are subject of this appeal." *Kimberly-Clark* at 146.

CONCLUSION:

It appears clear from these cases that absent explicit statutory authorization, actions of public agents in the operation of their governmental duties cannot estop the state from enforcing its statutes. In the case at hand, no declaratory ruling or written authorization was issued to the Respondent. In contrast, only general advice was given over the phone in response to a broad question.

Important objective writing points to remember include:

- Be clear of your goal before beginning your task. Always ask for clarification on an assignment if you are unsure what you are being asked to complete.
- Be mindful of your reader. Remember who you are writing for: is this an attorney who is intimately familiar with the facts of the case or will your memo be distributed to many readers who may not be as familiar with the facts and issues.
- Use clear and concise writing. Legalese is not good legal writing: if you can state it with less words, do so.
- Use signposts such as "There are three issues..." In legal writing you want your reader to be able to easily and quickly understand your reasoning and conclusions.

- Watch your sentence and paragraph structure. Avoid run-on sentences and long paragraphs. Use the IRAC framework discussed in Chapter 10. Begin with an issue statement and proceed to apply the rule to the facts of your case.

Discussion Point

Consult a thesaurus and identify words that are forceful. What words convey strength? Which are less persuasive?

Consider this example of structured writing based on writing assignment number two of this chapter.

Did Darcy "make payment" as contemplated by Bliss Revised Statute Sec. 22-15-992? [Issue statement]

There is a strong argument that Mr. Darcy did make payment for the shoes as contemplated by Sec. 22-15-992. [issue statement/topic sentence] After being released from the police station, Mr. Darcy immediately proceeded to Jane's shop and paid for the shoes he wore out of the store. [facts of our case] Clearly this action, Mr. Darcy paying for the shoes, satisfies the "making payment" element of the statute. There is no provision in Sec. 22-15-992 requiring *when* such payment must be made. Therefore, the fact that Mr. Darcy's payment occurred a few hours after leaving the store is irrelevant. [applying rule to our facts]

It may also be argued that Mr. Darcy "made payment" as contemplated by the statute by leaving his old pair of shoes at the store. [issue statement/topic sentence] There is no definition contained within the statute as to what constitutes a "payment" and its usage could be quite broad and could include an exchange of items. [rule to our facts] Further research as to this definition is required to complete an analysis.

Status Letter

A paralegal may be asked to draft a **status letter** to a client updating them on what has been done in their case. The letter should be written under the supervision of an attorney and should contain their signature because it may be construed as providing advice to a client, which may only be done by an attorney. In writing such a letter, proper business letter format should be followed. Clear and concise writing is preferred, keeping in mind that you are writing to a client without legal knowledge.

Fetzer & Ervin, LLC.
101 Cheatum Way
Manchester, CT 06001

Dear Mr. Darcy,

I am writing to update you on the status of the malicious prosecution civil action against Charles Bingley.

We have entered the discovery phase of the litigation, and have accordingly submitted the following discovery requests to the opposing side:

1. Interrogatories

Exhibit 15-1 Status Letter

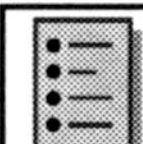

Discussion Point

Consider business letters you have received and written in the past. What makes a business letter easy to understand? Hard to understand?

Persuasive Writing

Persuasive writing presents an argument and attempts to convince the reader to agree with the position you are advocating. Most persuasive writing is presented to the court and is thus often performed mostly by attorneys. However, as a paralegal you may be asked to assist in the drafting of persuasive documents.

Motions

Motions are formal requests made to the court.

motion: Formal requests made to the court.

Motions must follow the particular rules of court of that jurisdiction. Motions generally must include:

- a caption
- legal reason for requesting granting of motion
- indication if oral argument is sought
- certification that copies have been mailed to all parties
- an order for the judge to indicate her decision

DOCKET NO. CV 05-000000 S	:	SUPERIOR COURT
WILLIAM DARCY	:	JUDICIAL DISTRICT
	:	OF TOLLAND
V.	:	AT ROCKVILLE
CHARLES BINGLEY	:	OCTOBER 19, 2004

MOTION TO STRIKE

Pursuant to Connecticut Practice Book Section 10-32, the defendant, Charles Bingley, hereby moves to strike the Fourth and Seventh counts of the Plaintiff's Complaint dated July 23, 2004 on the grounds that the said counts fail to state a claim upon which relief can be granted and are insufficient as a matter of law.

A memorandum of law in support of this motion is attached hereto.

THE DEFENDANT,
WILLIAM DARCY

BY____________________________

HER ATTORNEY
F.H. Fetzer, Esq.
Fetzer & Ervin, P.C.
101 Cheatum Way
Manchester, CT 06001

ORAL ARGUMENT NOT REQUESTED
TESTIMONY NOT REQUIRED

ORDER

The foregoing Motion having been duly presented and heard by the Court, it is hereby ORDERED: GRANTED/DENIED.

____
BY THE COURT

CERTIFICATION

I hereby certify that a copy of the above was mailed on October 19, 2004 to all counsel and pro se parties of record as follows: Benjamin D. Pap. Esq., of Pap and Pap, P.C., P.O. Box 1234, Canton, CT 06775.

____
F.H. Fetzer, Esq.

advocacy: Presentation of legal argument before a court on behalf of a client.

Motions are generally accompanied by a memorandum of law in support of the motion. This memorandum presents the legal argument to the court in an effort to persuade the judge to rule in your client's favor. This type of legal argument is called **advocacy.**

Memorandums in support of a motion are written with persuasive language. In such a memorandum, forceful language is used to advocate your position.

Important persuasive writing points remember include:

- Remember who you are writing for. The memorandum is written to a judge and your goal is to convince the judge to rule in your favor. Remember you are making an argument at all times.
- Use strong language. Not "The Plaintiff feels that the statute states…" but rather "The statutes state…"
- Use headings within your memorandum to highlight major points. Each heading should stand as a sentence and point the judge to a major argument you are presenting.
- Provide authority for all assertions. Every assertion you make in a persuasive document to a judge must be backed up by legal authority. Without such authority, the judge may dismiss your argument.

DOCKET NO. CV 05-000000 s	:	SUPERIOR COURT
WILLIAM DARCY	:	JUDICIAL DISTRICT
	:	OF TOLLAND
V.	:	AT ROCKVILLE
CHARLES BINGLEY	:	OCTOBER 19, 2005

MEMORANDUM OF LAW
IN SUPPORT OF MOTION TO STRIKE

I. BACKGROUND

The Plaintiff, William Darcy, was arrested on June 15, 2004 for shoplifting in violation of Section 37a-19. The Plaintiff subsequently filed the current action in a Complaint with this court dated June 15, 2005, alleging that he was maliciously prosecuted by the Defendant, Charles Bingley in violation of Section 54-34(b). The Defendant is the acting State's Attorney of this jurisdiction.

The Plaintiff's Complaint contains seven counts. In counts four and seven the Plaintiff ....

II. LAW AND ARGUMENT

A. The Plaintiff Failed to Meet the Burden Imposed By Section 54-34(b).

Section 54-34(b).provides: "Any public figure who uses his office's authority or resources to prosecute any person without proper statutory authority and for personal gain or retribution shall be in violation of this section."

In count four of the Plaintiff's complaint, ...

CONCLUSION

The allegations in the fourth and seventh counts of the Plaintiff's Complaint fail to state a cause of action against the Defendant under Section 54-34(v) and should therefore be stricken.

THE DEFENDANT,
CHARLES BINGLEY

BY________________________

HIS ATTORNEY
F.H. Fetzer, Esq.
Fetzer & Ervin, P.C.
101 Cheatum Way
Manchester, CT 06001

CERTIFICATION

A copy of the foregoing was sent, postage prepaid, to all counsel and pro se parties of record:

J.K Rowling, Esq.
Weasley, Potter and Malfoy, P.C.
18 Hogwarts Way
Hogsmeade, CT 06000

____

F.H. Fetzer, Esq.

Demand Letter

Another common type of persuasive writing encountered by the paralegal is the **demand letter.** A demand letter is a letter written in a civil case to persuade the opposing side to settle.

demand letter: A letter written in a civil case to persuade the opposing side to settle.

Such a letter emphasizes the strengths of your case in order to convince the other side to settle the case out of court in a manner most favorable to your client.

Fetzer & Ervin, LLC.
101CheatumWay
Manchester, CT 06001

Dear Attorney Rowling,

As you are aware, our office is representing Mr. Darcy in his claim of malicious prosecution against your client, Mr. Bingley. Our investigation has uncovered substantial evidence to support the malicious prosecution action. Accordingly, we offering a settlement in the amount of three hundred thousand dollars ($300,000).

Exhibit 15-2 Demand Letter

Key Terms

advocacy
demand letter
interoffice memorandum
motion
objective writing
persuasive writing
status letter

Exercises

I.

MEMORANDUM

To: Paralegal
From: Katherine Grace, Supervising Attorney
Re: Rodney Hagrid, File #2020

I recently met with a new client, Rodney Hagrid, regarding a pending civil suit against him. I have provided the facts of his case as gathered from his intake interview. I have also provided the statute under which Mr. Hagrid is being sued.

Please review these materials and write up an interoffice memorandum of law, which includes:

- a legal analysis of the strengths and weaknesses of the case against Mr. Hagrid based on the facts of the case and the statutory authority provided. Do not conduct any independent research;
- recommendations as to any further investigation or research you feel is needed;
- recommendations as to how to next proceed in the case and whether any counterclaims may be made by Mr. Hagrid.

FACTS:

Our client, Rodney Hagrid, owns a small house in a crowded subdivision neighborhood. One evening in late May , he returned from work and discovered a small dog of indeterminate breed on his back porch. Mr. Hagrid, an animal lover, fed the dog some leftover Chinese food and let him sleep on the back porch on an old quilt she provided for that purpose.

Every morning thereafter, the dog was gone when Mr. Hagrid left for work but always reappeared in the evening. The dog would wait on the back porch for dinner and its bed.

Early in the morning of June 30, approximately 2 months after the dog appeared, Mr. Hagrid was awakened by a loud noise emanating from his back porch. Upon investigating, Mr. Hagrid found the dog on the porch with its jaws clamped on the arm of a dark figure. Mr. Hagrid called the dog who then released the figure and sat by Hagrid's side. Hagrid then recognized the figure as Fred Weasley, his paperboy.

Both Hagrid and Weasley agree that Weasley customarily delivered the paper to the front door but Weasley claims that he occasionally delivered to the back door, depending upon the weather.

Weasley suffered numerous lacerations and bruises and was unable to complete his paper route for six months. Weasley has been delivering Hagrid's paper for over three years and is an altar boy and National Merit Scholar.

Weasley is suing Hagrid to recover for medical expenses and lost income.

Statutory Authority: Section 45b-11 Animal Control Statute

If a dog or other animal, without provocation, damages another's property or injures any person who is peaceably conducting himself in any place where the person may lawfully be, the owner of the dog or other animal is liable for the damage or injuries caused.

II.

To: Paralegal
From: Attorney Elizabeth Bennet
Re: William Darcy

ASSIGNMENT: We are defending William Darcy against larceny, fifth-degree charges brought by State's Attorney Charles "Chuck" Bingley. The charges stem from Darcy's alleged attempt to steal a pair of used Prince Albert brand shoes from Jane's Ye Olde Shoe Emporium on May 15, 2005 here in Netherfield, State of New Surrey. We have a meeting with Mr. Darcy scheduled for next week. Please analyze the strengths and weaknesses of the state's case in a written memorandum of law.

In drafting the memorandum, analyze whether the state will be able to convict Mr. Darcy. Additionally, if the state can obtain a conviction, provide analysis of Mr. Darcy's expected punishment. I have dictated a brief summary of the facts below. If you believe that your analysis requires further information, please set forth in your memorandum what additional information you will need to complete your analysis. Do not conduct any independent research at this time. Finally, if you have any suggestions as to possible litigation and/or plea bargain strategy, address this in your memorandum.

FACTS: Our client, William Darcy is an ex-detective of the Netherfield Police Department. He is currently a crime-story novelist who has written several books about famous murders in Netherfield. The locals know him as a "peculiar fellow" with many eccentricities. One of Mr. Darcy's eccentricities is that he will only wear black and white Prince Albert brand shoes while he working on a new book. Recently, Mr. Darcy has been working on a new book entitled "Shame and Acceptance."

On May 15, Mr. Darcy took a break from his writing endeavors and visited his favorite shoe store, Jane's Ye Olde Shoe Emporium to search for some high-quality, pre-owned Prince Albert shoes. A new salesperson, Catherine DeBourgh, was on the floor. Mr. Darcy asked if the store had any Prince Albert shoes in stock in a size 10. The salesperson brought a pair out. Mr. Darcy took off his very battered Prince Alberts and tried on the pair the salesperson brought to him. Mr. Darcy proceeded to walk around the store with the shoes on. While walking around the store with the shoes on, Mr. Darcy claims he "had a brainstorm" of an idea for his new book.

In his haste to get back to writing, Mr. Darcy left the store with the store's Prince Albert shoes on his feet. He also left his old Prince Albert shoes behind. According to an eyewitness, Bill Collins, when Mr. Darcy was outside Jane's on the sidewalk, he turned back to the store, looked down at his feet, and then proceeded to walk away. Mr. Darcy does not remember doing that. He does, however, remember Officer George Wickham of the Netherfield Police Department coming to his door and asking Mr. Darcy to "come with him." According to Mr. Darcy, Officer Wickham wanted to question him about a complaint from Jane's Ye Olde Shoe Emporium that he shoplifted a pair of size 10 Prince Albert shoes.

According to Mr. Darcy, he did go with Officer Wickham in Wickham's patrol car to Netherfield Police headquarters. Once there, Officer Wickham proceeded to interrogate Mr. Darcy for almost one hour about the Prince Albert shoes. Mr. Darcy claims that Officer Wickham "got hostile" and yelled at Mr. Darcy from six inches away from his face. According to our client, Officer Wickham was attempting to get him to sign a confession that said that Mr. Darcy intended to take the Prince Albert shoes from Jane's. Mr. Darcy also claims that Officer Wickham "hit a wall in he interrogation room with his baton." When Mr. Darcy asked if he could call me for legal advice, he claims that Officer Wickham refused to let him make the call. Officer Wickham then issued Mr. Darcy a summons for violating New Surrey Revised Statute Section 37a-19.

The Netherfield Police Department subsequently released Mr. Darcy. After returning home, Mr. Darcy claims that he called Jane, the shoe store's owner and explained the situation. He went down to the store, retrieved his old shoes, and paid for the size 10 Prince Albert shoes that he took from the store. According to Jane, she does not want to lose Darcy as a customer and has requested that State's Attorney Bingley drop the charges against Mr. Darcy. Bingley, who Mr. Darcy recently lampooned in one of his novels, has refused to do so. In fact, when I called him, Bingley said "this case is getting tried, and I'm trying it myself."

LEGAL AUTHORITY:

STATUTE: According to New Surrey Revised Statute Section 37a-19 (2004): "Any person that knowingly or intentionally takes property in excess of $200 in value belonging to another without making payment or otherwise providing adequate compensation, shall be guilty of larceny in the fifth degree..." The statute further states that "a person found guilty of larceny in the fifth degree shall receive a sentence of no more that ten days in jail or shall pay a fine of no more than $500."

CASELAW: *State v. McDonnell*, 240 A2d 35 (2002).

McDonnell was a fifteen-year-old boy observed by a plainclothes security guard shoplifting rare comic books at Herbie's Comics and Collectibles Shop. The guard handcuffed McDonnell, brought him to a closed room in the back of the store and questioned him for three hours before calling the police and releasing him into their custody. McDonnell was charged by the police with violating New Surrey Revised Statute 37a-19.

The New Surrey Supreme Court held: The length of detainment of McDonnell was excessive and therefore no jail time could be included in sentencing.

III.

MEMORANDUM

To: Paralegal
From: Attorney Oliver Slugworth
Re: Veruca Salt v. Wonka's World of Beauty, Inc.

We represent Wonka's in a product liability action. The plaintiff, Veruca Salt, through counsel, recently filed a single-count complaint against our client (see Chapter 5). Included in Paragraph 2 of the demand for relief is a claim for statutory punitive damages under Connecticut General Statute Sec. 52-240b. Your review of the complaint will show that it does not plead any facts to indicate that our client acted with reckless disregard for the plaintiff's safety in selling the hairdryer. Thus, I want to move to strike the demand for punitive damages.

Please draft a motion to strike the demand for punitive damages. Also draft a memorandum of law in support of the motion to strike the demand for punitive damages.

- Section I should be titled "FACTS" and should be based on the fact pleaded in the complaint. (Remember, a motion to strike admits all well-pleaded facts but not mere legal conclusions.)
- Section II shall be entitled "LAW & ARGUMENT" and shall contain a subsection governing the legal standard for deciding a motion to strike and another subsection arguing that the court should strike the demand for punitive damages.
- Finally, Section III shall be titled "CONCLUSION" and shall sum up the main points of the argument.
- Additionally, follow all appropriate formatting requirements as set forth in the Connecticut Practice Book. Your motion should, of course, include an order and certification to opposing counsel.

I have already done some of the research necessary for you to write the memorandum of law and have two on-point cases on the issue of when it is appropriate for a court to strike a demand for punitive damages under Connecticut's product liability act. You may locate these cases by accessing Westlaw. Here are their Westlaw citations: *Morin v. Troymac's Inc.*, 2000 WL 670040 (Conn.Super.2000); *Johnson v. Stop & Shop Companies, Inc.*, 1994 WL 271488 (Conn.Super.1994). Please perform additional research in the law library to determine whether there is other case law available to support the motion to strike.

Remember the following points:

- Even if there are no additional cases addressing the particular issue of motions to strike claims for punitive damages under the product statute, you will certainly want to conduct research under Connecticut law on the standard of when tortious conduct is "reckless." (There should be numerous CT Supreme Court and Appellate Court decisions addressing this standard.)
- You will also need to do research on the legal standard for deciding a motion to strike.
- Additionally, you will want to quote the relevant portions of the statute in your motion to strike and may want to consider a section of the memorandum addressing how courts generally attempt to construe statutes in accordance with their plain meaning.
- Finally, be sure to include copies of all legal authorities (statutes, reported cases, etc.) that you cite in your memorandum for my review.

I have attached a sample of a Motion to Strike and Memorandum in Support to assist you.

Library Resources

Legal Writing in Plain English: A Text with Exercises, Bryan A. Garner, University of Chicago Press, 2001.
An excellent concise text with helpful exercises.

Legal Research & Legal Writing: Structure, Strategy & Style (5th Ed), Richard K. Neumann, Aspen Publishing, 2001.
A great legal research and legal writing text.

Legal Writing By Design: A Guide to Great Briefs and Memos, Teresa J. Rambo & Leanne J. Pflaum, Carolina Academic Press, 2001.
This book contains nice examples and format.

Online Resources

Legal Information Institute at Cornell, http://www.law.cornell.edu/topics/legal_writing.html
This site provides an overview of legal writing.

University of Washington School of Law, http://Lib.law.washington.edu/ref/writing.htm
This site contains legal and general writing resources, including a thesaurus.

William H. Bowen School of Law at the University of Arkansas at Little Rock, http://www.ualr.edu/cmbarger/
Good links to other sites and helpful hints are available at this site.

PART 6

APPENDIX

APPENDIX A

The Constitution of the United States: A Transcription

Note: *The following text is a transcription of the Constitution in its* ***original*** *form.*
Items that are hyperlinked have since been amended or superseded.

We the People of the United States, in Order to form a more perfect Union, establish Justice, insure domestic Tranquility, provide for the common defence, promote the general Welfare, and secure the Blessings of Liberty to ourselves and our Posterity, do ordain and establish this Constitution for the United States of America.

Article. I.

Section. 1.

All legislative Powers herein granted shall be vested in a Congress of the United States, which shall consist of a Senate and House of Representatives.

Section. 2.

The House of Representatives shall be composed of Members chosen every second Year by the People of the several States, and the Electors in each State shall have the Qualifications requisite for Electors of the most numerous Branch of the State Legislature.

No Person shall be a Representative who shall not have attained to the Age of twenty five Years, and been seven Years a Citizen of the United States, and who shall not, when elected, be an Inhabitant of that State in which he shall be chosen.

Representatives and direct Taxes shall be apportioned among the several States which may be included within this Union, according to their respective Numbers, which shall be determined by adding to the whole Number of free Persons, including those bound to Service for a Term of Years, and excluding Indians not taxed, three fifths of all other Persons. The actual Enumeration shall be made within three Years after the first Meeting of the Congress of the United States, and within every subsequent Term of ten Years, in such Manner as they shall by Law direct. The Number of Representatives shall not exceed one for every thirty Thousand, but each State shall have at Least one Representative; and until such enumeration shall be made, the State of New Hampshire shall be entitled to chuse three, Massachusetts eight, Rhode-Island and Providence Plantations one, Connecticut five, New-York six, New Jersey four, Pennsylvania eight, Delaware one, Maryland six, Virginia ten, North Carolina five, South Carolina five, and Georgia three.

When vacancies happen in the Representation from any State, the Executive Authority thereof shall issue Writs of Election to fill such Vacancies.

The House of Representatives shall chuse their Speaker and other Officers; and shall have the sole Power of Impeachment.

Section. 3.

The Senate of the United States shall be composed of two Senators from each State, chosen by the Legislature thereof for six Years; and each Senator shall have one Vote.

Immediately after they shall be assembled in Consequence of the first Election, they shall be divided as equally as may be into three Classes. The Seats of the Senators of the first Class shall be vacated at the Expiration of the second Year, of the second Class at the Expiration of the fourth Year, and of the third Class at the Expiration of the sixth Year, so that one third may be chosen every second Year; and if Vacancies happen by Resignation, or otherwise, during the Recess of the Legislature of any State, the Executive thereof may make temporary Appointments until the next Meeting of the Legislature, which shall then fill such Vacancies.

No Person shall be a Senator who shall not have attained to the Age of thirty Years, and been nine Years a Citizen of the United States, and who shall not, when elected, be an Inhabitant of that State for which he shall be chosen.

The Vice President of the United States shall be President of the Senate, but shall have no Vote, unless they be equally divided.

The Senate shall chuse their other Officers, and also a President pro tempore, in the Absence of the Vice President, or when he shall exercise the Office of President of the United States.

The Senate shall have the sole Power to try all Impeachments. When sitting for that Purpose, they shall be on Oath or Affirmation. When the President of the United States is tried, the Chief Justice shall preside: And no Person shall be convicted without the Concurrence of two thirds of the Members present.

Judgment in Cases of Impeachment shall not extend further than to removal from Office, and disqualification to hold and enjoy any Office of honor, Trust or Profit under the United States: but the Party convicted shall nevertheless be liable and subject to Indictment, Trial, Judgment and Punishment, according to Law.

Section. 4.

The Times, Places and Manner of holding Elections for Senators and Representatives, shall be prescribed in each State by the Legislature thereof; but the Congress may at any time by Law make or alter such Regulations, except as to the Places of chusing Senators.

The Congress shall assemble at least once in every Year, and such Meeting shall be on the first Monday in December, unless they shall by Law appoint a different Day.

Section. 5.

Each House shall be the Judge of the Elections, Returns and Qualifications of its own Members, and a Majority of each shall constitute a Quorum to do Business; but a smaller Number may adjourn from day to day, and may be authorized to compel the Attendance of absent Members, in such Manner, and under such Penalties as each House may provide.

Each House may determine the Rules of its Proceedings, punish its Members for disorderly Behaviour, and, with the Concurrence of two thirds, expel a Member.

Each House shall keep a Journal of its Proceedings, and from time to time publish the same, excepting such Parts as may in their Judgment require Secrecy; and the Yeas and Nays of the Members of either House on any question shall, at the Desire of one fifth of those Present, be entered on the Journal.

Neither House, during the Session of Congress, shall, without the Consent of the other, adjourn for more than three days, nor to any other Place than that in which the two Houses shall be sitting.

Section. 6.

The Senators and Representatives shall receive a Compensation for their Services, to be ascertained by Law, and paid out of the Treasury of the United States. They shall in all Cases, except Treason, Felony and Breach of the Peace, be privileged from Arrest during their Attendance at the Session of their respective Houses, and in going to and returning from the same; and for any Speech or Debate in either House, they shall not be questioned in any other Place.

No Senator or Representative shall, during the Time for which he was elected, be appointed to any civil Office under the Authority of the United States, which shall have been created, or the Emoluments whereof shall have been encreased during such time; and no Person holding any Office under the United States, shall be a Member of either House during his Continuance in Office.

Section. 7.

All Bills for raising Revenue shall originate in the House of Representatives; but the Senate may propose or concur with Amendments as on other Bills.

Every Bill which shall have passed the House of Representatives and the Senate, shall, before it become a Law, be presented to the President of the United States: If he approve he shall sign it, but if not he shall return it, with his Objections to that House in which it shall have originated, who shall enter the Objections at large on their Journal, and proceed to reconsider it. If after such Reconsideration two thirds of that House shall agree to pass the Bill, it shall be sent, together with the Objections, to the other House, by which it shall likewise be reconsidered, and if approved by two thirds of that House, it shall become a Law. But in all such Cases the Votes of both Houses shall be determined by yeas and Nays, and the Names of the Persons voting for and against the Bill shall be entered on the Journal of each House respectively. If any Bill shall not be returned by the President within ten Days (Sundays excepted) after it shall have been presented to him, the Same shall be a Law, in like

Manner as if he had signed it, unless the Congress by their Adjournment prevent its Return, in which Case it shall not be a Law.

Every Order, Resolution, or Vote to which the Concurrence of the Senate and House of Representatives may be necessary (except on a question of Adjournment) shall be presented to the President of the United States; and before the Same shall take Effect, shall be approved by him, or being disapproved by him, shall be repassed by two thirds of the Senate and House of Representatives, according to the Rules and Limitations prescribed in the Case of a Bill.

Section. 8.

The Congress shall have Power To lay and collect Taxes, Duties, Imposts and Excises, to pay the Debts and provide for the common Defence and general Welfare of the United States; but all Duties, Imposts and Excises shall be uniform throughout the United States;

To borrow Money on the credit of the United States;

To regulate Commerce with foreign Nations, and among the several States, and with the Indian Tribes;

To establish an uniform Rule of Naturalization, and uniform Laws on the subject of Bankruptcies throughout the United States;

To coin Money, regulate the Value thereof, and of foreign Coin, and fix the Standard of Weights and Measures;

To provide for the Punishment of counterfeiting the Securities and current Coin of the United States;

To establish Post Offices and post Roads;

To promote the Progress of Science and useful Arts, by securing for limited Times to Authors and Inventors the exclusive Right to their respective Writings and Discoveries;

To constitute Tribunals inferior to the supreme Court;

To define and punish Piracies and Felonies committed on the high Seas, and Offences against the Law of Nations;

To declare War, grant Letters of Marque and Reprisal, and make Rules concerning Captures on Land and Water;

To raise and support Armies, but no Appropriation of Money to that Use shall be for a longer Term than two Years;

To provide and maintain a Navy;

To make Rules for the Government and Regulation of the land and naval Forces;

To provide for calling forth the Militia to execute the Laws of the Union, suppress Insurrections and repel Invasions;

To provide for organizing, arming, and disciplining, the Militia, and for governing such Part of them as may be employed in the Service of the United States, reserving to the States respectively, the Appointment of the Officers, and the Authority of training the Militia according to the discipline prescribed by Congress;

To exercise exclusive Legislation in all Cases whatsoever, over such District (not exceeding ten Miles square) as may, by Cession of particular States, and the Acceptance of Congress, become the Seat of the Government of the United States, and to exercise like Authority over all Places purchased by the Consent of the Legislature of the State in which the Same shall be, for the Erection of Forts, Magazines, Arsenals, dock-Yards, and other needful Buildings;--And

To make all Laws which shall be necessary and proper for carrying into Execution the foregoing Powers, and all other Powers vested by this Constitution in the Government of the United States, or in any Department or Officer thereof.

Section. 9

The Migration or Importation of such Persons as any of the States now existing shall think proper to admit, shall not be prohibited by the Congress prior to the Year one thousand eight hundred and eight, but a Tax or duty may be imposed on such Importation, not exceeding ten dollars for each Person.

The Privilege of the Writ of Habeas Corpus shall not be suspended, unless when in Cases of Rebellion or Invasion the public Safety may require it.

No Bill of Attainder or ex post facto Law shall be passed.

No Capitation, or other direct, Tax shall be laid, unless in Proportion to the Census or enumeration herein before directed to be taken.

No Tax or Duty shall be laid on Articles exported from any State.

No Preference shall be given by any Regulation of Commerce or Revenue to the Ports of one State over those of another; nor shall Vessels bound to, or from, one State, be obliged to enter, clear, or pay Duties in another.

No Money shall be drawn from the Treasury, but in Consequence of Appropriations made by Law; and a regular Statement and Account of the Receipts and Expenditures of all public Money shall be published from time to time.

No Title of Nobility shall be granted by the United States: And no Person holding any Office of Profit or Trust under them, shall, without the Consent of the Congress, accept of any present, Emolument, Office, or Title, of any kind whatever, from any King, Prince, or foreign State.

Section. 10.

No State shall enter into any Treaty, Alliance, or Confederation; grant Letters of Marque and Reprisal; coin Money; emit Bills of Credit; make any Thing but gold and silver Coin a Tender in Payment of Debts; pass any Bill of Attainder, ex post facto Law, or Law impairing the Obligation of Contracts, or grant any Title of Nobility.

No State shall, without the Consent of the Congress, lay any Imposts or Duties on Imports or Exports, except what may be absolutely necessary for executing it's inspection Laws: and the net Produce of all Duties and Imposts, laid by any State on Imports or Exports, shall be for the Use of the Treasury of the United States; and all such Laws shall be subject to the Revision and Controul of the Congress.

No State shall, without the Consent of Congress, lay any Duty of Tonnage, keep Troops, or Ships of War in time of Peace, enter into any Agreement or Compact with another State, or with a foreign Power, or engage in War, unless actually invaded, or in such imminent Danger as will not admit of delay.

Article. II.

Section. 1.

The executive Power shall be vested in a President of the United States of America. He shall hold his Office during the Term of four Years, and, together with the Vice President, chosen for the same Term, be elected, as follows:

Each State shall appoint, in such Manner as the Legislature thereof may direct, a Number of Electors, equal to the whole Number of Senators and Representatives to which the State may be entitled in the Congress: but no Senator or Representative, or Person holding an Office of Trust or Profit under the United States, shall be appointed an Elector.

The Electors shall meet in their respective States, and vote by Ballot for two Persons, of whom one at least shall not be an Inhabitant of the same State with themselves. And they shall make a List of all the Persons voted for, and of the Number of Votes for each; which List they shall sign and certify, and transmit sealed to the Seat of the Government of the United States, directed to the President of the Senate. The President of the Senate shall, in the Presence of the Senate and House of Representatives, open all the Certificates, and the Votes shall then be counted. The Person having the greatest Number of Votes shall be the President, if such Number be a Majority of the whole Number of Electors appointed; and if there be more than one who have such Majority, and have an equal Number of Votes, then the House of Representatives shall immediately chuse by Ballot one of them for President; and if no Person have a Majority, then from the five highest on the List the said House shall in like Manner chuse the President. But in chusing the President, the Votes shall be taken by States, the Representation from each State having one Vote; A quorum for this purpose shall consist of a Member or Members from two thirds of the States, and a Majority of all the States shall be necessary to a Choice. In every Case, after the Choice of the President, the Person having the greatest Number of Votes of the Electors shall be the Vice President. But if there should remain two or more who have equal Votes, the Senate shall chuse from them by Ballot the Vice President.

The Congress may determine the Time of chusing the Electors, and the Day on which they shall give their Votes; which Day shall be the same throughout the United States.

No Person except a natural born Citizen, or a Citizen of the United States, at the time of the Adoption of this Constitution, shall be eligible to the Office of President; neither shall any Person be eligible to that Office who shall not have attained to the Age of thirty five Years, and been fourteen Years a Resident within the United States.

In Case of the Removal of the President from Office, or of his Death, Resignation, or Inability to discharge the Powers and Duties of the said Office, the Same shall devolve on the Vice President, and the Congress may by Law provide for the Case of Removal, Death, Resignation or Inability, both of the President and Vice President, declaring what Officer shall then act as President, and such Officer shall act accordingly, until the Disability be removed, or a President shall be elected.

The President shall, at stated Times, receive for his Services, a Compensation, which shall neither be increased nor diminished during the Period for which he shall have been elected, and he shall not receive within that Period any other Emolument from the United States, or any of them.

Before he enter on the Execution of his Office, he shall take the following Oath or Affirmation:--"I do solemnly swear (or affirm) that I will faithfully execute the Office of President of the United States, and will to the best of my Ability, preserve, protect and defend the Constitution of the United States."

Section. 2.

The President shall be Commander in Chief of the Army and Navy of the United States, and of the Militia of the several States, when called into the actual Service of the United States; he may require the Opinion, in writing, of the principal Officer in each of the executive Departments, upon any Subject relating to the Duties of their respective Offices, and he shall have Power to grant Reprieves and Pardons for Offences against the United States, except in Cases of Impeachment.

He shall have Power, by and with the Advice and Consent of the Senate, to make Treaties, provided two thirds of the Senators present concur; and he shall nominate, and by and with the Advice and Consent of the Senate, shall appoint Ambassadors, other public Ministers and Consuls, Judges of the supreme Court, and all other Officers of the United States, whose Appointments are not herein otherwise provided for, and which shall be established by Law: but the Congress may by Law vest the Appointment of such inferior Officers, as they think proper, in the President alone, in the Courts of Law, or in the Heads of Departments.

The President shall have Power to fill up all Vacancies that may happen during the Recess of the Senate, by granting Commissions which shall expire at the End of their next Session.

Section. 3.

He shall from time to time give to the Congress Information of the State of the Union, and recommend to their Consideration such Measures as he shall judge necessary and expedient; he may, on extraordinary Occasions, convene both Houses, or either of them, and in Case of Disagreement between them, with Respect to the Time of Adjournment, he may adjourn them to such Time as he shall think proper; he shall receive Ambassadors and other public Ministers; he shall take Care that the Laws be faithfully executed, and shall Commission all the Officers of the United States.

Section. 4.

The President, Vice President and all civil Officers of the United States, shall be removed from Office on Impeachment for, and Conviction of, Treason, Bribery, or other high Crimes and Misdemeanors.

Article. III.

Section. 1.

The judicial Power of the United States shall be vested in one supreme Court, and in such inferior Courts as the Congress may from time to time ordain and establish. The Judges, both of the supreme and inferior Courts, shall hold their Offices during good Behaviour, and shall, at stated Times, receive for their Services a Compensation, which shall not be diminished during their Continuance in Office.

Section. 2.

The judicial Power shall extend to all Cases, in Law and Equity, arising under this Constitution, the Laws of the United States, and Treaties made, or which shall be made, under their Authority;--to all Cases affecting Ambassadors, other public Ministers and Consuls;--to all Cases of admiralty and maritime Jurisdiction;--to Controversies to which the United States shall be a Party;--to Controversies between two or more States;--between a State and Citizens of another State;--between Citizens of different States;--between Citizens of the same State claiming Lands under Grants of different States, and between a State, or the Citizens thereof, and foreign States, Citizens or Subjects.

In all Cases affecting Ambassadors, other public Ministers and Consuls, and those in which a State shall be Party, the supreme Court shall have original Jurisdiction. In all the other Cases before mentioned, the supreme Court shall have appellate Jurisdiction, both as to Law and Fact, with such Exceptions, and under such Regulations as the Congress shall make.

The Trial of all Crimes, except in Cases of Impeachment, shall be by Jury; and such Trial shall be held in the State where the said Crimes shall have been committed; but when not committed within any State, the Trial shall be at such Place or Places as the Congress may by Law have directed.

Section. 3.

Treason against the United States, shall consist only in levying War against them, or in adhering to their Enemies, giving them Aid and Comfort. No Person shall be convicted of Treason unless on the Testimony of two Witnesses to the same overt Act, or on Confession in open Court.

The Congress shall have Power to declare the Punishment of Treason, but no Attainder of Treason shall work Corruption of Blood, or Forfeiture except during the Life of the Person attainted.

Article. IV.

Section. 1.

Full Faith and Credit shall be given in each State to the public Acts, Records, and judicial Proceedings of every other State. And the Congress may by general Laws prescribe the Manner in which such Acts, Records and Proceedings shall be proved, and the Effect thereof.

Section. 2.

The Citizens of each State shall be entitled to all Privileges and Immunities of Citizens in the several States.

A Person charged in any State with Treason, Felony, or other Crime, who shall flee from Justice, and be found in another State, shall on Demand of the executive Authority of the State from which he fled, be delivered up, to be removed to the State having Jurisdiction of the Crime.

No Person held to Service or Labour in one State, under the Laws thereof, escaping into another, shall, in Consequence of any Law or Regulation therein, be discharged from such Service or Labour, but shall be delivered up on Claim of the Party to whom such Service or Labour may be due.

Section. 3.

New States may be admitted by the Congress into this Union; but no new State shall be formed or erected within the Jurisdiction of any other State; nor any State be formed by the Junction of two or more States, or Parts of States, without the Consent of the Legislatures of the States concerned as well as of the Congress.

The Congress shall have Power to dispose of and make all needful Rules and Regulations respecting the Territory or other Property belonging to the United States; and nothing in this Constitution shall be so construed as to Prejudice any Claims of the United States, or of any particular State.

Section. 4.

The United States shall guarantee to every State in this Union a Republican Form of Government, and shall protect each of them against Invasion; and on Application of the Legislature, or of the Executive (when the Legislature cannot be convened), against domestic Violence.

Article. V.

The Congress, whenever two thirds of both Houses shall deem it necessary, shall propose Amendments to this Constitution, or, on the Application of the Legislatures of two thirds of the several States, shall call a Convention for proposing Amendments, which, in either Case, shall be valid to all Intents and Purposes, as Part of this Constitution, when ratified by the Legislatures of three fourths of the several States, or by Conventions in three fourths thereof, as the one or the other Mode of Ratification may be proposed by the Congress; Provided that no Amendment which may be made prior to the Year One thousand eight hundred and eight shall in any Manner affect the first and fourth Clauses in the Ninth Section of the first Article; and that no State, without its Consent, shall be deprived of its equal Suffrage in the Senate.

Article. VI.

All Debts contracted and Engagements entered into, before the Adoption of this Constitution, shall be as valid against the United States under this Constitution, as under the Confederation.

This Constitution, and the Laws of the United States which shall be made in Pursuance thereof; and all Treaties made, or which shall be made, under the Authority of the United States, shall be the supreme Law of the Land; and the Judges in every State shall be bound thereby, any Thing in the Constitution or Laws of any State to the Contrary notwithstanding.

The Senators and Representatives before mentioned, and the Members of the several State Legislatures, and all executive and judicial Officers, both of the United States and of the several States, shall be bound by Oath or Affirmation, to support this Constitution; but no religious Test shall ever be required as a Qualification to any Office or public Trust under the United States.

Article. VII.

The Ratification of the Conventions of nine States, shall be sufficient for the Establishment of this Constitution between the States so ratifying the Same.

The Word, "the," being interlined between the seventh and eighth Lines of the first Page, the Word "Thirty" being partly written on an Erazure in the fifteenth Line of the first Page, The Words "is tried" being interlined between the thirty second and thirty third Lines of the first Page and the Word "the" being interlined between the forty third and forty fourth Lines of the second Page.

Attest William Jackson Secretary

Done in Convention by the Unanimous Consent of the States present the Seventeenth Day of September in the Year of our Lord one thousand seven hundred and Eighty seven and of the Independence of the United States of America the Twelfth In witness whereof We have hereunto subscribed our Names,

G. Washington
Presidt and deputy from Virginia

Delaware
Geo: Read
Gunning Bedford jun
John Dickinson
Richard Bassett
Jaco: Broom

Maryland
James McHenry
Dan of St Thos. Jenifer
Danl. Carroll

Virginia
John Blair
James Madison Jr.

North Carolina
Wm. Blount
Richd. Dobbs Spaight
Hu Williamson

South Carolina
J. Rutledge
Charles Cotesworth Pinckney
Charles Pinckney
Pierce Butler

Georgia
William Few
Abr Baldwin

New Hampshire
John Langdon
Nicholas Gilman

Massachusetts
Nathaniel Gorham
Rufus King

Connecticut
Wm. Saml. Johnson
Roger Sherman

New York
Alexander Hamilton

New Jersey
Wil: Livingston
David Brearley
Wm. Paterson
Jona: Dayton

Pennsylvania
B Franklin
Thomas Mifflin
Robt. Morris
Geo. Clymer
Thos. FitzSimons
Jared Ingersoll
James Wilson
Gouv Morris

For biographies of the non-signing delegates to the Constitutional Convention, see the Founding Fathers page.

Page URL: http://www.archives.gov/national-archives-experience/charters/constitution_transcript.html

---

U.S. National Archives & Records Administration
8601 Adelphi Road, College Park, MD, 20740-6001 • 1-86-NARA-NARA • 1-866-272-6272

APPENDIX B

NFPA Code of Ethics

NFPA MODEL DISCIPLINARY RULES AND ETHICAL CONSIDERATIONS

1.1 A PARALEGAL SHALL ACHIEVE AND MAINTAIN A HIGH LEVEL OF COMPETENCE.

Ethical Considerations

EC-1.1(a) A paralegal shall achieve competency through education, training, and work experience.

EC-1.1(b) A paralegal shall aspire to participate in a minimum of twelve (12) hours of continuing legal education, to include at least one (1) hour of ethics education, every two (2) years in order to remain current on developments in the law.

EC-1.1(c) A paralegal shall perform all assignments promptly and efficiently.

1.2 A PARALEGAL SHALL MAINTAIN A HIGH LEVEL OF PERSONAL AND PROFESSIONAL INTEGRITY.

Ethical Considerations

EC-1.2(a) A paralegal shall not engage in any ex parte communications involving the courts or any other adjudicatory body in an attempt to exert undue influence or to obtain advantage or the benefit of only one party.

EC-1.2(b) A paralegal shall not communicate, or cause another to communicate, with a party the paralegal knows to be represented by a lawyer in a pending matter without the prior consent of the lawyer representing such other party.

EC-1.2(c) A paralegal shall ensure that all timekeeping and billing records prepared by the paralegal are thorough, accurate, honest, and complete.

EC-1.2(d) A paralegal shall not knowingly engage in fraudulent billing practices. Such practices may include, but are not limited to: inflation of hours billed to a client or employer; misrepresentation of the nature of tasks performed; and/or submission of fraudulent expense and disbursement documentation.

EC-1.2(e) A paralegal shall be scrupulous, thorough, and honest in the identification and maintenance of all funds, securities, and other assets of a client and shall provide accurate accounting as appropriate.

EC-1.2(f) A paralegal shall advise the proper authority of non-confidential knowledge of any dishonest or fraudulent acts by any person pertaining to the handling of the funds, securities, or other assets of a client. The authority to whom the report is made shall depend on the nature and circumstances of the possible misconduct, (e.g., ethics committees of law firms, corporations and/or paralegal associations, local or state bar associations, local prosecutors, administrative agencies, etc.). Failure to report such knowledge is in itself misconduct and shall be treated as such under these rules.

A PARALEGAL SHALL MAINTAIN A HIGH STANDARD OF PROFESSIONAL CONDUCT. 1.3

Ethical Considerations

A paralegal shall refrain from engaging in any conduct that offends the dignity and decorum of proceedings before a court or other adjudicatory body and shall be respectful of all rules and procedures. EC-1.3(a)

A paralegal shall avoid impropriety and the appearance of impropriety and shall not engage in any conduct that would adversely affect his/her fitness to practice. Such conduct may include, but is not limited to: violence, dishonesty, interference with the administration of justice, and/or abuse of a professional position or public office. EC-1.3(b)

Should a paralegal's fitness to practice be compromised by physical or mental illness, causing that paralegal to commit an act that is in direct violation of the Model Code/Model Rules and/or the rules and/or laws governing the jurisdiction in which the paralegal practices, that paralegal may be protected from sanction upon review of the nature and circumstances of that illness. EC-1.3(c)

A paralegal shall advise the proper authority of non-confidential knowledge of any action of another legal professional that clearly demonstrates fraud, deceit, dishonesty, or misrepresentation. The authority to whom the report is made shall depend on the nature and circumstances of the possible misconduct, (e.g., ethics committees of law firms, corporations and/or paralegal associations, local or state bar associations, local prosecutors, administrative agencies, etc.). Failure to report such knowledge is in itself misconduct and shall be treated as such under these rules. EC-1.3(d)

A paralegal shall not knowingly assist any individual with the commission of an act that is in direct violation of the Model Code/Model Rules and/or the rules and/or laws governing the jurisdiction in which the paralegal practices. EC-1.3(e)

If a paralegal possesses knowledge of future criminal activity, that knowledge must be reported to the appropriate authority immediately. EC-1.3(f)

A PARALEGAL SHALL SERVE THE PUBLIC INTEREST BY CONTRIBUTING TO THE IMPROVEMENT OF THE LEGAL SYSTEM AND DELIVERY OF QUALITY LEGAL SERVICES, INCLUDING PRO BONO PUBLICO SERVICES. 1.4

Ethical Considerations

A paralegal shall be sensitive to the legal needs of the public and shall promote the development and implementation of programs that address those needs. EC-1.4(a)

A paralegal shall support efforts to improve the legal system and access thereto and shall assist in making changes. EC-1.4(b)

A paralegal shall support and participate in the delivery of Pro Bono Publico services directed toward implementing and improving access to justice, the law, the legal system or the paralegal and legal professions. EC-1.4(c)

A paralegal should aspire annually to contribute twenty-four (24) hours of Pro Bono Publico services under the supervision of an attorney or as authorized by administrative, statutory or court authority to: EC-1.4(d)

1. persons of limited means; or
2. charitable, religious, civic, community, governmental and educational organizations in matters that are designed primarily to address the legal needs of persons with limited means; or
3. individuals, groups or organizations seeking to secure or protect civil rights, civil liberties, or public rights.

The twenty-four (24) hours of Pro Bono Publico services contributed annually by a paralegal may consist of such services as detailed in this EC-1.4(d), and/or administrative matters designed to develop and implement the attainment of this aspiration as detailed above in EC-1.4(a) B (c), or any combination of the two.

1.5 A PARALEGAL SHALL PRESERVE ALL CONFIDENTIAL INFORMATION PROVIDED BY THE CLIENT OR ACQUIRED FROM OTHER SOURCES BEFORE, DURING, AND AFTER THE COURSE OF THE PROFESSIONAL RELATIONSHIP.

Ethical Considerations

EC-1.5(a) A paralegal shall be aware of and abide by all legal authority governing confidential information in the jurisdiction in which the paralegal practices.

EC-1.5(b) A paralegal shall not use confidential information to the disadvantage of the client.

EC-1.5(c) A paralegal shall not use confidential information to the advantage of the paralegal or of a third person.

EC-1.5(d) A paralegal may reveal confidential information only after full disclosure and with the client's written consent; or, when required by law or court order; or, when necessary to prevent the client from committing an act that could result in death or serious bodily harm.

EC-1.5(e) A paralegal shall keep those individuals responsible for the legal representation of a client fully informed of any confidential information the paralegal may have pertaining to that client.

EC-1.5(f) A paralegal shall not engage in any indiscreet communications concerning clients.

1.6 A PARALEGAL SHALL AVOID CONFLICTS OF INTEREST AND SHALL DISCLOSE ANY POSSIBLE CONFLICT TO THE EMPLOYER OR CLIENT, AS WELL AS TO THE PROSPECTIVE EMPLOYERS OR CLIENTS.

Ethical Considerations

EC-1.6(a) A paralegal shall act within the bounds of the law, solely for the benefit of the client, and shall be free of compromising influences and loyalties. Neither the paralegal's personal or business interest, nor those of other clients or third persons, should compromise the paralegal's professional judgment and loyalty to the client.

EC-1.6(b) A paralegal shall avoid conflicts of interest that may arise from previous assignments, whether for a present or past employer or client.

EC-1.6(c) A paralegal shall avoid conflicts of interest that may arise from family relationships and from personal and business interests.

EC-1.6(d) In order to be able to determine whether an actual or potential conflict of interest exists a paralegal shall create and maintain an effective recordkeeping system that identifies clients, matters, and parties with which the paralegal has worked.

EC-1.6(e) A paralegal shall reveal sufficient non-confidential information about a client or former client to reasonably ascertain if an actual or potential conflict of interest exists.

EC-1.6(f) A paralegal shall not participate in or conduct work on any matter where a conflict of interest has been identified.

In matters where a conflict of interest has been identified and the client consents to continued representation, a paralegal shall comply fully with the implementation and maintenance of an Ethical Wall. EC-1.6(g)

A PARALEGAL'S TITLE SHALL BE FULLY DISCLOSED. 1.7

Ethical Considerations

A paralegal's title shall clearly indicate the individual's status and shall be disclosed in all business and professional communications to avoid misunderstandings and misconceptions about the paralegal's role and responsibilities. EC-1.7(a)

A paralegal's title shall be included if the paralegal's name appears on business cards, letterhead, brochures, directories, and advertisements. EC-1.7(b)

A paralegal shall not use letterhead, business cards, or other promotional materials to create a fraudulent impression of his/her status or ability to practice in the jurisdiction in which the paralegal practices. EC-1.7(c)

A paralegal shall not practice under color of any record, diploma, or certificate that has been illegally or fraudulently obtained or issued or which is misrepresentative in any way. EC-1.7(d)

A paralegal shall not participate in the creation, issuance, or dissemination of fraudulent records, diplomas, or certificates. EC-1.7(e)

A PARALEGAL SHALL NOT ENGAGE IN THE UNAUTHORIZED PRACTICE OF LAW. 1.8

Ethical Considerations

A paralegal shall comply with the applicable legal authority governing the unauthorized practice of law in the jurisdiction in which the paralegal practices. EC-1.8(a)

NFPA GUIDELINES FOR THE ENFORCEMENT OF THE MODEL CODE OF ETHICS AND PROFESSIONAL RESPONSIBILITY §2.

BASIS FOR DISCIPLINE 2.1

Disciplinary investigations and proceedings brought under authority of the Rules shall be conducted in accord with obligations imposed on the paralegal professional by the Model Code of Ethics and Professional Responsibility. 2.1(a)

STRUCTURE OF DISCIPLINARY COMMITTEE 2.2

The Disciplinary Committee ("Committee") shall be made up of nine (9) members including the Chair. 2.2(a)

Each member of the Committee, including any temporary replacement members, shall have demonstrated working knowledge of ethics/professional responsibility-related issues and activities. 2.2(b)

The Committee shall represent a cross-section of practice areas and work experience. The following recommendations are made regarding the members of the Committee. 2.2(c)

1. At least one paralegal with one to three years of law-related work experience.
2. At least one paralegal with five to seven years of law related work experience.
3. At least one paralegal with over ten years of law related work experience.

4. One paralegal educator with five to seven years of work experience; preferably in the area of ethics/professional responsibility.
5. One paralegal manager.
6. One lawyer with five to seven years of law-related work experience.
7. One lay member.

2.2(d) The Chair of the Committee shall be appointed within thirty (30) days of its members' induction. The Chair shall have no fewer than ten (10) years of law-related work experience.

2.2(e) The terms of all members of the Committee shall be staggered. Of those members initially appointed, a simple majority plus one shall be appointed to a term of one year, and the remaining members shall be appointed to a term of two years. Thereafter, all members of the Committee shall be appointed to terms of two years.

2.2(f) If for any reason the terms of a majority of the Committee will expire at the same time, members may be appointed to terms of one year to maintain continuity of the Committee.

2.2(g) The Committee shall organize from its members a three-tiered structure to investigate, prosecute, and/or adjudicate charges of misconduct. The members shall be rotated among the tiers.

2.3 OPERATION OF COMMITTEE

2.3(a) The Committee shall meet on an as-needed basis to discuss, investigate, and/or adjudicate alleged violations of the Model Code/Model Rules.

2.3(b) A majority of the members of the Committee present at a meeting shall constitute a quorum.

2.3(c) A Recording Secretary shall be designated to maintain complete and accurate minutes of all Committee meetings. All such minutes shall be kept confidential until a decision has been made that the matter will be set for hearing as set forth in Section 6.1 below.

2.3(d) If any member of the Committee has a conflict of interest with the Charging Party, the Responding Party, or the allegations of misconduct, that member shall not take part in any hearing or deliberations concerning those allegations. If the absence of that member creates a lack of a quorum for the Committee, then a temporary replacement for the member shall be appointed.

2.3(e) Either the Charging Party or the Responding Party may request that, for good cause shown, any member of the Committee not participate in a hearing or deliberation. All such requests shall be honored. If the absence of a Committee member under those circumstances creates a lack of a quorum for the Committee, then a temporary replacement for that member shall be appointed.

2.3(f) All discussions and correspondence of the Committee shall be kept confidential until a decision has been made that the matter will be set for hearing as set forth in Section 6.1 below.

2.3(g) All correspondence from the Committee to the Responding Party regarding any charge of misconduct and any decisions made regarding the charge shall be mailed certified mail, return receipt requested, to the Responding Party's last known address and shall be clearly marked with a "Confidential" designation.

2.4 PROCEDURE FOR THE REPORTING OF ALLEGED VIOLATIONS OF THE MODEL CODE/DISCIPLINARY RULES

2.4(a) An individual or entity in possession of non-confidential knowledge or information concerning possible instances of misconduct shall make a confidential written report to the Committee within thirty (30) days of obtaining same. This report shall include all details of the alleged misconduct.

The Committee so notified shall inform the Responding Party of the allegation(s) of misconduct no later than ten (10) business days after receiving the confidential written report from the Charging Party. 2.4(b)

Notification to the Responding Party shall include the identity of the Charging Party, unless, for good cause shown, the Charging Party requests anonymity. 2.4(c)

The Responding Party shall reply to the allegations within ten (10) business days of notification. 2.4(d)

PROCEDURE FOR THE INVESTIGATION OF A CHARGE OF MISCONDUCT 2.5

Upon receipt of a Charge of Misconduct ("Charge"), or on its own initiative, the Committee shall initiate an investigation. 2.5(a)

If, upon initial or preliminary review, the Committee makes a determination that the charges are either without basis in fact or, if proven, would not constitute professional misconduct, the Committee shall dismiss the allegations of misconduct. If such determination of dismissal cannot be made, a formal investigation shall be initiated. 2.5(b)

Upon the decision to conduct a formal investigation, the Committee shall: 2.5(c)

1. mail to the Charging and Responding Parties within three (3) business days of that decision notice of the commencement of a formal investigation. That notification shall be in writing and shall contain a complete explanation of all Charge(s), as well as the reasons for a formal investigation and shall cite the applicable codes and rules;
2. allow the Responding Party thirty (30) days to prepare and submit a confidential response to the Committee, which response shall address each charge specifically and shall be in writing; and
3. upon receipt of the response to the notification, have thirty (30) days to investigate the Charge(s). If an extension of time is deemed necessary, that extension shall not exceed ninety (90) days.

Upon conclusion of the investigation, the Committee may: 2.5(d)

1. dismiss the Charge upon the finding that it has no basis in fact;
2. dismiss the Charge upon the finding that, if proven, the Charge would not constitute Misconduct;
3. refer the matter for hearing by the Tribunal; or
4. in the case of criminal activity, refer the Charge(s) and all investigation results to the appropriate authority.

PROCEDURE FOR A MISCONDUCT HEARING BEFORE A TRIBUNAL 2.6

Upon the decision by the Committee that a matter should be heard, all parties shall be notified and a hearing date shall be set. The hearing shall take place no more than thirty (30) days from the conclusion of the formal investigation. 2.6(a)

The Responding Party shall have the right to counsel. The parties and the Tribunal shall have the right to call any witnesses and introduce any documentation that they believe will lead to the fair and reasonable resolution of the matter. 2.6(b)

2.6(c) Upon completion of the hearing, the Tribunal shall deliberate and present a written decision to the parties in accordance with procedures as set forth by the Tribunal.

2.6(d) Notice of the decision of the Tribunal shall be appropriately published.

2.7 SANCTIONS

2.7(a) Upon a finding of the Tribunal that misconduct has occurred, any of the following sanctions, or others as may be deemed appropriate, may be imposed upon the Responding Party, either singularly or in combination:

1. letter of reprimand to the Responding Party; counseling;
2. attendance at an ethics course approved by the Tribunal; probation;
3. suspension of license/authority to practice; revocation of license/authority to practice;
4. imposition of a fine; assessment of costs; or
5. in the instance of criminal activity, referral to the appropriate authority.

2.7(b) Upon the expiration of any period of probation, suspension, or revocation, the Responding Party may make application for reinstatement. With the application for reinstatement, the Responding Party must show proof of having complied with all aspects of the sanctions imposed by the Tribunal.

2.8 APPELLATE PROCEDURES

2.8(a) The parties shall have the right to appeal the decision of the Tribunal in accordance with the procedure as set forth by the Tribunal.

DEFINITIONS

"Appellate Body" means a body established to adjudicate an appeal to any decision made by a Tribunal or other decision-making body with respect to formally-heard Charges of Misconduct.

"Charge of Misconduct" means a written submission by any individual or entity to an ethics committee, paralegal association, bar association, law enforcement agency, judicial body, government agency, or other appropriate body or entity, that sets forth non-confidential information regarding any instance of alleged misconduct by an individual paralegal or paralegal entity.

"Charging Party" means any individual or entity who submits a Charge of Misconduct against an individual paralegal or paralegal entity.

"Competency" means the demonstration of: diligence, education, skill, and mental, emotional, and physical fitness reasonably necessary for the performance of paralegal services.

"Confidential Information" means information relating to a client, whatever its source, that is not public knowledge nor available to the public. ("Non-Confidential Information" would generally include the name of the client and the identity of the matter for which the paralegal provided services.)

"Disciplinary Hearing" means the confidential proceeding conducted by a committee or other designated body or entity concerning any instance of alleged misconduct by an individual paralegal or paralegal entity.

"Disciplinary Committee" means any committee that has been established by an entity such as a paralegal association, bar association, judicial body, or government agency to: (a) identify, define, and investigate general ethical considerations and concerns with respect to paralegal practice; (b) administer and enforce the Model Code and Model Rules and; (c) discipline any individual paralegal or paralegal entity found to be in violation of same.

"Disclose" means communication of information reasonably sufficient to permit identification of the significance of the matter in question.

"Ethical Wall" means the screening method implemented in order to protect a client from a conflict of interest. An Ethical Wall generally includes, but is not limited to, the following elements: (1) prohibit the paralegal from having any connection with the matter; (2) ban discussions with or the transfer of documents to or from the paralegal; (3) restrict access to files; and (4) educate all members of the firm, corporation, or entity as to the separation of the paralegal (both organizationally and physically) from the pending matter. For more information regarding the Ethical Wall, see the NFPA publication entitled "The Ethical Wall - Its Application to Paralegals."

"Ex parte" means actions or communications conducted at the instance and for the benefit of one party only, and without notice to, or contestation by, any person adversely interested.

"Investigation" means the investigation of any charge(s) of misconduct filed against an individual paralegal or paralegal entity by a Committee.

"Letter of Reprimand" means a written notice of formal censure or severe reproof administered to an individual paralegal or paralegal entity for unethical or improper conduct.

"Misconduct" means the knowing or unknowing commission of an act that is in direct violation of those Canons and Ethical Considerations of any and all applicable codes and/or rules of conduct.

"Paralegal" is synonymous with "Legal Assistant" and is defined as a person qualified through education, training, or work experience to perform substantive legal work that requires knowledge of legal concepts and is customarily, but not exclusively performed by a lawyer. This person may be retained or employed by a lawyer, law office, governmental agency, or other entity or may be authorized by administrative, statutory, or court authority to perform this work.

"Pro Bono Publico" means providing or assisting to provide quality legal services in order to enhance access to justice for persons of limited means; charitable, religious, civic, community, governmental and educational organizations in matters that are designed primarily to address the legal needs of persons with limited means; or individuals, groups or organizations seeking to secure or protect civil rights, civil liberties or public rights.

"Proper Authority" means the local paralegal association, the local or state bar association, Committee(s) of the local paralegal or bar association(s), local prosecutor, administrative agency, or other tribunal empowered to investigate or act upon an instance of alleged misconduct.

"Responding Party" means an individual paralegal or paralegal entity against whom a Charge of Misconduct has been submitted.

"Revocation" means the recision of the license, certificate, or other authority to practice of an individual paralegal or paralegal entity found in violation of those Canons and Ethical Considerations of any and all applicable codes and/or rules of conduct.

"Suspension" means the suspension of the license, certificate, or other authority to practice of an individual paralegal or paralegal entity found in violation of those Canons and Ethical Considerations of any and all applicable codes and/or rules of conduct.

"Tribunal" means the body designated to adjudicate allegations of misconduct.

Glossary

Acceptance: The intent by the acceptor to be bound by the terms and conditions of the offer.

Acquit: Decision made by the jury finding the defendant not guilty in a criminal case.

Actual damages: Lost wages, medical costs, and other tangible damages suffered by the plaintiff.

Actus reus: The agreement to commit an unlawful act.

Ad damnum: Portion of the complaint in which the plaintiff asks for money damages. Also known as the "wherefore clause" and "prayer for relief."

Admissible evidence: Evidence that the judge determines may be considered by the jury.

Adversarial system: Provides that both sides have a chance to be heard, to present evidence, and to prove or disprove legal arguments.

Advocacy: Presentation of legal argument before a court on behalf of a client.

Affidavit of Service: Sworn statement that party has been served completed by the sheriff or marshal who served the papers and returned to the court to prove that personal service has been completed.

Affirm: Decision made by an appellate court in which the court agrees with the decision of the lower court.

Affirmative defenses: Responses filed by the defendant based on new allegations raised by the defendant that the defendant must prove.

Allegations: Charges made by the defendant against the plaintiff.

Answer: The defendant's formal response to the plaintiff's complaint. In the answer, the defendant will respond to each allegation contained in the complaint by admitting, denying, or leaving the plaintiff to her proof.

Appeal: Request by the losing party that the appellate court review the trial court record for error.

Appellant: The party making an appeal.

Appellate court: The court that reviews the record of the trial court and rules on decisions made by the trial judge.

Appellee: The person being brought on appeal.

Arson: The act of intentionally causing a dangerous fire or explosion, especially for the purpose of destroying a building of another.

Assault: The creation of the fear of imminent physical harm or intentional touching without physical contact.

Assumption of risk: For cases in which it is proven that the plaintiff knew and understood the danger of the activity that resulted in the tort claim and voluntarily engaged in the activity anyway, the plaintiff may not recover damages from someone else for a resulting injury.

Attempt: A serious and substantial but unsuccessful effort to commit a particular crime.

Attorney-client privilege: An attorney and his paralegal may not disclose any information regarding the client nor forced to disclose such information.

Authentication: Proof that a document or other piece of evidence is genuine and authentic.

Authority: Something a court may rely on in making a decision.

Battery: The intentional infliction of a harmful or offensive touching of another person.

Best evidence rule: An exception made when the original document has been destroyed through no fault of the person now attempting to enter it into evidence.

Beyond a reasonable doubt: A very high standard of proof required in a criminal trial. If the state does not prove the defendant guilty beyond a reasonable doubt, the jury may acquit the defendant.

Biases: Prejudices of potential jurors that may affect their decision-making capabilities.

Bilateral contract: A contract in which promises are made by both parties.

Bill: A new piece of proposed legislation.

Boolean language: Language that the computer understands.

Breach of contract: When a party to a contract fails to perform as promised in the contract, without legal justification.

Brief: A written summary of the important elements of an opinion.

Burden of proof: Requirement in a civil trial whereby the plaintiff must prove that the defendant is liable for the injuries suffered by the plaintiff by a preponderance of the evidence. In a criminal trial, the state must prove that the defendant committed the crime he has been accused of beyond a reasonable doubt.

Burglary: Breaking and entering into the dwelling of another with the intent to commit a crime therein.

"But for" test: In a negligence action, the test applied to determine cause in fact by proving that "but for" the defendant's actions, no injury to the plaintiff would have resulted.

CALR: Computer assisted legal research

Capacity: The legal qualification to engage in or perform an act that has legal consequences.

Cartwheel strategy: A brainstorming exercise developed by William Statsky that helps you identify many possible descriptive words.

Causation: In a negligence action, the plaintiff must prove that the defendant's actions were the probable and sufficiently direct cause of the plaintiff's injuries.

Cause of action: A legally acceptable reason for suing.

Circumstantial evidence: Evidence that must be inferred from another fact and is not based on personal observation or knowledge.

Citation: Listing of the location an opinion may be found in a reporter.

Cited material: The law you are shepardizing.

Citing material: The law cited in Shepard's.

Client counseling: The act, that only an attorney may do, of giving advice to a client.

Comparative negligence: Modern doctrine that allows that liability for damages be proportionately divided among the parties.

Compensatory damages: Damages awarded to compensate for the loss of benefits the plaintiff would have received had the defendant performed in conformance with the contract.

Competency: Using the necessary skills and knowledge to reasonably assist in representing a client.

Concurring opinion: Opinion written by a judge when a judge agrees with the final outcome of the majority's decision but disagrees with its reasoning supporting that decision.

Confidentiality: Legal protection that allows the client to speak freely and honestly to her counsel and thereby ensure that her attorney and legal team can most effectively represent her interests.

Conflict of interest: The paralegal has competing interests against those of her client that may compromise her ability to provide unbiased judgment and loyalty to that client.

Connectors: Words used to link search words into sentences in Boolean language.

Consequential damages: Damages awarded to compensate for expenses or other losses besides compensatory damages that occur as a result of the breach of contract.

Consideration: Anything of value.

Conspiracy: The agreement between two or more individuals to commit an unlawful act or a lawful act in an unlawful manner.

Contract: A legally enforceable agreement between two or more individuals or entities. The symbol of a lower case "**k**" is often used by lawyers and paralegals as an abbreviation for contract.

Contributory negligence: Seldom applied doctrine that holds that if any negligence by the plaintiff is proven, the plaintiff is then barred from any recovery.

Conversion: The intentional, permanent taking of another's personal property.

Counter-offer: A conditional acceptance of an offer in which the terms and conditions of the offer are changed.

Counterclaim: Claim filed by the defendant against the plaintiff that alleges a separate cause of action against the plaintiff arising from the same event. The counterclaim is not a defense, such as comparative negligence but a separate cause of action.

Crossclaim: A claim filed by a defendant against a co-defendant.

Damages: The plaintiff's request for a sum of money to be paid by the defendant for civil wrongs committed by the defendant.

Deep pockets: Term used to describe the defendant with the most money.

Defamation: The communication of a false, embarrassing and/or damaging message about another's reputation to a third party.

Default judgment: Judgment whereby the plaintiff's allegations are deemed to be proven due to lack of response from the defendant and the defendant is liable for damages requested.

Defendant: The party being sued in a legal matter or the person being tried for a criminal offense.

Demand letter: A letter written in a civil case to persuade the opposing side to settle.

Deposition: Oral questioning under oath recorded by reporter or video during the discovery phase of litigation.

Depositions: Oral questioning under oath.

Descriptive word index: Part of West's Digests that lists which volume of the digest contains a brief description of the case relating to that descriptive word heading. The digests do not contain the full text of the opinion; instead they provide a brief description of the contents of the opinion and the citation of the case.

Digesting depositions: The process of summarizing the content of a deposition in order to make the information contained therein easy to access.

Direct evidence: Evidence based on personal observation or knowledge, which proves or disproves a fact without the need of inference.

Directed verdict: A verdict in which the judge determines that based on the evidence presented at trial, there is by law only one way the jury can decide and therefore decides for the jury.

Directories: Organize Web sites into logical categories. A group of editors at a Web site determine certain broad subject categories and then break those broad categories into specific subcategories.

Discovery: The formal process of fact gathering prior to commencement of trial.

Disposition: Describes what the court orders for the case.

Dissenting opinion: Opinion written by a judge when a judge or judges disagree with the majority's reasoning and decision.

Due process: Ensures criminal defendants a range of constitutional protections including prohibition of unreasonable search and seizure and a right against self-incrimination.

Eighth Amendment of the U.S. Constitution: States that "Excessive bail shall not be required, nor excessive fines imposed, nor cruel and unusual punishments inflicted."

Elements analysis: Technique that allows you to apply the individual elements of a statute to the particular facts of your case.

Embezzlement: Unlawful conversion of the personal property of another by one who has lawful possession of the property.

Ethical or Chinese wall: A method to isolate a paralegal from any work in a firm that could create a conflict.

Ethics: A set of rules that provide a standard of conduct and behavior for a certain set of people.

Evidence: Anything that makes a fact more or less probable.

Expert testimony: Expert witnesses may testify without first-hand knowledge of the matter and may express an opinion on that matter. This exception allows both parties in litigation to present technical and/or specialized information.

Express contract: A contract that is expressed in words, either orally or in written form.

False imprisonment: The restriction of a person by physical restraint or through threat to a person or his property.

Federal Rules of Evidence: Formal rules of evidence that are introduced and certain types of evidence can be excluded by the presiding judge.

Felony murder: A statutory offense that provides that any death resulting from a dangerous felony is murder.

Fifth Amendment of the U.S. Constitution: Requires indictment by a grand jury for persons held for "capital" or "otherwise infamous" crime. The Fifth Amendment prohibits double jeopardy and requiring a criminal defendant to "be a witness against himself" and provides that no citizen shall "be deprived of life, liberty, or property without due process of law."

For cause: Type of challenge attorneys may make against potential jurors when they can demonstrate biases exist.

Foreseeability: In a negligence action, the duty of a reasonable person to foresee the probable consequences of his actions.

Fourteenth Amendment of the U.S. Constitution: Prohibits the states from making or enforcing any law that abridges the "privileges or immunities" of citizens of the United States and further holds that no state shall "deprive any person of life, liberty, or property, without due process of law; nor deny to any person within its jurisdiction the equal protection of the laws."

Headnotes: Brief summaries of key points of an opinion written by a private publisher.

Hearsay: Testimony offered in court, about an out of court statement made by someone else, offered to prove the truth of the matter asserted.

Hearsay exceptions: Rule of evidence that allows certain types of hearsay evidence to be admissible based on the rationale that circumstances give an inherent credibility to the statement thereby relieving the concern regarding lack of cross examination.

Holding: In a court opinion, the answer to the issues presented in the case.

Homicide: An act or omission resulting in the death of another person. Homicide can be further classified into degrees depending upon the intent and acts of the perpetrator.

Homicide: An act or omission resulting in the death of another person.

IME: Acronym for Independent Medical Examination.

Immaterial breach: A breach of minor terms or provisions of the contract that does not materially change the nature or value of that contract.

Impeach: To question a witness's veracity and credibility. The goal is to make the jury question the credibility of the witness's testimony.

Implied contract: A contract in which the essential elements of the contract are expressed through conduct of the parties.

In personam jurisdiction: The court has jurisdiction over a party to the litigation.

In rem jurisdiction: The court has jurisdiction over property that is the subject of the litigation.

Inchoate crimes: "Attempt-type" crimes, such as conspiracy and solicitation.

Indifferent person: Party who must serve the complaint and is uninvolved in the legal matter; usually a marshal or sheriff.

Intake interview: The initial interview the client has when hiring a firm.

Intent: A "meeting of the minds;" all parties to the contract share the same understanding regarding the terms and conditions of the contract they are entering.

Intentional infliction of emotional distress: The defendant intends to cause severe emotional distress upon the plaintiff through his outrageous conduct.

Intentional misrepresentation: The false representation of facts to the plaintiff that the defendant knows to be false and supplied with the expectation that the plaintiff will rely on those falsehoods to his detriment.

Interrogatories: During the discovery phase of litigation; written questions answered under oath, in writing.

Intervening cause: In a negligence action, an unforeseeable, independent act that destroys the chain of proximate cause.

Invasion of privacy: The unauthorized use of the plaintiff's likeness or name, or the unreasonable disclosure of the plaintiff's private affairs, for the pecuniary advantage of the defendant.

Issue statement: Identifies the issue in sentence form.

Issues: Matters and elements discussed by the court.

Judgment: The jury's decision as to the amount of damages awarded in a civil case.

Judicial notice: Evidence that is admitted without question because it is such a well-accepted fact that the judge will acknowledge it in the record.

Jurisdiction: A courts' power to consider a case and decide the outcome.

Jurisdictional statement: A statement included in the complaint that informs the court that they have jurisdiction over the lawsuit.

Jury instructions: Instructions given to the jury by the judge before the jury deliberates. These instructions are written by the judge with input from both parties and include information the jury may use to guide its deliberations.

Kidnapping: Forcible removal of a person against his or her will for ransom, use as a hostage, or harming or terrorizing that person or others.

Larceny: The wrongful taking of personal property of another with the intent to convert it to one's own use.

Larceny by deception and fraud: Includes a variety of offenses like forgery, mail fraud, and larceny by trick.

Lay opinion: The opinion of a non-expert.

Legal interviewing: The process of obtaining relevant information from an individual for a specific case.

Legal investigator: An employee dedicated to conducting investigations.

Legal memorandum: Written communication that often takes the form of an interoffice memorandum and is used to discuss the strengths and weaknesses of a particular case and is written specifically for use within the law office only.

Liable: Responsible or accountable under the law.

Libel: The written form of defamation.

Litigation: Legal action against certain defendants in order to recover damages for one's injuries.

Majority opinion: The opinion of the majority of the justices considering a case and the ruling upon which later courts may rely as precedent.

Malice aforethought homicide: A type of homicide that includes the most heinous acts and carries the most severe penalties.

Mandatory authority: Any law the court must rely on in making its decision. Mandatory authority is always primary authority because a court is never required to rely on non-law in making its decisions.

Manslaughter: The crime of causing the death of another person under circumstances falling short of murder.

Material breach: A breach of major and material terms and conditions of the contract.

Mens rea: The state of mind that makes the performance of a particular act a crime.

Mitigate: To make less severe.

Motion: A formal request to a judge.

Motion to compel: A motion requesting that the judge require the other party to comply with discovery requests.

NALA: National Association of Legal Assistants

NFPA: National Federation of Paralegal Associations

Non-pecuniary damages: Damages that cannot be quantified economically, such as pain and mental anguish.

Negligence: Failure to act in a manner that a reasonable person under similar circumstances would, involving an unreasonable risk of injury to others.

Negligence per se: Negligence determined by the fact that the defendant violated a statute that incorporates the elements of negligence.

Object: The goal or purpose of the contract.

Objective writing: Discusses the strengths and weaknesses of a position and often includes recommendations for further investigation as well as negotiation strategies.

Offer: The act that initiates the contract.

Opinion: Written document issued by a court that explains its decision in a case.

Parallel cite: The citation of the other reporter in which the full text of the cited material may be found.

Parties: The plaintiff and the defendant in a legal matter.

Peremptory challenges: Limited type of challenge attorneys may make against potential jurors whereby they may excuse a juror for any reason at all.

Perpetrator: One who commits a crime.

Personal service: The delivery of the summons and complaint to the defendant ordering him to appear or answer the complaint.

Persuasive authority: An element that a court may rely on but is not required to do so. Secondary authority is always persuasive authority.

Persuasive writing: Style of writing in which the writer presents an argument and authority to sustain that argument.

Plaintiff: The injured party seeking relief in a legal matter.

Plea bargain: An agreement in which a criminal defendant agrees to plead guilty and avoid a trial in exchange for a lesser sentence.

Pleadings: The initial documents filed in a lawsuit and begin with the complaint.

Prayer for relief: The portion of the complaint that requests-damages be awarded to the plaintiff. Also known as ad damnum clause or wherefore clause.

Precedent: Requirement that judges follow ruling made by higher court judges, in the same jurisdiction on a case that is factually analogous.

Presumption: A fact inferred to be true once another fact has been proven.

Pretrial conference: A meeting during which both parties to a civil action meet to attempt to settle or come to a mutual agreement without trial. If pretrial conferences fail to produce a settlement, the court will set a date for trial.

Prima facie case: A showing of evidence sufficient to satisfy a party's burden of proof. In Latin it translates to "At first sight."

Primary authority: Any law the court can rely on in making its decisions. This includes statutes, constitutions, administrative regulations, and case law.

Private nuisance: A nuisance that affects and unreasonably interferes with the use and enjoyment of property by a limited amount of people.

Privilege: The right to refuse to testify or to prevent someone else from testifying.

Proof by preponderance of the evidence: Standard of proof in a civil action that provides that the evidence presented must make it "more likely than not" that the defendant is liable for the harm suffered by the plaintiff.

Proximate cause: In a negligence action, an act that, unbroken by another cause, produces injury and without which the injury would not have occurred.

Public nuisance: A nuisance that affects and unreasonably interferes with the use and enjoyment of property of a large amount of people.

Punitive damages: Civil damages assessed to punish the defendant for outrageous behavior.

Query: Question used to search the Internet. This query can be phrased as a "natural word search" or a Boolean language search.

"Reasonable man" standard: In a negligence action, the duty to exercise reasonable care where circumstances would indicate to any reasonable or prudent person that such care is required.

Reasoning: Explains how the court justifies its holding in a court opinion.

Relevant evidence: Any evidence that has a reasonable connection or relationship to the truth or falsity of a fact.

Remand: Decision made by an appellate court in which the court sends back the case to the trial court for further proceedings.

Reporters: Contain full text of court opinions.

Request for admissions: Written statements sent to the opposing party that must be admitted or denied during the discovery phase of litigation.

Request for physical or mental examination: A written request to allow a physician to conduct an examination of the opposing party during the discovery phase of litigation.

Request for production and inspection of documents: Written request to inspect or copy documents and other tangible items under the opposing party's control during the discovery phase of litigation.

Res ipsa loquitor: Doctrine that holds that if the plaintiff in a negligence action can prove that the instrument that caused the damage was in the exclusive control or possession of the defendant at the time the injury occurred, negligence is thereby established. In Latin it translates to "The thing speaks for itself."

Res judicata: The doctrine that provides that litigation must end at some point and once the parties have been given a full opportunity to have their case heard, they can no longer litigate.

Rescission: A remedy in which the court cancels the contract and relieves the defendant of any economic benefit he derived as a result of his breach because such a result would be unjust.

Reverse: Decision made by an appellate court in which the court does not agree with the decision of the lower court.

Robbery: The taking of someone's money or other personal property from the victim's person or in the victim's presence by force or threat of imminent harm.

Rules: Guidelines being applied in the case, including statutes, regulations, and or case law.

Rules of civil procedure. The rules of court in a given jurisdiction that ensure that all practice before the court conforms to standards set by the court.

Sanctions: Punishment or penalties for failing to conform to the ethical standard.

Search engines: Internet devices that search for specific words or phrases you, as the researcher, provide. Using descriptive words, the researcher inputs a command to the engine to search for Web sites that contain those specific words contained in the command.

Secondary authority: Any non-law a court may rely on in making its decisions. This includes treatises, legal periodicals, and law review articles.

Sexual offense: The intentional touching of another person in a sexual way without that person's consent, or when that person lacks the capacity to legally give effective consent.

Simple breach: One or more parties to a contract fails to fulfill one or more of the terms and conditions of the valid contract.

Slander: The oral or spoken form of defamation.

Slip law: Small pamphlet that contains the text of a statute immediately after it has been passed by the legislature.

Specific performance: When the plaintiff sues to recover for the actual performance called for in the contract.

Stare decisis: Doctrine which holds that judges are reluctant to overturn their own rulings.

Statute: A law written by a legislature.

Statute of Frauds: Doctrine requiring certain contracts to be in writing and adopted through the UCC in most states.

Statute of limitations: The amount of time in which a civil or criminal action must be initiated

Statutes at large: Bound volumes containing statutes at the end of a session of Congress.

Statutory duty: A duty set forth and encoded in a statute.

Subject matter jurisdiction: The court has jurisdiction because of the subject matter of the litigation.

Summary judgment: Motion requesting that the court dismiss the case on the grounds that the plaintiff has failed to provide enough evidence to support her cause of action.

Summons: A formal notice from the court telling the defendant to appear or answer; usually accompanied by the complaint.

Subpoena: An order from the court to appear for questioning in a legal matter.

Subpoena duces tecum: An order from the court to appear for questioning in a legal matter that requires that the person bring specified documents with him or her.

Subscription: The signature of the attorney who prepared the complaint, represents the plaintiff, and is affixed at the end of the complaint.

Third-party complaint: Complaint against a person not originally named as a party to the lawsuit.

Tort: A civil wrong or omission by one individual against another.

Tort law: The area of civil law wherein individuals seek compensation for injuries or harm caused by another individual's action or lack of action.

Tortfeasor: The person or entity who commits a tort.

Trespass to personal property: The use of another's personal property without authorization.

Trespass to property: The entering onto another's land without authorization.

Trial court: The court that hears evidence and a jury is often the finder of fact.

Unauthorized practice of law: Practicing law without a license or special authorization. Includes providing legal advice and representing clients before the court and is a criminal offense in most states.

Unilateral contract: A contract in which only one party makes a promise.

Venue: The actual court that considers the litigation.

Verdict: The decision of the finder of fact in a trial.

Vicarious liability: The extension of liability for a tortious act based on the legal relationship of the parties.

Voir dire: The process of jury selection in which potential jurors are questioned in a group setting or individually.

West's Digests: West's Publishing's digest for each state's judicial opinions. These digests take all opinions issued by that state's appellate courts and assemble them in categories to be accessed by the researcher.

Wherefore clause: The portion of the complaint that requests damages be awarded to the plaintiff. Also known as ad damnum clause or prayer for relief.

With prejudice: Type of motion whereby the case is dismissed and the plaintiff may not file another complaint from the same cause of action.

Without prejudice: Type of motion whereby the plaintiff may file another complaint.

Index

D

K

L

M

N

O

P